D1826772

ALLEGED NON-PAST USES OF *QATAL* IN CLASSICAL HEBREW

STUDIA SEMITICA NEERLANDICA

edited by

Prof. dr. W.J. van Bekkum
Prof. dr. W.A.M. Beuken s.j.
Dr. M.L. Folmer
Prof. dr. J. Hoftijzer
Prof. dr. T. Muraoka
Prof. dr. K.A.D. Smelik
Prof. dr. H.J. Stroomer
Prof. dr. K. van der Toorn
Prof. dr. K.R. Veenhof

Submission of manuscripts

- Manuscripts should be submitted to the editor of Van Gorcum
  Publishers, P.O. Box 43, 9440 AA Assen, The Netherlands.
  E-Mail: info@vangorcum.nl

- Each manuscript submitted is reviewed by two reviewers.

- The reviewers will not be identified to the authors.

Max Rogland

ALLEGED NON-PAST USES OF *QATAL* IN CLASSICAL HEBREW

2003 ⋙ ROYAL VAN GORCUM

© 2003 Koninklijke Van Gorcum, P.O. Box 43, 9400 AA Assen, The Netherlands

All rights reserved. No part of this publication may be reproduced, stored in a retrieval system, or transmitted, in any form or by any means, electronic, mechanical, photocopying, recording, or otherwise, without the prior permission of the Publisher.

ISBN 90 232 3973 3

Printed by: Royal Van Gorcum, Assen, The Netherlands

CONTENTS

This book is a very slightly edited version of my doctoral dissertation that was defended in October of 2001 at Leiden University. I am grateful to Dr. M. Folmer, Prof. Dr. J. Hoftijzer, Prof. Dr. E. Talstra, Prof. Dr. K. Veenhof, and Prof. Dr. E. van Wolde for the comments, corrections and suggestions they gave as members of my *promotiecommissie*. Many helpful comments were also given by the Rev. Dr. W. B. Aucker, Drs. M. F. J. Baasten, Prof. Dr. C. J. Collins, Dr. M. Malessa, and Dr. W. Th. van Peursen. Most of all, I am indebted to my advisor, Prof. Dr. T. Muraoka, for his superb guidance of this project. It has been a true privilege to have worked under his supervision.

Finally, it goes without saying that I owe an inestimable debt to my wife Lara – thankfully, she is too gracious to ask me to pay it back.

ברוך יהוה לעולם
אמן ואמן

§ 1. INTRODUCTION

§ 1.1 Preliminary Remarks

The basic task in the study of the Hebrew verbal system is, as Gentry states, "correlating an adequate and simple description of the form and function of the verb together with the realities of all its usage – whether common or marginal."[1] Such a task, to put it in a slightly different way, seeks to address two distinct problems, one of a theoretical and one of an interpretive nature. On a theoretical level one is faced with the challenge of developing a descriptive model of the verbal system and, taking Occam's Razor into account, the simpler it is the better. A number of factors can contribute to the development of such a model, such as diachronic observations, cross-linguistic data, comparative Semitics, past grammatical tradition and, of course, empirical study of the Hebrew verb. On an interpretive level one must deal with the question of whether or not the proposed model of the verbal system is actually capable of explaining the use of the verb as we encounter it in Hebrew texts. To address this issue necessarily involves one in matters of exegesis and interpretation.[2] The theoretical and interpretive issues, though distinguishable, are naturally inseparable: One's theoretical model of the verbal system affects one's interpretation of individual verbs, yet one's perception of the actual use of the verb typically plays a large role in the development of one's theory.[3]

---

[1] Gentry (1998: 7f.). Gentry takes the term "marginal" from Hendel, who also speaks of "statistically less frequent" uses (1996: 152).

[2] Cf. Hoftijzer (1985: 5, 98 n.28), Isaksson (1987: 15f.), Talstra (1992: 270). That being said, I am inclined to agree with Talstra (1997: 101) when he argues that "an analysis [of verbal forms] based on language as a *system* should have priority over an analysis based on the language used in an *individual text.*"

[3] Cf. Waltke and O'Connor § 29.3 *h*, Dempsey (1988: 6f.), Groß (1976: 8 n.20). Some scholars would downplay the importance of having any sort of working theory and would apparently lay exclusive emphasis on the interpretive, inductive issue. Cf. e.g. McFall (1982: 184): "Every care must be taken in future studies of the [Hebrew verbal system] not to approach it with any preconceived ideas regarding the nature of its verbal system." Similarly Michel (1960: 13): "wir müssen die Psalmen untersuchen, als sei die Bedeutung der Verbformen, die in ihnen vorkommen, völlig unbekannt." While I do not at all dispute the importance of empirical observation, I think it very doubtful whether anyone can approach a subject which has been discussed as much as the Hebrew verbal system as a *tabula rasa*. See further Goldfajn (1998: 21ff.) and Furuli (1997: 90).

It may fairly be said that the two most popular models for describing the indicative functions of the Hebrew verbal forms, namely the "tense" model (much more accurately: tense *and* aspect model[4]) and the (exclusively) "aspect" model,[5] are relatively simple and coherent on a theoretical level. Furthermore, as Hendel points out, on an interpretive level both seem to work reasonably well in explaining the usage of the verb a good deal of the time.[6] However, both theories encounter enough apparent exceptions to call their general validity into question and thereby to keep scholarly opinions sharply divided on the matter. We may thus say that the objections to these two models lie primarily on the interpretive level rather than the theoretical.

The present study will examine a number of uncommon ("marginal") uses of *qatal* in Classical Hebrew which appear to refer to non-past situations, namely the so-called "gnomic", "performative" and "prophetic" perfects. Although such uses are not extremely common, for many scholars they play a significant role in the semantic description of the function(s) of *qatal*. In his discussion of the prophetic perfect, for example, Hendel claims that "in these instances there is no ambiguity concerning an aspectual vs. relative tense interpretation; contextually aspect is the only relevant possibility."[7] Similarly, in regard to the performative perfect Tropper states: "diese Funktion kann eindeutig dem [perfektiven] Aspekt zugeordnet werden."[8] Statements such as these could easily be multiplied.[9] It hardly needs to be added that one's view of the semantics of *qatal* has far-reaching consequences for one's view of the verbal system as a whole.

There is already a vast literature devoted to the Hebrew verb, and there are no signs at present that interest in the subject is on the wane. We believe that the current study is justified, however, by the surprising lack of systematic investigation of these allegedly non-past uses of *qatal*. While they are mentioned in the standard grammars and are frequently invoked by exegetes, to the best of my knowledge there has been no discussion devoted to the gnomic perfect in the periodical literature and only one such treatment of the prophetic perfect, despite S. R. Driver's opinion that it is "the most special and remarkable use of the tense".[10] This lacuna in

---

[4] Such as that found in e.g. Joüon and Muraoka § 111. The concepts of "tense" and "aspect" will be discussed below (§ 1.2, § 1.3).
[5] E.g. Waltke and O'Connor § 29.6, Tropper (1998).
[6] Hendel (1996: 152).
[7] Hendel (1996: 183).
[8] Tropper (1998: 183).
[9] See e.g. Kottsieper (1999: 70), Hatav (1997: 12), Baayen (1997: 278), Waltke and O'Connor § 29.2 *f*, Junger (1989: 73), McFall (1982: 18f.), Ben-Ḥayyim (1977: 68), Kustár (1972: 5f.), Cohen (1924: 14ff.); cf. Binnick (1991: 434ff.).
[10] Driver § 14.

the scholarly literature is nothing less than astonishing given the important conclusions that are frequently drawn from these examples of *qatal*.

Further justification for the present study is supplied by the remarkable fact that, despite the widespread acceptance of the existence of these different "types" of perfects, there is often considerable disagreement when it comes to the interpretation of individual examples. One can only partially agree when Binnick writes:

> It seems puzzling, given the huge amount of study applied to the Bible ... that there can be such divergent opinion as to the analysis of the verb systems. In fact there is no *real* controversy in regard to the interpretation of *particular* verbs; the problem arises only in regard to the two types of verbs [viz., *qatal* and *yiqtol*] *in general*.[11]

To be sure, as a general rule there is no controversy regarding the interpretation of particular verbs, but the alleged non-past uses of *qatal* to be examined here are a notable exception. To mention only one example, consider Pr 4.2:

כִּי לֶקַח טוֹב נָתַתִּי לָכֶם תּוֹרָתִי אַל־תַּעֲזֹבוּ׃

"For I give/will give/have given (?) you good teaching; do not abandon my instruction."

The verb נָתַתִּי, though sometimes rendered as a past tense,[12] has been considered by some scholars to be prophetic,[13] gnomic[14] as well as performative![15] Such conflicting exegetical opinions point to the serious need for a more systematic investigation of these examples of *qatal*.

The diversity of opinion concerning Pr 4.2 is, in fact, merely symptomatic of a larger problem noted by Bergsträsser:

> In der Dichtung, vor allem der späteren, hat eine weitere Ausdehnung der präsentischen und futurischen Gebrauchsweisen des Perf. zu einer völligen Verwischung der Bedeutungsunterschiede der Tempora und einem regellosen Promiscuegebrauch sämtlicher Tempusbezeichnungen (einschließlich Perf. cons., Imperf. cons. und auch Nominalsatz) im Sinne

---

[11] Binnick (1991: 436).

[12] E.g. Plöger and the Peshitta. Unless otherwise noted, in the present work commentaries are always cited *ad loc.*

[13] Gesenius-Kautzsch-Cowley § 106 *n*, Böttcher § 947 *f.*

[14] Klein (1990: 57).

[15] Bergsträsser's interpretation (§ 6 *e*) is clearly performative in nature, though his grammar predated the introduction of the concept in general linguistics (cf. § 4); see also Delitzsch.

der Gegenwart und Zukunft geführt... Dabei macht es oft Schwierigkeiten festzustellen, welche Zeitstufe in Wirklichkeit gemeint ist.[16]

Anyone who has seriously attempted to make sense of the verb tenses in some of the passages mentioned by Bergsträsser will no doubt feel a great deal of sympathy for this statement. Yet it is nevertheless, as Groß points out, "eine syntaktische Bankrotterklärung":

> Die Sprache ist ein Zeichensystem, und ein Zeichensystem, in dem alle Zeichen dasselbe bezeichnen können, ist ein Widerspruch... Dieser Promiscuegebrauch besteht also höchstens quoad nos, für unsere syntaktische Einsicht, nicht aber für den in dieser Sprache dichtenden Autor und sein Zielpublikum.[17]

Groß is surely correct that the difficulty only exists "quoad nos." Unfortunately, one is still left with the very real problem of interpreting the tense forms in a number of extremely difficult passages.

It is our hope that we will be able to present solutions to some of the theoretical and interpretive problems presented by these allegedly non-past uses of *qatal* and thereby to make a useful contribution to the larger debate over the Hebrew verbal system. The limited scope of the current study thus stands in contrast to many others which attempt to tackle the entire verbal system as a whole. Joosten writes:

> even if the elaboration of a comprehensive model [of the verbal system] is legitimate – it is in a sense the ultimate goal of all research in this field – it is more prudent, and no less correct methodologically, provisorily to limit our research to those parts of the BH verbal system which remain obscure, or which have not hitherto received much attention.[18]

The outline of this study is as follows: In this introductory chapter we will provide some general discussion of tense (§ 1.2) and aspect (§ 1.3), followed by our working theory of how these concepts relate to the Hebrew verbal system (§ 1.4). Chapters two through four are devoted to the gnomic, prophetic and performative perfects, respectively. The concluding chapter (§ 5) will review the results and suggest some avenues for further research.[19]

---

[16] Bergsträsser § 6 *i*; cf. Buth (1986: 26).

[17] Groß (1976: 3); cf. also *idem* (1977: 37): "Die absurde Vorstellung, alle hebräischen Verbformen könnten gleichermaßen für alle Zeitstufen stehen, ist einer Widerlegung nicht bedürftig."

[18] Joosten (1992:1).

[19] The *Forschungsgeschichte* has already been surveyed a number of times; see e.g. Jenni (2000: 26ff.), DeCaen (1996), Pascual (1993: 41ff., 1995), Buth (1992), Waltke and O'Connor § 29, McFall (1982), Groß (1982), Fensham (1978), Fleisch (1975), Mettinger

§ 1.2 Tense

By "tense" I mean the "grammaticalised expression of location in time".[20] Tense is therefore a deictic category and "tensed" languages are languages in which temporal location is encoded in the verb itself. This is to be contrasted with the expression of temporal location by other means (e.g. adverbials) as well as with the expression of "aspect" (§ 1.3). It is of course possible for a tensed language also to utilize temporal adverbials and for verbal forms to encode both tense and aspect.[21]

The work of Hans Reichenbach has been very influential on discussions of tense,[22] and the present study will make use of his method of tense analysis. Reichenbach analyzed tenses in terms of three time-points: The moment of speaking (S), the event referred to (E), and a point of reference (R). R indicates "the vantage point from which the speaker views the situation referred to".[23] In addition to these three points, there are two possible relations: "overlapping"[24] (symbolized here by "=") and "precedence" (symbolized by "<"). Thus the notation E<S means "E precedes S" (this necessarily indicates the converse: "S follows E"). He provides some typical relations:

S=R=E	present	*I see John*
S<R=E	future[25]	*I shall see John*
E=R<S	past	*I saw John*
E<S=R	present perfect[26]	*I have seen John*

(1973: 70ff.), Brockelmann (1951). We will only review the scholarly literature as it relates to the particular function of *qatal* under discussion.

[20] Comrie (1985: 9); similarly Chung and Timberlake (1985: 202ff.), Dik (1987: 59): "Tense distinctions locate some State of Affairs on the temporal axis in relation to the moment of speaking (absolute Tense) or to a reference point defined by some other State of Affairs (relative Tense)." On "absolute" vs. "relative" tense see below. See further C. Smith (1991: 136f.), Lyons (1995: 312), Ljungberg (1995: 87).

[21] Cf. C. Smith (1991: 135), Chung and Timberlake (1985: 206), Lyons (1977: 682), Comrie (1976: 9), Hatav (1997: 1).

[22] Reichenbach (1947: 287ff.).

[23] Comrie (1981: 24); cf. Reichenbach (1947: 288), C. Smith (1991: 141f.), Hamann (1987). Hatav, who considers R to be an interval rather than a point, defines R as "the time-unit responsible for the temporal interpretation of the clause" (1997: 5); cf. also *idem* (1989).

[24] Comrie (1981: 24) prefers "overlapping" to the commonly used "simultaneous", since the latter implies "coterminous", which is often not the case.

[25] On the debate over whether or not the future tense should properly be viewed as a "tense" or a "mood" see e.g. Lyons (1977: 677), Comrie (1985: 43ff.), Bache (1986: 66f.), Chung and Timberlake (1985: 206, 243), and with particular reference to Classical Hebrew see Hoftijzer (2001). In this study I will discuss the future tense strictly in deictic terms, without attempting to answer this question.

[26] Reichenbach viewed the difference between the English present perfect and the simple past to be one of R, though other scholars argue that the difference relates to aspect or

E<R<S	pluperfect	*I had seen John*
R<E<S	future-in-the-past	*I would see John*

Reichenbach's system requires some modifications.[27] Most important is that there are cases in which it is not necessary to specify S[28] or R,[29] and in the present study I will attempt to analyze tenses with the smallest number of points possible. In other words, if either S or R appears to be dispensable then I will not include it in my analyses. Furthermore, there are two important subjects not treated by Reichenbach. First, while Reichenbach assumes that temporal divisions are tripartite (past, present, future), there are also tense systems with a binary temporal distinction of e.g. past vs. non-past.[30] This type of system requires a symbol to indicate "overlapping or preceding". In this study I will indicate this relation with "≤". Thus:

E<S	past	*I saw John*
S≤E	non-past	*I (will) see John*

Second, Reichenbach does not discuss the difference between absolute and relative tense systems. According to Comrie, the former type of system locates situations in time from the perspective of the present moment (S), whereas the latter locates situations in regard to a reference point (R) which is potentially variable.[31] An absolute tense system expresses e.g. "past" and "future", whereas the corresponding terms in a relative tense system would be "anterior" and "posterior."[32] Compare:

---

some other semantic parameter. For discussion see e.g. Bache (1994), C. Smith (1991: 146ff.), Bybee and Dahl (1989: 55), Comrie (1976: 52ff.). Whatever the answer to this question may be, at the very least I think it is safe to say that it makes reference in some way to a past event and thus may legitimately be discussed in terms of temporal deixis.

[27] For a full discussion see Comrie (1981). One such correction which is worth mentioning, though it cannot be pursued in detail here, is that in complex sequences of tenses it is possible to have more than one reference point (see also Harder 1994: 62 and Vet 1981: 159ff.). Dahl (1985: 30f.) argues for the necessity of another parameter which he calls the "temporal frame", yet it seems to me that this can probably be understood as an additional reference point (it should be noted that this parameter has not been adopted in the general literature).

[28] I have demonstrated elsewhere that this is the case with the Hebrew "epistolary perfect", in which only E and R are necessary; see Rogland (2000).

[29] This applies in particular to the simple tenses (thus e.g. present: S=E; past: E<S; future: S<E). See also Hamann (1987: 28 n.5).

[30] Lyons (1995: 314), Chung and Timberlake (1985: 204f.).

[31] Comrie (1985: 56); cf. Fanning (1990: 17), Dik (1987: 59), Ljungberg (1995: 87). In a relative system R can be S, of course, and it is for this reason that it can be difficult to determine whether a tense system with only one set of verb forms is primarily absolute or relative in nature (Comrie 1985: 22).

[32] It appears that absolute tense can be subsumed under relative tense (Comrie 1985: 63).

| | |
| *absolute* | *relative* |

absolute	*relative*
past: $E<S$	anterior: $E<R$
present: $S=E$	overlapping: $R=E$
future: $S<E$	posterior: $R<E$

These distinctions apply, *mutatis mutandis*, to binary relative tense systems:

absolute	*relative*
past: $E<S$	anterior: $E<R$
non-past: $S \leq E$	non-anterior: $R \leq E$

Just as R is optional for absolute simple tenses (see n.29), so is S optional in a relative tense system.[33] In my discussion I will provide analyses in terms of absolute and relative tense when both appear to be possible.[34]

§ 1.3 Aspect

In contrast to tense, "aspect" does not relate to the location of a situation in time but rather to its "internal temporal structure".[35] More specifically, a speaker may view a situation as either "perfective" or "imperfective". Imperfective forms "make explicit reference to the internal temporal constituency of the situation,"[36] whereas perfective forms lack such an explicit reference; rather, perfectives view a situation as "one single whole, regardless of its internal complexity".[37] This semantic parameter is most familiar to us in the contrasting past tense forms found in a number of languages (though a perfective-imperfective aspectual opposition can occur in any temporal sphere):

---

[33] Comrie (1981: 25f.). In the absence of contrary evidence, however, it will usually be assumed that S is the same as R (Comrie 1976: 2, Chung and Timberlake 1985: 203).

[34] It should be mentioned that some scholars call absolute tenses "deictic" and relative tenses "non-deictic", yet this is largely a question of definition. A number of scholars define "deixis" in terms of the moment of speaking; so e.g. Fanning (1990: 17f.), C. Smith (1991: 136ff., 164 n.5), Lyons (1968: 304f.; 1977: 682, 689; 1995: 313), Bache (1985: 3; 1986: 68f.; 1995: 315f.). Obviously, with such a definition relative tenses cannot be considered "deictic". However, I agree with Comrie that relative tenses can legitimately be considered deictic since, just like absolute tenses, they do express location in time (Comrie 1985: 16, 22; cf. Fanning 1990: 85).

[35] Chung and Timberlake (1985: 202, 213ff.). Aspect is to be contrasted with *Aktionsart*, which is a lexical, rather than a grammatical, category (Creason 1995, Ljungberg 1995: 88; cf. Bache 1982, Dik 1987: 59).

[36] Comrie (1976: 3).

[37] Cuvalay-Haak (1997: 32).

French	*il lut* :: *il lisait*
Greek	ἐποίησεν :: ἐποίει
Latin	*laudavi* :: *laudabam*

Both forms are marked as past tenses, but the second form also expresses imperfective aspect, which adds various notions such as continuous, progressive, iterative or habitual activity.[38] Comrie summarizes as follows:

> ...the perfective looks at the situation from outside, without necessarily distinguishing any of the internal structure of the situation, whereas the imperfective looks at the situation from inside, and as such is crucially concerned with the internal structure of the situation...[39]

§ 1.4 The Hebrew Verbal System

Our interest in the present study is primarily a semantic one: What indicative function(s) does *qatal* possess in relation to the other members of the verbal system? The question as such relates to the verbal system as viewed synchronically. Before addressing this synchronic question, however, a few remarks of a diachronic nature are in order.

I agree with the generally accepted view that Hebrew, as several other Semitic languages, possessed two distinct prefix conjugations: a "long" form derived from *yaqtulu* and a "short" form *yaqtul*.[40] The latter form possessed modal (jussive) as well as indicative (preterite or perfective) functions. In its indicative function it occurs in Biblical Hebrew most frequently in the ubiquitous *wayyiqtol* form, although it also occurs without the conjunction (primarily in poetry). The long form *yaqtulu* possessed a variety of functions which are typically described as either aspectual (imperfective) or temporal (present/future).[41] In many cases the formal opposition between the long and short forms no longer exists in Hebrew due to the loss of the final *-u* vowel from the long imperfect, making the "short/long" terminology not entirely felicitous,[42] though a

---

[38] Cf. Comrie (1985: 25ff.).

[39] Comrie (1976: 4); Bache (1995: 269f.) is largely in agreement with Comrie's definition, yet he does suggest some minor corrections.

[40] See e.g. Rainey (1986), Tropper (1998). To be strictly accurate, there were other prefix conjugations as well, such as *yaqtula*. The functions of this form are modal, rather than indicative, and hence fall outside the scope of this study. We do not accept the existence of a *yaqattal* form in Classical Hebrew (cf. Kottsieper 2000); see Tropper (2000: 460f.), T. Andersen (2000: 14), Schüle (2000: 96ff.), Groß (1976: 21f.), Rainey (1975: 423), Fenton (1970).

[41] In the present study these parameters are considered indicative in nature. For a different analysis in regard to the long imperfect in Hebrew, see n.57 below.

[42] Cf. Hoftijzer (1985: 96 n.7).

distinct morphology has been preserved in some verb classes.[43] In contrast to the situation regarding the prefix conjugations, we believe that there was originally only one suffix conjugation in proto-Semitic.[44] The origin of the Hebrew "inverted perfect" (*weqatalti*) is admittedly somewhat obscure, but the most likely explanation seems to be that it arose from the use of *qatal* in the apodosis of conditional sentences.[45] Regardless of its origin, we think it necessary to treat it as a separate member of the verbal system.[46] The analysis of verb forms in Hebrew texts has been complicated to a certain extent by the fact that the formal opposition between the short and long *yiqtol* has been neutralized in many cases, as well as by the fact that in many cases of *weqatal* there is no possibility for an accent shift. In the present study I will assume that the functional oppositions which correspond to the observable formal oppositions,[47] and which are supported by historical-comparative evidence (in the case of the prefix conjugations), continue to exist even in cases in which a formal distinction cannot be observed; in these cases we must rely upon non-formal criteria such as textual interpretation. This assumption is not without its dangers[48] and should be considered somewhat provisional in the absence of a comprehensive treatment of these issues. Nevertheless, a structuralist approach to the study of the Hebrew verb requires at least a basic working theory regarding the members of the verbal system which can stand in opposition to *qatal* (such as *yiqtol* and *weqatal*). Hence a model for the entire system is presented here,[49] though the only element

---

[43] There is also a morphosyntactic distinction regarding the use of certain pronominal suffixes; see Muraoka (1975), Rainey (1986: 10ff.).

[44] Two separate suffix conjugations, namely a past tense *qatál* (*qatíl/qatúl*) and a present-future *qátal*, are argued for by e.g. G. R. Driver (1936: 88; 1969: 50) and Zevit (1998: 49ff.). For discussion of the historical development of the *qatala* morpheme in Semitic see e.g. T. Andersen (2000), Rainey (1996: 5f.), Tropper (1995), Priebatsch (1978), Rundgren (1965-66), Gelb (1965).

[45] Gentry (1998: 12 n.21), Bombeck (1997: 232), Hendel (1996: 153 n.5), M. Smith (1991: 6ff.), Gropp (1991: 46f.), Waltke and O'Connor § 32.1.2, Moran (1961: 64f.). This view is disputed by T. Andersen (2000: 33), who argues that both the "perfect" *qatal* and the "imperfective" *weqatal* developed from an originally progressive *qatala.

[46] See Joosten (1992), Gropp (1991: 48); contrast Tropper (1998: 185): "[es gibt] keinen Grund, *qatal* und *w°qatalti* morphologisch oder funktional zu trennen". The clear opposition between *weqatalti* as an iterative and *qatal* as a non-iterative past provides more than enough reason to do so from a functional standpoint.

[47] On these functional oppositions, see below.

[48] Cf. Hoftijzer (1985: 1).

[49] In contrast to many recent studies which do not take the participle into account (e.g. Tropper 1998, Gentry 1998), we think that it is to be considered an integral member of the verbal system (Muraoka 1999: 191f., Joosten 1989, 1997, Hoftijzer 1991: 649f.; cf. Driver § 135). In the current study *qatal*, *yiqtol*, *qotel* and the "inverted" tenses *wayyiqtol* and *weqatalti* are treated as the primary members of this system. This definition of "the verbal system" is clearly somewhat arbitrary and incomplete, as it does not include e.g. the periphrastic participle (cf. Muraoka 1999, Van Peursen 1997) and certain uses of infinitival forms (cf. Solá-Solé 1961: 79ff.). Indeed, the entire range of forms which could poten-

that the current study will attempt to argue in detail concerns the semantic value of *qatal*.

As we turn more directly to the synchronic/semantic question, we must first mention some limitations to our working theory regarding the verbal system: The system to be described is concerned with the indicative function[50] of lexically fientive verbs[51] and applies to Standard and Late Biblical Hebrew texts.[52] The theory is as follows: fientive *qatal* is semantically marked as a past tense[53] (either relative or absolute) but unmarked aspectually. As a past tense it stands in opposition to (long) *yiqtol* and *qotel*, which refer to various types of non-past situations.[54]

---

tially stand in opposition to *qatal* could be much more complex than is typically supposed; cf. Hoftijzer (1991: 648ff.). It is nonetheless hoped that our definition of "the verbal system", though perhaps incomplete, will still prove sufficient for our present purposes.

[50] Consequently we will not discuss the debated question of the so-called "precative" perfect in the present study (but see our concluding chapter, § 5), since this would be most properly analyzed as an expression of deontic modality (see Hoftijzer 2001, Warren 1998: 89ff., Gianto 1998: 194, Hendel 1996: 171). Likewise, sentence types which are by definition non-indicative (e.g. interrogatives) are excluded here.

[51] Cf. Gropp (1991: 51f.). For some of the reasons for this see § 2.5 and § 4.4.2.

[52] The precise relation of early or "archaic" Hebrew texts to this system is uncertain. It is quite likely that a different system of morphosyntactic oppositions existed in an early phase of Hebrew, and it would be imprudent simply to assume that these different morphosyntactic systems were semantically identical. In order to keep the present discussion within reasonable bounds, "archaic" Hebrew texts will be excluded. On a practical level one is faced with the considerable difficulty of attempting to identify what marks a text as "archaic" and what is simply "archaizing"; see Hurvitz (2000: 147), Waltke and O'Connor § 1.4 and especially Young (1998). Despite Young's helpful caution on this point, I have chosen to follow the majority opinion in viewing the following texts as actually archaic (cf. Kutscher 1982: 12): Gen 49, Ex 15, Nu 23-24, Dt 32-33, Ju 5, 1 Sam 2.1-10. A further complication is that the uses of *qatal* to be examined here are often considered remnants of "archaic" meanings possessed by the form; see e.g. T. Andersen (2000: 52ff.), Baayen (1997: 281), Blau (1971: 25), G. R. Driver (1936: 12ff., 18, 88). This is certainly possible, but it would be extremely difficult to prove on the basis of this fairly small corpus of "archaic" texts (assuming, moreover, that one accepts them as genuinely archaic). In most cases I do not think it is necessary to appeal to an "archaic" meaning of the form, but cf. § 2.6 below.

[53] It should be remembered that it is possible for the meaning of a verbal form to be neutralized by its syntactic environment (Comrie 1985: 31f., 102ff.). This could be the case in conditional statements, as the perfect appears to be regularly used with a non-past meaning in such statements in several Semitic languages. See e.g. Muraoka and Porten § 84 *i*, Sivan (1997: 98; 1998: 91f.), Rainey (1996: 355ff.), Tropper (1993: 236), Hug (1993: 117), M. Smith (1991: 8), Folmer (1991: 58f., 1995: 394ff.), Krahmalkov (1986), Fitzmyer (1956: 187f.). In my judgment, conditional statements require a separate syntactic-semantic study, and hence will be excluded here.

[54] It is possible to draw further distinctions in the non-past sphere, though they cannot be argued in detail here. One of the important points emphasized by Joosten (1989, 1997; cf. Bartelmus 1982: 54ff.) is that *yiqtol* is practically non-existent in Biblical Hebrew as an indicative actual present and that this function is fulfilled by the participle. Consequently it appears that a fairly neat opposition can be established between *yiqtol* as a general present and *qotel* as an actual present (though *qotel* does occur in some general statements; according to Driver 1892: § 135 (2) *obs.* this is a mark of a later period of the language).

Tense:

past (E<S)/anterior (E<R)	*qatal*
non-past (S≤E)/non-anterior (R≤E)	*yiqtol, qotel*

Being aspectually unmarked, *qatal* stands in opposition to *yiqtol* and *qotel*, which, when used in a past context,[55] function as iterative-habitual and progressive pasts, respectively.[56] In this study I have opted to label these functions as aspectually imperfective, though other descriptions are possible.[57]

Aspect:

aspectually unmarked past	*qatal*
imperfective past	
iterative-habitual past[58]	*yiqtol*
progressive past	*qotel*

As far as the parameters of tense and aspect are concerned, the inverted forms *wayyiqtol* (<*yaqtul) and *weqatalti* are treated here as syntactic variants for *qatal* and *yiqtol*, respectively.[59]

In opting for this particular theory I have been guided by the following factors:[60]

Likewise, when referring to future time we can establish the opposition future vs. *futurum instans* (on degrees of remoteness in tense systems see Fleischman 1989, Chung and Timberlake 1985: 207ff., Dahl 1983, Comrie 1981, Denz 1971: 15).

[55] This is not inconsistent with the fact that they refer to non-past situations if we understand *qatal* to be the marked term in regard to the expression of tense; in other words, "non-past" is to be understood as a neutral, rather than a negative, value. Cf. Kurylowicz (1972: 80).

[56] On this functional difference between past *yiqtol* and *qotel* see Joosten (1999); cf. Bombeck (1997: 124, 185).

[57] See e.g. Comrie (1985: 25ff.); cf. Binnick (1991: 155), Lyons (1977: 681). Joosten (1997, 1999) has presented some stimulating arguments for viewing all of the functions of *yiqtol* as essentially modal, including its iterative-habitual function. Muraoka (1999: 192) has also come into question the traditional view (as represented by e.g. Joüon and Muraoka § 121 *c, h*) that the participle marks durative aspect, preferring to characterize it as indicating "concomitance" (cf. D. Cohen 1984: 302). (If I am not mistaken, this is equivalent to the "overlapping" relation discussed in § 1.2 above.) Neither of these alternative analyses significantly affects our working theory regarding the semantic value of *qatal*, which is the primary concern of this study, and hence we will not pursue these questions in detail here.

[58] *Yiqtol* can also function as a future-in-the-past; cf. Joosten (1999).

[59] Cf. e.g. Rabin (1984: 394f.), Blau (1971: 24f.); contrast Pascual (1995: 109f.). This description is a provisional one, for it is quite likely that a complete description of these forms would involve discourse-oriented parameters such as "sequence" (cf. Gropp 1991, Gentry 1998: 13, Groß 1976: 163ff., Bartelmus 1982: 43).

First, I feel obliged to adopt a theory which makes use of the standard linguistic categories of tense and aspect. While the indicative functions of the verbal forms may involve other semantic parameters, I find it *a priori* unlikely that tense and/or aspect would not be expressed to some extent. Consequently I think that one must eschew theories which do not involve at least one of these parameters in a significant way.[61]

Second, as mentioned above (§ 1.1), an exclusively aspectual analysis of the Hebrew verb is not without its difficulties. Cross-linguistic evidence indicates that Classical Hebrew would possess an atypical aspectual system.[62] For example, the future tense is typically perfective rather than imperfective, and the use of Hebrew *yiqtol* for the future would be peculiar if it were only marked for "imperfective" aspect.[63]

Third, an approach based on a combination of tense and aspect is sufficient in the overwhelming amount of instances in prose and a considerable number of cases in poetry as well.[64] This is, without a doubt, largely the reason why tense has been considered an important element of the verbal system since the beginning of formal linguistic reflection on Biblical Hebrew by the medieval Jewish grammarians: It is a reasonably simple and coherent theory which is capable of explaining a significant amount of data (cf. § 1.1). This combination of simplicity and explanatory power should make us reluctant to give it up on the basis of a com-

---

[60] In contrast to Tropper (1998: 155), comparative Semitic data plays a relatively small role in our synchronic understanding of the Hebrew verb (though it is very significant for our diachronic understanding of the verbal system). This is not because we feel that such data is irrelevant or uninteresting, but is due in the first place to the simple fact that the semantics of the verbal system is a matter of debate for practically every ancient Semitic language (cf. Nebes 1999), which naturally makes cross-Semitic comparison extremely precarious. Moreover, in my judgment, an approach such as Tropper's fails to do justice to the significant structural differences between the various Semitic verbal systems. Cf. Kurylowicz (1972: 80): "It would be an elementary error to speak of a *Common Semitic* verbal system since the functions depend on the number of the forms represented in the conjugational system." See also Hoftijzer (1974: 12f.).

[61] Such as e.g. Michel (1960) and Kustár (1972). Baayen goes so far as to argue that *qatal* has no semantic value of its own and that it is to be understood entirely in pragmatic terms, though he admits that this is "exceptional" for a verb form (1997: 281); cf. also Peckham (1997).

[62] See especially DeCaen (1995: 61, 175ff.).

[63] Hughes (1993: 134); cf. Kurylowicz (1972: 79). It is indeed possible for imperfective forms to be used to refer to future events (Givón 1984: 277), yet it must be remembered that such forms are often marked for tense as well as aspect. Tropper (1998: 160f.) argues that in Semitic (including Hebrew) this use of "imperfective" *yaqtulu* for the future is an extension of its use for the present (compare e.g. "I'm leaving for Chicago tomorrow"). Such an explanation does not apply to Hebrew *yiqtol*, however, as it does not mark the indicative actual present (n.54 above); Tropper's analysis applies to the participle as *futurum instans* instead. Compare e.g. Baayen (1997: 255): "it is impossible to analyze the function of the *yiqtol* as either perfective or imperfective... its semantic function cannot be an aspectual one."

[64] Cf. Blau (1971: 25f.).

paratively small number of exceptions. An attempt should certainly be made to explain these exceptions more adequately, and that is precisely what we consider the present study to be.[65]

The third reason just mentioned assumes in its turn that prose texts provide a reasonable starting point for the study of the verbal system. O'Connor rightly observes that "the most complex segment of poetic diction involves the verbal system",[66] and, given the greater ambiguity of poetry and its much wider range of interpretive possibilities,[67] it is methodologically preferable to begin one's examination of the functions of the verb with the clearer instances of prose and then to move to the study of poetic texts. It is for this reason that many studies of the Hebrew verbal system deal exclusively with prose, and given the number and complexity of problems involved in analyzing the verb this decision is a very practical one. However, some unfortunate problems can arise when poetry and prose are too widely separated. It has been noted that most of the difficult or uncommon uses of verbal forms (such as allegedly non-past *qatals*) occur in poetry,[68] and this has led some scholars to claim that the functions of the verb in poetry radically differ from its functions in prose.[69] Such is the claim, for example, of Michel's important monograph *Tempora und Satzstellung in den Psalmen*. While it is of course theoretically possible that a language could possess a single morphosyntactic system with completely different semantic values in poetry and prose, it does not strike me as very likely (I am not aware of any other language for which this has been demonstrated to be the case).[70] In any event, such a hypothesis would require some unequivocal evidence to support it. Other

---

[65] See DeCaen (1995: 236); cf. Dempsey (1988: 12) and Heimerdinger (1999: 16 n.9): "A more systematic examination of the counter-examples [to aspectual or tense-based theories] would cause the numer [sic] of peremptory statements made by scholars to be reduced."

[66] O'Connor (1980: 145).

[67] Craigie (1983: 111), Bergsträsser § 6 *i*.

[68] Bergsträsser § 6 *i*, Dempsey (1988: 7ff.), Gropp (1991: 46), Joüon and Muraoka § 111 *a*. However, Bergsträsser also claims (§ 6 *g*): "Obgleich die Mehrzahl der Beispiele aus poetischen Stücken stammt, ist doch die Zahl der prosaischen Belege groß genug zu zeigen, daß es sich nicht nur um dichterisch freien Gebrauch der Tempora handelt."

[69] Cf. e.g. Hatav (1997: 24), Gosling (1992), Niccacci (1990: 10, 194ff.), Segert (1984: 88), Fensham (1978), Michel (1960).

[70] It is naturally not being claimed here that the language of poetry and of prose are identical in every respect, for there are clear differences between the two genres in many languages. As far as I am aware, however, these differences do not involve the *semantic value* of verbal forms but rather to other linguistic features (word order, lexicon, etc.). Even an observable difference between Hebrew poetry and prose such as the use of the free-standing preterital *yiqtol* (**yaqtul*) relates not to the semantic value of the verbal form itself but rather to its frequency of use and distribution in different literary genres. Furthermore, in many languages a speaker has some freedom to ignore grammatical rules for stylistic or rhetorical reasons ("poetic license"). I consider this to be a question of poetics, not grammar.

scholars do not go so far as to claim that the Hebrew verb possesses a different semantic value in poetry as opposed to prose, but nonetheless draw significant conclusions regarding the verb on the basis of a relatively small number of poetic examples.[71] As we have already pointed out, however, the interpretation of these examples is frequently open to debate, and consequently I would argue that the utmost caution is necessary when attempting to integrate them into a description of the verbal system as a whole.[72] This is of course not to say that the verbal system in poetic texts should be neglected. Taking Occam's razor again into account (cf. § 1.1), it is clear that a unified model of the Hebrew verb which applies to poetry as well as prose is to be preferred to two separate models for each literary genre.[73] The present investigation is thus very much interested in the question of whether or not such a model is possible for Classical Hebrew, though to address this question completely would require much more than one monograph. Nevertheless, it is hoped that this study will be able to provide at least a partial answer by focusing on alleged examples of non-past *qatal*.[74]

---

[71] E.g. Tropper (1998).

[72] See Groß (1976: 5ff., 10f.), Hendel (1996: 153), Buth (1986: 32).

[73] Cf. § 1.1; see also Dempsey (1988: 10ff.), Groß (1976: 13).

[74] It would be impossible to anticipate every possible example of a non-past *qatal* that could be cited. The examples discussed in the following chapters are drawn from the grammatical and exegetical literature and our own reading of the Hebrew Bible. A complete catalogue of *qatal* forms, such as Dempsey (1988) provides for every verbal form occurring in Isaiah 40-55, could not be attempted, given the much wider corpus of the present study. Nevertheless, I believe that a significant amount of examples have been dealt with, and certainly the ones most frequently cited.

§ 2. THE GNOMIC PERFECT

In Greek one encounters aorist verbal forms in proverbs and gnomic statements which do not appear to refer to the past but rather to the present. In Reichenbachian terms the present tense is analyzed as follows (cf. § 1.2):

$$
\begin{array}{ll}
\textit{absolute}: & S=E \\
\textit{relative}: & R=E
\end{array}
$$

Yet this should not be taken to mean that the situations referred to in such statements are thought to be occurring precisely at the moment of utterance.[1] We can express this difference by distinguishing between a "general present" and an "actual present"; this so-called "gnomic aorist" expresses the former, not the latter.

The gnomic aorist has been the subject of a number of grammatical studies,[2] and though it is generally agreed that it is distinct from an aorist which simply reports a past event,[3] there nonetheless remains disagreement as to how this use is to be understood. Some grammarians describe it as expressing a general truth which is based on a past observation or experience. According to Smyth, for example, "The aorist simply states a past occurrence and leaves the reader to draw the inference from a concrete case that what has occurred once is typical of what often occurs".[4] Similarly, Kühner and Gerth state:

> Wahrheiten und allgemeine Urteile, welche auf Erfahrung gegründet sind, sowie Erscheinungen, welche in der Vergangenheit öfters wahrgenommen sind, werden von den Griechen häufig durch den Indikativ des Aorists als etwas einfach Geschehenes, als etwas, das sich einmal in der Vergangenheit ereignete, ausgesprochen, indem sie in objektiver Sinnlichkeit den einzelnen konkreten Fall, in dem sich jene allgemeinen Gedanken und Erscheinungen bethätigten, auffassen und es dem Hörer überlassen, aus der einzelnen Beobachtung das allgemeine Urteil zu ziehen... Dass es gegebenenfalls jederzeit wieder vorkommen kann, ist

---

[1] Cf. Lyons (1977: 681), Binnick (1991: 129).
[2] For a survey of the discussion see Porter (1989: 218ff.).
[3] E.g. Smyth (§§ 1930, 1931), J. Humbert (1945: 124ff.).
[4] Smyth (§ 1931).

nicht ausgesprochen, wird aber vom Hörer ebenso wie vom Redenden hinzuergänzt.[5]

Humbert, on the other hand, denies any temporal value to the gnomic aorist, attributing it rather to aspect alone. He comments:

> Il est certain que l'aoriste d'expérience a aidé au développement de l'aoriste gnomique, et qu'on pouvait passer facilement de « *on a toujours vu* » à « *on voit* (toujours) ». Cependant, malgré des échanges entre ces deux types d'aoriste, rien n'est, dans son principe, plus différent de l'aoriste gnomique que l'aoriste d'expérience.[6]

An aspectual explanation has been accepted by a number of other scholars.[7] Nevertheless, despite the numerous studies devoted to the subject, at present no consensus exists as to how the Greek gnomic aorist is to be explained.

§ 2.1 Previous Discussion

A number of Hebrew grammarians have argued that in certain instances fientive *qatal* does not refer to the past but rather appears to have the meaning of a general present.[8] The similarity to the Greek gnomic aorist has not gone unnoticed, and hence one occasionally encounters the term "gnomic perfect".[9] In contrast to the situation in Greek grammar, however, there has been no study devoted exclusively to the Hebrew gnomic perfect.

According to many scholars, the gnomic perfect expresses a truth known from experience. Thus Driver states that *qatal* "is used to express general truths known to have actually occurred, and so proved from experience: here again the idiomatic rendering in English is by means of the present".[10] Others relate the gnomic perfect to the use of *qatal* as a "global" past tense. Joüon and Muraoka write:

---

[5] Kühner and Gerth (§ 386 7).

[6] J. Humbert (1945: 124ff.).

[7] See Porter (1989: 211ff.). Other explanations have been proposed which do not relate to either tense or aspect but rather to stylistic issues (e.g. Elmer 1894).

[8] E.g. Ewald § 135 *b*, Böttcher § 940, Gesenius-Kautzsch-Cowley § 106 *k*, Driver § 12, Davidson § 40 *c*, Bergsträsser § 6 *f*, Gibson § 57 *c*, Waltke and O'Connor § 30.5.1 *c*, Isaksson (1987: 75ff.).

[9] Van der Merwe-Naudé-Kroeze (1999: 146), Kottsieper (1999: 70), Müller (1986: 368 n.16).

[10] Driver § 12. See also Gesenius-Kautzsch-Cowley § 106 *k*, Davidson § 40 *c*, Bergsträsser § 6 *f*, DeCaen (1995: 13).

The *unity* of the action can, and sometimes must, be emphasised in our languages. Thus ... Jdg 19.30 means: "such a thing has not been done (*not even once*), has *never* been done" (Vulg. *nunquam*) ... Therein lies the explanation of the use of qatal to express a permanent truth: ... Ps 9.11 "you have *never* abandoned those who look for you, O Yahweh!," which is more or less equivalent to *you do not abandon*.

On the other hand all the actions of a series or of a category can be considered in a global way...; thus one can explain the use of qatal in certain cases, especially for truths of experience...[11]

For the idea of a "global" past tense one may compare the comments of Zerwick on the Greek aorist:

the action expressed by the aorist may have occupied a long time, or the reference may be to an act frequently repeated; the aorist will be used so long as the writer wishes simply to record the fact of the act or acts, and not to represent the action as in progress or habitual, i.e. so long as the whole activity expressed by the verb is regarded «globally».[12]

König had already expressed views similar to Joüon's. He takes a case such as Ps 84.4 מָצְאָה as "hat (schon und noch immer) gefunden" and argues: "Dies ist temporale Characteristik a potiori, mit dem Blick auf die Vergangenheit als die grundlegende Zeitsphäre, von der allein die Beobachtung hergenommen sein kann, wie beim Aoristus gnomicus".[13] A similar approach, though from an aspectual point of view, is taken by Irsigler:

Ist der ausgedrückte Sachverhalt generell, so wird durch [Suffixkonjugation] die Abgeschlossenheit der 'Globalaktion' bezeichnet: Rückschauend wird ein gewohnheitsmäßiges Geschehen als Erfahrung konstatiert, die auch eine künftige Fortsetzung folgern läßt. (Typ: "Er hat das bisher noch immer getan").[14]

---

[11] Joüon and Muraoka § 112 *d*.

[12] Zerwick § 253: Compare also Fanning (1990: 166): "The present gives emphasis to the iterative nature of the occurrence. The *aorist* gives a summary or composite view of the multiple situations, with no emphasis on the repetition."

[13] König § 126. In his Psalms commentary he makes continual reference to his discussion of Ps 115.3 (כֹּל אֲשֶׁר־חָפֵץ עָשָׂה), where he comments, "alles, woran er Gefallen findet, auch von jeher getan hat (Sy. § 126: ein Aoristus gnomicus), deshalb auch zu tun pflegt." That he does not understand this as a present-referring *qatal* is clear from his discussion of Ps 14, where he takes issue with Gunkel's view that the perfect of fientive verbs may be understood as a present. Similar comments can be found in his commentary on Job.

[14] Irsigler (1978: 159); similarly Groß (1982: 63 n.148) on the "Erfahrungssatz". Cf. also Denz (1971: 18ff.). This analysis is disputed by Kottsieper (1999: 70 n.66); cf. Mayer (1992).

Despite the disagreement as to the basic semantic value of the verbal forms, it seems to me that these two explanations are quite similar in attributing the gnomic perfect to a type of global reference to the past. Other scholars also explain this use in terms of perfective aspect,[15] though without the temporal factor mentioned by Irsigler. For example, Waltke and O'Connor contrast the gnomic perfective with the "habitual non-perfective" (i.e. *yiqtol*):

> By *habitual non-perfective* we mean the representation of a repeated general, non-specific situation. Rarely in prose, but rather frequently in poetry and proverbial expressions, the non-perfective is used to denote habitual activity with no specific tense value. It forms a fitting parallel with the gnomic perfective... Whereas the gnomic perfective conceives of a universal state or event as a single event, the habitual non-perfective represents the internal temporal phases of the general situation as occurring over and over again, including the time present to the act of speaking.[16]

Andersen also attributes this use of *qatal* to aspect but, interestingly, takes it as supporting an imperfective rather than a perfective analysis of the verb form.[17] Others attempt to explain the gnomic perfect diachronically. G. R. Driver, for example, argued that *qatal* was originally a "universal present" (cf. Akkadian *paris*) and that the use of *qatal* in gnomic statements is a survival from an older stage of the language.[18]

§ 2.2 Post-Biblical Hebrew

The gnomic perfect does not appear to be attested in Qumran or Mishnaic Hebrew.[19] Van Peursen has noted a number of examples of "truths of experience" in Ben Sira in which *qatal* is "used for a series of actions or for a number of actions belonging to a category".[20] For example:

1. 8.2 (ms. A)

כי רבים הפחיז זהב

---

[15] Tropper (1998: 183, cf. 172ff.), Hendel (1996: 156 n.20), Waltke and O'Connor § 30.5.1 *c*, Cohen (1924: 29f.).

[16] Waltke and O'Connor § 31.3 *e*.

[17] T. Andersen (2000: 54).

[18] G. R. Driver (1936:12ff.; 18, 88). See also Gibson § 56 and § 57 *c*, Joosten (1989: 157), Eskhult (1990: 21), Isaksson (1987: 83), Meyer § 101 2b, Müller (1986: 368 n.16); cf. Fensham (1978).

[19] Kesterson (1984: 6f.), Thorion-Vardi (1985), DeVries (1964: 412), Segal § 306, Pérez-Fernández (1997: 115ff.), Sharvit (1980: 111).

[20] Van Peursen (1999: 63f.).

"for gold has unsettled many".

2.   9.8 (ms. A)

בעד אשה [ה]שחתו רבים

"through a woman, many have been ruined".[21]

This use is then related to the "gnomic" perfect:

3.   30.22 (ms. B)

וגיל אדם האריך אפו

"and a man's cheerfulness makes him patient".

4.   12.3 (ms. A)

וגם צדקה לא עשה

"it is no act of mercy that he does".

5.   20.13 (ms. C)

חכם במעט דבר נפשו

"a wise man with a little utters his desire".[22]

On this latter function, however, Van Peursen comments:

> It is a debatable issue whether we can really say that *qatal* has (general) present tense meaning when it is used in maxims, proverbs, general rules and the like. It is also possible to classify the gnomic use of *qatal* under the 'truths of experience' discussed in the preceding paragraph... The verb form itself has past tense value, but the statement is valid for all time spheres, since 'a fact of the past is exhibited as a rule for all time'.[23]

§ 2.3 Comparative Semitics

A gnomic perfect is attested in Ugaritic,[24] Aramaic,[25] Arabic[26] and Ethiopic.[27] As an analogy one should also note that Akkadian attests a "gnomic preterite".[28]

---

[21] See also: 11.5, 6 (ms. A); 30.23 (ms. B); 31[34].6, 25 (ms. B); 37.31 (ms. D).

[22] See also: 4.11 (ms. A); 6.13[14] (ms. A); 10.14 (ms. A); 39.22 (ms. B).

[23] Van Peursen (1999: 63); the concluding citation is from Driver § 12.

[24] Tropper (2000: 715) only mentions two examples, however, and they are questionable. One example (1.15:I:2 *mẓma yd mṭkt* "dem Dürstenden reicht sie die Hand") occurs in a broken context, and is rendered as a past by e.g. Aistleitner (1959: 95) and Jirku (1962: 95). The other example (1.16:VI:32 *šqlt b glt ydk* "Bei Ungerechtigkeit hängt dein Arm (tatenlos) herab") is rendered as a past by e.g. Greenstein (1997: 41), Del Olmo Lete

§ 2.4 "Gnomic" Statements

It should first be remarked that the term "gnomic" is sometimes used in a formal sense and sometimes in a semantic one.[29] As a formal description, a "gnomic statement" is typically understood to refer to a proverb or a proverb-like utterance. As a semantic description, a "gnomic statement" is often understood to refer to an utterance which expresses e.g. a general, "eternal" or "timeless truth" or a generic situation which holds for all time (past, present and future).[30] There is obviously a connection between the formal and semantic uses of the term: Proverbs as a literary form are typically understood as expressing general or timeless truths, i.e. as expressing semantically "gnomic" propositions.[31] Two cautions are necessary here, however. First, it should be pointed out that a precise definition of a "proverb" as a literary form has proved elusive.[32] Hence the term "gnomic" lacks precision even when used in a strictly formal sense. Second, the term "gnomic" also lacks clarity as a semantic description, as is clear from the varying ways in which the term is defined (cf. above). Lyons writes,

> It is in the nature of things that the term 'gnomic' cannot be given a very precise definition. But it is a useful term, the more so as it is often much

---

(1981: 321), Caquot-Sznycer-Herdner (1974: 572), Gordon (1965: 464), J. Gray (1964: 28), Jirku (1962: 113).

[25] See e.g. Fitzmyer (1956: 172, 177f.), Segert (1975: § 6.6.3.2.2 *l*), Lindenberger (1974: 200; 1983: 95), Muraoka and Porten § 51 *d*; cf. Rogland (2003: 422f.). Müller (1991:15) argues for a gnomic perfect in the Deir 'Alla texts (e.g. I 13 *wšm'w* "und sie hören", I 14 *hzw* "sie sehen"), yet it is debated whether these are to be parsed as imperatives or perfects (so Müller originally, see 1982: 227 and cf. Hoftijzer and Van der Kooij 1976: 208ff.). McCarter (1980: 51f.) interprets these as past tenses (cf. Caquot and Lemaire 1977: 199f.), though according to Sasson (1986: 286) and Garbini (1979: 179, 181f.) these are prophetic perfects (contrast Müller 1991: 15).

[26] Cohen (1924: 29f.), Reckendorf (1921: 56f.), G. R. Driver (1936: 116), Aartun (1963: 68ff.).

[27] Dillmann § 152 b.

[28] Mayer (1992). As with Greek and Hebrew, it is debated how this use of the preterite is to be explained: Mayer (1992: 390) argues that *iprus* "dient hier *direkt* für zeitstellenwertlose Aussagen und hat keine Vergangenheitsbedeutung", whereas Streck (1995: 145ff.) disputes this and thinks that a general statement is being made on the basis of a past experience. These differing analyses are undoubtedly due, at least in part, to opposing views concerning the semantics of the Akkadian verbal system (cf. above, p.12 n.60).

[29] Cf. Lyons (1977: 681).

[30] See e.g. Binnick (1991: 129), Bybee-Perkins-Pagliuca (1994: 126, 319).

[31] See e.g. Isaksson (1987: 90).

[32] See e.g. Nel (1982: 14 n.40), Wehrle (1993: 14f.), Röhrich and Mieder (1977: 2).

easier to decide that an utterance is gnomic than that it is to decide whether it expresses a timeless or omnitemporal proposition.[33]

In my judgment, this lack of precision makes the term a rather infelicitous one, though it appears to be too firmly entrenched in the literature to avoid it entirely. My own preference is to speak of "proverbs" on a formal level and of "general truths" on a semantic one.

Of primary interest to the present study is the question of tenses used in general truths or proverbs. Some argue that the present tense is the normal one with which to express general truths.[34] Accordingly, given the common assumption that proverbs express general truths, it should come as no surprise that some have argued that proverbs *require* a present tense. For example, in discussing Qoh 7.19 Isaksson remarks, "Since the verse is a proverb, a present tense rendering of *hayu* is inevitable".[35] On the other hand, some scholars think that general truths have nothing to do with time at all:

> we should not be misled by the implications of the traditional term 'present tense' into thinking that the so-called general truths embodied in gnomic utterances have anything to do with present time. Their temporal status, if they are time-bound, is non-deictic.[36]

It is not the purpose of the present study to attempt to provide a comprehensive discussion of such issues. It is suggested here, however, that some commonly accepted generalizations about proverbs are not, in fact, valid in all cases. Consider the following examples taken from some collections of proverbs:[37]

---

[33] Lyons (1977: 681). Both Lyons (*ibid.*) and Dahl (1975: 100 n.1) argue that the terms "generic" and "gnomic", though overlapping to some degree, are not equivalent. Both admit that this is a vague distinction, however.

[34] Lawler describes "gnomic", "timeless", "habitual", or "generic" statements as a "present tense construction" (1972: 247); see also Bybee-Perkins-Pagliuca (1994: 126). Porter (1989: 217) considers "omnitemporal reference" to belong to the non-past sphere.

[35] Isaksson (1987: 90). Being a stative verb, הָיָה may naturally refer to the present; the point is that Isaksson argues for a present tense meaning on the basis of genre alone. Cf. Zuber (1986: 97 n.8).

[36] Lyons (1977: 681); cf. also Binnick (1991: 129). However, it should be noted that Lyons (1968: 304f.; 1977: 682, 689; 1995: 313) defines "deixis" in terms of the moment of speaking (S), which by definition appears to deny that relative tenses are "deictic". For our objections to this definition see above, p.7 n.34; see further § 2.5.4 below.

[37] Cf. the appendix to this chapter.

6.   Seeing his friend being disemboweled, he asked "Will you give me some for my cat?" (Arabic)

7.   Too much water drowned the miller. (English)

Such proverbs are not describing general truths but rather refer to extraordinary or uncommon situations. Scott points out that proverbs not only express what happens generally but also "what is *contrary to right order*: the irregular, absurd, paradoxical, and impossible."[38] It is therefore an oversimplification to view all proverbs as statements of general truths. It is also important to observe that the two examples just cited demonstrate that past tense forms can occur in proverbs. In fact, this occurs much more frequently than is generally recognized, and in the appendix to this chapter we have collected a number of past tense proverbs from various languages. While it is perhaps statistically the case that proverbs most frequently utilize the present tense, it cannot be maintained that this is the "proper" tense for them.

It should also be pointed out that "general truths" are not restricted to the present tense, but can be found in other temporal spheres. Binnick mentions the following examples:

8.   Two and two make four.

9.   Men were deceivers ever.

10.   The poet will go to any end to make a rhyme.

He points out that "in many languages there seems to be great latitude in the use of tenses to make such [viz., gnomic] statements."[39] General statements can be made in any of the temporal spheres, and it would thus be possible to express the same basic idea with different tense forms. Compare example 11 with some hypothetical versions of the same proverb:

11.   Never a duck was hatched by a drake.

12.   *Never a duck is hatched by a drake.

13.   *Never a duck will be hatched by a drake.

---

[38] Scott (1965: 6); cf. Röhrich and Mieder (1977: 2).
[39] Binnick (1991: 129); see also Lyons (1977: 680), Dahl (1975: 103), Denz (1971: 18ff.).

All of these examples are expressing very similar ideas, yet this can hardly mean that the English tenses are simply interchangeable or have lost their semantic marking.[40] The verbal forms are still to be understood as *tense* forms: example 12 indicates *the way things typically happen now*, example 13 indicates the way things *will typically happen*, and example 11 indicates *the way things have typically happened*. In all of these cases there is of course an implication that what holds true for the one temporal sphere holds true for the others. At least, it is very difficult to imagine that someone could affirm "Never a duck *was* hatched by a drake" but also deny "Never a duck *is* hatched by a drake." Yet this is a question of what may be legitimately *inferred* from an utterance, i.e. it is primarily a matter of pragmatics rather than semantics.[41] I would therefore argue that examples such as 9 and 11 make it necessary to speak of a "general past" just as one speaks of a "general present".[42] Lyons remarks that "we can base our assertion of a general truth upon the evidence of our past experience: hence the use of the past, rather than the non-past, tense for the expression of gnomic propositions in certain languages."[43]

§ 2.5 Textual Studies

The preceding discussion has attempted to demonstrate that some common assumptions regarding proverbs, though of course valid in many cases, do not apply to a number of examples and can occasionally prove misleading. Most importantly, we have seen that the assumption that proverbs do not utilize past tenses is unfounded. Hence it must be emphasized that one should not automatically assume that a *qatal* form which occurs in Hebrew proverbs has a general present meaning. In order to avoid being misled by some of these common assumptions concerning "gnomic statements", I have collected examples of past tense usage in proverbs from a variety of languages (see the appendix) in order to compare them with the Biblical examples. This is a limited sampling and is not meant to be anything like a comprehensive linguistic examination of proverbial expressions, yet even a brief investigation has revealed a sig-

---

[40] Contrast Binnick, who claims that gnomic tenses "do not relate ... to any definite times at all" (1991: 129; see also the quote by Lyons above). I think it would be more accurate to say that they do not point to a specific *situation* or *occurrence*; i.e. they are not deictic with regard to a particular event or individual.

[41] Cf. Denz (1971: 20), Kühner and Gerth § 386 7, Elmer (1894: lx). It should be observed that there are very few proverbs (I am not aware of any, in fact) which explicitly state that they have held, hold, and will hold true for all time, *pace* the definition of "gnomic statements" of e.g. Bybee-Perkins-Pagliuca (1994: 319; cf. Lyons' "omnitemporal statement", 1977: 680f.).

[42] Cf. Denz (1971: 18ff.).

[43] Lyons (1977: 681).

nificant amount of past tense proverbs with a wide range of tense usage, and this will be incorporated into the following textual studies.

The examples to be examined below have been drawn primarily from the standard grammars and specialized studies. In many cases one could legitimately question whether or not the example cited is in fact a proverb. I have nevertheless chosen to include these in the discussion because our concern here is not so much one of genre but whether or not fientive *qatal* has a general present meaning. I have excluded textually problematic examples,[44] conditional statements,[45] interrogatives[46] and possible prophetic[47] or performative[48] perfects. Furthermore, stative verbs are excluded here since it is well-established that the *qatal* of stative verbs can refer to the present, and a general present meaning is therefore not problematic in regard to the semantics of the form.[49]

§ 2.5.1 *Proverbs Reporting an Experience or Observation*

We have already seen some examples of proverbs which utilize past tenses (§ 2.4):

14.   Seeing his friend being disemboweled, he asked "Will you give me some for my cat?"

15.   Too much water drowned the miller.

Such examples purport to be relating a particular experience or observation, and the verb is consequently to be understood as having a past reference. The situations described in these proverbs are not to be viewed as regular, habitual, or frequent occurrences.[50] This is typically clear on

---

[44] 1 S 20.2 (read *Qere* עשה); Ps 10.3; 49.15; 73.7; 90.5 (see Bartelmus 1982: 132); Pr 14.1. Joel 2.6 is too uncertain lexically to function as a useful example.

[45] Ezek 33.15; Job 7.13.

[46] Cf. above, p.10 n.50. Excluded here are: Ps 2.1; 11.3; 14.4; Job 10.3; 36.23.

[47] See § 3. Possible examples: Is 18.5; 26.9f.; 31.2; 57.1; Job 5.20; 11.20; Ps 20.7; 37.20, 38; 64.8ff.; 110.5f; 146.4; Pr 4.11 (הִדְרַכְתִּיךָ, הִרְתִּיךָ); prophetic according to Böttcher § 947).

[48] Some alleged gnomics are taken as performatives by other scholars (cf. chapter 4), but most could be understood as past tenses: Pr 22.19 (הוֹדַעְתִּיךָ; cf. RSV); 30.7 (שָׁאַלְתִּי; cf. *Traduction œcuménique*); Ps 31.15 (אָמַרְתִּי; cf. König).

[49] היה (Ps 14.3); ידע (Is 1.3; Jer 8.7a); זכר (Ps 9.13; 88.6); שכח (Ps 9.13; Pr 2.17); רוש (Ps 34.11); תאב (Ps 119.40); שאן (Job 3.18a); שגב (Job 5.11); שכב (Qoh 2.23); רבב (Qoh 5.10); גבר (Ps 103.11).

[50] This is not necessarily to say that they could not be *translated* as general occurrences, however. It is quite possible that these situations, which are presented as specific occur-

pragmatic grounds, i.e. the nature of the situation described is too extraordinary to be considered a common occurrence. As Lawler points out, for a statement to be considered a general truth it needs to be true "more often than only occasionally".[51]

Examples:

16.　Pr 22.13

אָמַר עָצֵל אֲרִי בַחוּץ

"A lazy one said, 'There's a lion outside!'"[52]

17.　Pr 21.22

עִיר גִּבֹּרִים עָלָה חָכָם וַיֹּרֶד עֹז מִבְטֶחָה

"A wise man went up against a city of warriors, and brought down the strength in which it trusted."

18.　Pr 14.6

בִּקֶּשׁ־לֵץ חָכְמָה וָאָיִן

"A scoffer sought wisdom but there wasn't any."[53]

19.　Pr 19.24

טָמַן עָצֵל יָדוֹ בַּצַּלָּחַת גַּם־אֶל־פִּיהוּ לֹא יְשִׁיבֶנָּה:

"A lazy one buried his hand in the pot; he would not bring it back even to his mouth."[54]

20.　Pr 28.1

נָסוּ וְאֵין־רֹדֵף רָשָׁע וְצַדִּיקִים כִּכְפִיר יִבְטָח:

"The wicked fled, but there was no pursuer; but the righteous are as confident as a lion."

---

rences, are understood to have a normative or exemplary character. Precisely how these examples should be translated will depend to a certain extent on the structure of the target language.

[51] Lawler (1972: 254).

[52] Also Pr 26.13. In Joüon and Muraoka § 112 *d* it is pointed out that examples such as this are not gnomic but "are better explained as due to the author having a typical case in mind." Compare the examples of the "Sagte-Sprichtwort" in Röhrich and Mieder (1977: 11ff.), e.g. "Aller Anfang ist schwer, sagte der Dieb, da stahl er einen Amboß", "Was ich nicht weiss, macht mich nicht heiss, sagte der Ochse, als er gebraten wurde."

[53] Despite Delitzsch's present tense translation he remarks, "The general sentence is concrete, composed in the common historical form." See also his remarks *ad* 11.2, 8 (examples 22 and 23 below).

[54] Also Pr 26.15.

Although we find *qatal* in parallelism to *yiqtol* here, we could simply be dealing with a contrast between a particular observation and a general statement.

21. Ps 7.16

בּוֹר כָּרָה וַיַּחְפְּרֵהוּ וַיִּפֹּל בְּשַׁחַת יִפְעָל׃

"He dug a pit and hollowed it out, and he fell into the pit which he made."[55]

The poet could have a particular enemy in mind in this case, and hence a simple preterital meaning is fitting.

In other examples it seems to be primarily the narrative style which indicates that a particular event in the past is being described, rather than the unusualness of the situation described:

22. Pr 11.2

בָּא־זָדוֹן וַיָּבֹא קָלוֹן

"Pride came, and then came disgrace."[56]

23. Pr 11.8

צַדִּיק מִצָּרָה נֶחֱלָץ וַיָּבֹא רָשָׁע תַּחְתָּיו׃

"A righteous man was delivered from trouble, and a wicked man came in his place."[57]

24. Pr 18.22

מָצָא אִשָּׁה מָצָא טוֹב וַיָּפֶק רָצוֹן מֵיהוָה׃

"He found a wife, he found a good thing, and he received favor from YHWH."

25. Pr 27.12

עָרוּם רָאָה רָעָה נִסְתָּר פְּתָאיִם עָבְרוּ נֶעֱנָשׁוּ׃

"A smart one saw evil, hid; simple ones went over, were punished."[58]

---

[55] The use of *yiqtol* has caused some discussion; see Groß (1976: 131). A preterital interpretation seems most likely (Vulgate: *quam fecit*; LXX: ὃν εἰργάσατο). It is worth observing that preterital *yiqtols* not infrequently occur in subordinate clauses; see Van Peursen (1999: 272), Joüon and Muraoka § 113 *ga*.

[56] Cf. Groß (1976: 140).

[57] Cf. *Traduction œcuménique*, Groß (1976: 120). I read נֶחֱלָץ as a perfect in pause (so Brown-Driver-Briggs) rather than as a participle (so Gesenius-Buhl).

[58] Also Pr 22.3.

In other examples the situation is not necessarily strange or extraordinary, but there is nonetheless no particular reason to take *qatal* as non-past:

26.   Pr 11.7

בְּמוֹת אָדָם רָשָׁע תֹּאבַד תִּקְוָה וְתוֹחֶלֶת אוֹנִים אָבָדָה:

"In the death of a wicked man, (his) hope perished; and the hope of strength (wealth?) perished."

Held has argued that תֹּאבַד is a case of the preterital *yiqtol* and not the **yaqtulu* imperfect.[59] This juxtaposition of the preterite and *qatal* of the same verbal root is an attested phenomenon not only in Biblical Hebrew but also in Ugaritic poetry.[60]

27.   Pr 16.26

נֶפֶשׁ עָמֵל עָמְלָה לּוֹ כִּי־אָכַף עָלָיו פִּיהוּ:

"The appetite of a laborer labored for him, for his mouth impelled him."

28.   Pr 22.2

עָשִׁיר וָרָשׁ נִפְגָּשׁוּ עֹשֵׂה כֻלָּם יְהוָה:

"A rich man and a poor man encountered/fought (?) each other; the maker of both of them is YHWH."

The typical interpretation of this example (and Pr 29.13) understands it to refer to the common or general occurrence[61] of a rich man and a poor one "meeting" or "encountering" each other. That an antagonistic relationship is being described here, however, is suggested by Pr 29.13, which speaks of a poor man and a אִישׁ תְּכָכִים "oppressor". Bearing this in mind, it should be noted that in Mishnaic Hebrew the *nifal* of פגשׁ (as well as the *hithpael* and *nithpael*) can have a more violent notion of "to wrestle, fight".[62] Indeed, in Biblical Hebrew itself the *qal* is occasionally used in contexts expressive of hostility (Ex 4.24; Hos 13.8; Pr 17.12). It is possible that this proverb refers to a rich man/oppressor "fighting" or "struggling" with a poor one; one should note that the Peshitta's ܦܓܥ can also have a violent notion (cf. Hebrew פגע). If this is the case then it does not seem necessary to understand this as referring to a general occurrence but rather to a particular example.

---

[59] Held (1962: 281).

[60] Held (1962), Watson (1994: 240ff.; 1984: 279f.).

[61] Cf. Cohen (1924: 29), Driver § 12.

[62] See Jastrow, *s.v.*

29.   Ps 84.4

גַּם־צִפּוֹר מָצְאָה בַיִת וְגוֹ'

"Even a swallow has found a home..."

The psalmist could simply be reporting something he had observed.

In the Biblical literature some alleged gnomic perfects should be understood as allusions to particular acts of God in the past, such as the creation,[63] rather than as references to a common or habitual activity:

30.   Job 28.25

לַעֲשׂוֹת לָרוּחַ מִשְׁקָל וּמַיִם תִּכֵּן בְּמִדָּה:

"When he gave the wind its weight, and meted out the waters with a measure."

Possibly also the following, though they are more difficult:

31.   Am 5.8

עֹשֵׂה כִימָה וּכְסִיל וְהֹפֵךְ לַבֹּקֶר צַלְמָוֶת וְיוֹם לַיְלָה
הֶחְשִׁיךְ הַקּוֹרֵא לְמֵי־הַיָּם וַיִּשְׁפְּכֵם עַל־פְּנֵי הָאָרֶץ יְהוָה שְׁמוֹ:

"He who made the Pleiades and Orion, and who changed deepest darkness to morning and darkened day to night, who summoned the waters of the sea and poured them out upon the surface of the earth— YHWH is his name."

עֹשֵׂה is most naturally understood as a reference to the creation, and hence it seems possible to take the following וְהֹפֵךְ ... הֶחְשִׁיךְ in a similar fashion. Instead of referring to the constant alternation of day and night, this is perhaps a past tense (cf. Peshitta: ܐܚܫܟ) which alludes to Gen 1.3-5, i.e. to God's original distinguishing between light and darkness/day and night.[64]

32.   Jer 10.12-13 (=51.15-16)

12 עֹשֵׂה אֶרֶץ בְּכֹחוֹ מֵכִין תֵּבֵל בְּחָכְמָתוֹ וּבִתְבוּנָתוֹ נָטָה שָׁמָיִם:
13 לְקוֹל תִּתּוֹ הֲמוֹן מַיִם בַּשָּׁמַיִם וַיַּעֲלֶה נְשִׂאִים מִקְצֵה
הָאָרֶץ בְּרָקִים לַמָּטָר עָשָׂה וַיּוֹצֵא רוּחַ מֵאֹצְרֹתָיו:

---

[63] Cf. Pr 3.19f.; 8.25f.; 16.4; 20.12; Qoh 7.29.

[64] Finley (1981: 262 n.59) appears to suggest this, despite his acceptance of a general present meaning for *qatal* here. It is also possible that this example should be explained according to § 2.5.2 below.

"The one who made the earth by his power, who established the world by his wisdom, and by his understanding stretched out the heavens. When he gave his voice there was a roar of waters in the heavens (?), and he made clouds arise from the ends of the earth, he made lightning for rain, and he brought wind out of his storehouses."

33. Ps 135.7

מַעֲלֶה נְשִׂאִים מִקְצֵה הָאָרֶץ בְּרָקִים לַמָּטָר עָשָׂה
מוֹצֵא־רוּחַ מֵאוֹצְרוֹתָיו:

"The one who made clouds rise from the ends of the earth, who made lightning for rain, who brought wind out of his storehouses."

I think a convincing case can be made that examples 32 and 33 are allusions to Biblical creation imagery, though this can only be briefly sketched out here. The decisive factor is one's interpretation of Gen 2.5-6, which has puzzled commentators:[65]

5 וְכֹל שִׂיחַ הַשָּׂדֶה טֶרֶם יִהְיֶה בָאָרֶץ וְכָל־עֵשֶׂב הַשָּׂדֶה טֶרֶם
יִצְמָח כִּי לֹא הִמְטִיר יְהוָה אֱלֹהִים עַל־הָאָרֶץ וְאָדָם אַיִן לַעֲבֹד
אֶת־הָאֲדָמָה: 6 וְאֵד יַעֲלֶה מִן־הָאָרֶץ וְהִשְׁקָה אֶת־כָּל־פְּנֵי־הָאֲדָמָה:

"And no shrub of the field was yet on the earth, and no grass of the field had yet sprouted, for YHWH God had not caused it to rain upon the earth and there was no man to work the ground. And a rain cloud kept rising/he [viz., YHWH] kept bringing up a rain cloud from the earth and it/he watered all the surface of the ground."

Futato has recently argued that the obscure אֵד should be understood as "rain cloud"[66] and that יַעֲלֶה is to be parsed as *hifil* with God as the subject.[67] If one accepts this interpretation of Gen 2.5-6 then it is not difficult to understand examples 32 and 33 as allusions to this passage. I think

---

[65] See Barr (1987: 423).

[66] Futato (1998). The Targum renders אֵד with עֲנָנָא here and the LXX renders it with νεφέλην in Job 36.27. A point not mentioned by Futato is that this meaning of אֵד is attested in Mishnaic Hebrew (see Jastrow, *s.v.*). For further discussion of אֵד see e.g. Hasel and Hasel (2000), Ellenbogen (1962: 13), Dahood (1981), Barr (1987: 421ff.), Tsumura (1989: 94ff.).

[67] See Futato (1998) for a full treatment. He interprets יַעֲלֶה as inceptive (cf. Waltke and O'Connor § 31.2 c) and takes the clause as consecutive (Gesenius-Kautzsch-Cowley § 166 a; disputed by Tsumura 1989: 96), though he admits that an adversative rendering is possible (cf. Gesenius-Kautzsch-Cowley § 163 a; so Tsumura 1989: 88 n.11, with reference to Andersen 1974: 183). It is quite possible that the inceptive notion is determined by narrative context (cf. Fanning 1990: § 3.5.2; see also § 4.2.4).

this is true even if one parses יַעֲלֶה as *qal* with אֵד as the subject; in that case these examples would be a more explicitly theological reflection on Gen 2.5-6. It should be noted that Jer 10.12 clearly refers to the creation, and this could be the case in Ps 135.6 as well (taking עשׂה in the sense of "make" rather than "do"; cf. König's "er hat gemacht"). Hence it makes excellent contextual sense to view these examples as allusions to the Genesis passage.

Other possible allusions to events in the past:

34.   Ps 111.4-5

4 זֵכֶר עָשָׂה לְנִפְלְאֹתָיו חַנּוּן וְרַחוּם יְהוָה:
5 טֶרֶף נָתַן לִירֵאָיו יִזְכֹּר לְעוֹלָם בְּרִיתוֹ:

"He made a memorial for his wonders; gracious and compassionate is YHWH. He gave food to those who feared him. He will remember/may he remember (?) his covenant forever."

This refers to the institution of the Passover and God's feeding of Israel during the Exodus. The collocation of לְעוֹלָם with the verb יִזְכֹּר in this context most likely indicates futurity,[68] for the general present would probably have been expressed by a stative *qatal* as in Ps 105.8 זָכַר לְעוֹלָם בְּרִיתוֹ (assuming the MT is correct here). The writer thus makes an assertion about the future on the basis of past events. It would also be possible, however, to interpret the *yiqtol* in initial position as jussive.[69]

35.   Nah 1.4

גּוֹעֵר בַּיָּם וַיַּבְּשֵׁהוּ וְכָל־הַנְּהָרוֹת הֶחֱרִיב אֻמְלַל בָּשָׁן
וְכַרְמֶל וּפֶרַח לְבָנוֹן אֻמְלָל:

"He rebuked the sea and dried it up; he made all the rivers dry. Bashan and Carmel withered and the sprout of Lebanon withered."

This could be an allusion to the drying up of the Sea of Reeds[70] or, alternatively, a description of a theophany.[71] Compare the following example:

36.   Ps 97.4-9

4 הֵאִירוּ בְרָקָיו תֵּבֵל רָאֲתָה וַתָּחֵל הָאָרֶץ: 5 הָרִים כַּדּוֹנַג נָמַסּוּ
מִלִּפְנֵי יְהוָה מִלִּפְנֵי אֲדוֹן כָּל־הָאָרֶץ: 6 הִגִּידוּ הַשָּׁמַיִם צִדְקוֹ וְרָאוּ

---

[68] Cf. Brown-Driver-Briggs 762, 2 *a*; LXX: μνησθήσεται.
[69] Cf. Niccacci (1987).
[70] Cf. Keil, Clark and Hatton, Spronk.
[71] Cf. Roberts.

כָּל־הָעַמִּים כְּבוֹדוֹ: 7 יֵבֹשׁוּ כָּל־עֹבְדֵי פֶסֶל הַמִּתְהַלְלִים בָּאֱלִילִים
הִשְׁתַּחֲווּ ־לוֹ כָּל־אֱלֹהִים: 8 שָׁמְעָה וַתִּשְׂמַח צִיּוֹן וַתָּגֵלְנָה בְּנוֹת
יְהוּדָה לְמַעַן מִשְׁפָּטֶיךָ יְהוָה: 9 כִּי־אַתָּה יְהוָה עֶלְיוֹן עַל־כָּל־הָאָרֶץ
מְאֹד נַעֲלֵיתָ עַל־כָּל־אֱלֹהִים:

"His lightning lit up the world; the earth saw and trembled. The mountains melted like wax before YHWH, before the Lord of all the earth. The heavens declared his righteousness, and all the peoples saw his glory. May all who worship images be put to shame, those who boast in idols. Worship him, all you gods! Zion heard and rejoiced, and the daughters of Judah rejoiced on account of your judgments, O YHWH. For you, O YHWH, are the Most High over all the earth, you have been much exalted over all the gods."

The *qatals* in vv.4-9 are easily understood as describing a theophany as an historical occurrence. In v.6 וַיִּרְאוּ can be understood as a conjunctive *weqatal*, and v.7 יֵבֹשׁוּ is most likely a jussive (LXX: αἰσχυνθήτωσαν).[72]

In the following examples we could be dealing with a reference to some sort of historical event, yet the precise referent is uncertain:

37. Ps 46.7

הָמוּ גוֹיִם מָטוּ מַמְלָכוֹת נָתַן בְּקוֹלוֹ תָּמוּג אָרֶץ:

"Volkeren woedden, koninkrijken wankelden, Hij verhief zijn stem, de aarde versmolt" (NBG).

38. Ps 33.10

יְהוָה הֵפִיר עֲצַת־גּוֹיִם הֵנִיא מַחְשְׁבוֹת עַמִּים:

"YHWH scattered the counsel of the nations, he frustrated the thoughts of the peoples."

Delitzsch understands this to refer to a particular act of God in the past, though König argues that this is a global/general past (see § 2.5.2 below).

39. Is 40.23-24

23 הַנּוֹתֵן רוֹזְנִים לְאָיִן שֹׁפְטֵי אֶרֶץ כַּתֹּהוּ עָשָׂה: 24 אַף בַּל־נִטָּעוּ
אַף בַּל־זֹרָעוּ אַף בַּל־שֹׁרֵשׁ בָּאָרֶץ גִּזְעָם וְגַם־נָשַׁף בָּהֶם וַיִּבָשׁוּ
וּסְעָרָה כַּקַּשׁ תִּשָּׂאֵם:

"He who turns/turned[73] rulers into nothing made the judges of the earth as a void: They were hardly planted, they were hardly sown, their

---

[72] Note that it occurs in the first position in the clause; cf. Niccacci (1987).

32

stem was hardly rooted in the earth, and he also blew upon them and they dried up, while the storm carried them away like stubble."[74]

In other examples, as several scholars have noted, we are dealing with past tenses which refer to an imaginary scene. Some obvious examples of this are the descriptions of "Wisdom" (Pr 1.20-33; 8.1-9.6) and of an adulteress (Pr 7.5-27). So also:

40.   Pr 30.20

כֵּן דֶּרֶךְ אִשָּׁה מְנָאָפֶת אָכְלָה וּמָחֲתָה פִיהָ וְאָמְרָה לֹא־פָעַלְתִּי אָוֶן:

"This is the way of an adulterous woman: She ate, and wiped her mouth, and said, 'I've done no wrong'."

The *weqatals* can be understood as conjunctive.

41.   Pr 31.10-31

10 אֵשֶׁת־חַיִל מִי יִמְצָא וְרָחֹק מִפְּנִינִים מִכְרָהּ:
11 בָּטַח בָּהּ לֵב בַּעְלָהּ וְשָׁלָל לֹא יֶחְסָר:
12 גְּמָלַתְהוּ טוֹב וְלֹא־רָע כֹּל יְמֵי חַיֶּיהָ:
13 דָּרְשָׁה צֶמֶר וּפִשְׁתִּים וַתַּעַשׂ בְּחֵפֶץ כַּפֶּיהָ:
14 הָיְתָה כָּאֳנִיּוֹת סוֹחֵר מִמֶּרְחָק תָּבִיא לַחְמָהּ:
15 וַתָּקָם בְּעוֹד לַיְלָה וַתִּתֵּן טֶרֶף לְבֵיתָהּ וְחֹק לְנַעֲרֹתֶיהָ:
16 זָמְמָה שָׂדֶה וַתִּקָּחֵהוּ מִפְּרִי כַפֶּיהָ נָטְעָה כָּרֶם:
17 חָגְרָה בְעוֹז מָתְנֶיהָ וַתְּאַמֵּץ זְרוֹעֹתֶיהָ:
18 טָעֲמָה כִּי־טוֹב סַחְרָהּ לֹא־יִכְבֶּה בַלַּיְלָה נֵרָהּ:
19 יָדֶיהָ שִׁלְּחָה בַכִּישׁוֹר וְכַפֶּיהָ תָּמְכוּ פָלֶךְ:
20 כַּפָּהּ פָּרְשָׂה לֶעָנִי וְיָדֶיהָ שִׁלְּחָה לָאֶבְיוֹן:
21 לֹא־תִירָא לְבֵיתָהּ מִשָּׁלֶג כִּי כָל־בֵּיתָהּ לָבֻשׁ שָׁנִים:
22 מַרְבַדִּים עָשְׂתָה־לָּהּ שֵׁשׁ וְאַרְגָּמָן לְבוּשָׁהּ:
23 נוֹדָע בַּשְּׁעָרִים בַּעְלָהּ בְּשִׁבְתּוֹ עִם־זִקְנֵי־אָרֶץ:
24 סָדִין עָשְׂתָה וַתִּמְכֹּר וַחֲגוֹר נָתְנָה לַכְּנַעֲנִי:

---

[73] The time reference of הַנּוֹתֵן is not entirely certain, since the non-predicative participle can be used in the sphere of the past, present or future (Joüon and Muraoka § 121 *i*; Van Peursen 1999: 200f.). Dempsey argues for past (1988: 37), but cf. LXX: ὁ διδούς; Vulgate: *qui dat*.

[74] תִּשָּׂאֵם is capable of various explanations: Saydon (1959: 296) takes it as a preterital *yiqtol* (though cf. Múgica 1971), while Dempsey (1988: 37) takes it as durative past ("then the wind bore them on and on like straw"). On the occurrence of preterital *yiqtol* in subordinate clauses, see n.55 above.

25 עֹז־וְהָדָר לְבוּשָׁהּ וַתִּשְׂחַק לְיוֹם אַחֲרוֹן:
26 פִּיהָ פָּתְחָה בְחָכְמָה וְתוֹרַת־חֶסֶד עַל־לְשׁוֹנָהּ:
27 צוֹפִיָּה הֲלִיכוֹת בֵּיתָהּ וְלֶחֶם עַצְלוּת לֹא תֹאכֵל:
28 קָמוּ בָנֶיהָ וַיְאַשְּׁרוּהָ בַּעְלָהּ וַיְהַלְלָהּ:
29 רַבּוֹת בָּנוֹת עָשׂוּ חָיִל וְאַתְּ עָלִית עַל־כֻּלָּנָה:
30 שֶׁקֶר הַחֵן וְהֶבֶל הַיֹּפִי אִשָּׁה יִרְאַת־יְהוָה הִיא תִתְהַלָּל:
31 תְּנוּ־לָהּ מִפְּרִי יָדֶיהָ וִיהַלְלוּהָ בַשְּׁעָרִים מַעֲשֶׂיהָ:

"Who can find a woman of valor? Her value is far beyond pearls. The heart of her husband trusted in her, and he did not lack a valuable thing. She did him good and not harm all the days of her life…"

Joüon argues that several features in this passage, including the verbal forms used, indicate that this is to be understood as a past tense description (compare the versions), rather than as gnomic or general present statements: The level of detail given suggests that a particular person is being described, and certain expressions (e.g. vv.12, 25, 28-29) imply that the person is no longer living.[75] The *yiqtols* can be explained as habitual-iterative (v.14 תָּבִיא) or as modal pasts (לֹא + *yiqtol* in vv.18, 21, 27).[76]

42.   Job 6.19-20

19 הִבִּיטוּ אָרְחוֹת תֵּמָא הֲלִיכֹת שְׁבָא קִוּוּ־לָמוֹ:
20 בֹּשׁוּ כִּי־בָטָח בָּאוּ עָדֶיהָ וַיֶּחְפָּרוּ:

"The caravans of Tema looked, the convoys of Sheba waited for them; they were ashamed because they had hoped, they came unto them and were ashamed."[77]

43.   Job 28.3-11

1 כִּי יֵשׁ לַכֶּסֶף מוֹצָא וּמָקוֹם לַזָּהָב יָזֹקּוּ:
2 בַּרְזֶל מֵעָפָר יֻקָּח וְאֶבֶן יָצוּק נְחוּשָׁה:
3 קֵץ שָׂם לַחֹשֶׁךְ וּלְכָל־תַּכְלִית הוּא חוֹקֵר אֶבֶן אֹפֶל וְצַלְמָוֶת:
4 פָּרַץ נַחַל מֵעִם־גָּר הַנִּשְׁכָּחִים מִנִּי־רָגֶל דַּלּוּ מֵאֱנוֹשׁ נָעוּ:
5 אֶרֶץ מִמֶּנָּה יֵצֵא־לָחֶם וְתַחְתֶּיהָ נֶהְפַּךְ כְּמוֹ־אֵשׁ:
6 מְקוֹם־סַפִּיר אֲבָנֶיהָ וְעַפְרֹת זָהָב לוֹ:

---

[75] See Joüon (1922).

[76] Perhaps also in v.11, though it might be preferable to analyze this *yiqtol* as preterital. Joosten (1999: 19ff.) notes that most of his examples of past modal *yiqtols* in narrative prose occur with the negative לֹא.

[77] Driver and Gray: "The poet, in using the past tenses, pictures a particular scene." Similarly G. R. Driver (1936: 136), Groß (1976: 133).

34

7 נָתִיב לֹא־יְדָעוֹ עָיִט וְלֹא שְׁזָפַתּוּ עֵין אַיָּה:
8 לֹא־הִדְרִיכֻהוּ בְנֵי־שָׁחַץ לֹא־עָדָה עָלָיו שָׁחַל:
9 בַּחַלָּמִישׁ שָׁלַח יָדוֹ הָפַךְ מִשֹּׁרֶשׁ הָרִים:
10 בַּצּוּרוֹת יְאֹרִים בִּקֵּעַ וְכָל־יְקָר רָאֲתָה עֵינוֹ:
11 מִבְּכִי נְהָרוֹת חִבֵּשׁ וְתַעֲלֻמָהּ יֹצִא אוֹר:

"For silver has a source, and gold a place where it is purified. One
takes iron from the dry earth and melts the ore into copper. He made an
end to darkness, and to the farthest limit was searching out ore in gloom
and deepest darkness…"

The passage begins with general statements in vv.1-2, and in v.3 begins
an imaginary narrative description of mining activity.[78] The participle
חֹקֵר expresses the progressive past (cf. § 1.4). On the negated *qatals* in
vv.7-8, cf. § 2.5.2 below.[79] There are two verbal forms which pose some
difficulty. In v.5 יֵצֵא is probably a general present,[80] and it is tempting to
interpret נֶהְפַּךְ in a similar manner on account of the parallelism. However, I do not think this is necessary. The verse could simply be drawing
a contrast between everyday agricultural activities above ground and the
particular scene of mining activity which is taking place beneath it; hence
a juxtaposition of a general present and a past tense is not problematic:
"Food comes forth from the earth, but underneath it was changed as fire".
In v.11 the verb יֹצִא is open to various interpretations. It could perhaps
have a modal/final nuance ("He bound up rivers from trickling, that he
might bring the hidden thing to light"), an iterative past ("he kept bringing
the hidden things to light")[81] or perhaps even a simple preterite.[82]

44. Is 40.7-8

7 יָבֵשׁ חָצִיר נָבֵל צִיץ כִּי רוּחַ יְהוָה נָשְׁבָה בּוֹ אָכֵן חָצִיר הָעָם:
8 יָבֵשׁ חָצִיר נָבֵל צִיץ וּדְבַר־אֱלֹהֵינוּ יָקוּם לְעוֹלָם:

---

[78] I take שָׂם in v.3 as a perfect (so e.g. Bobzin, König, LXX: ἔθετο, Peshitta: ܣܡ, Vulgate:
posuit) rather than a participle (so Driver and Gray).
[79] Cf. Bobzin (1974: 357f.): "auf einem Pfad, den der Raubvogel nicht kennt, und den das
Auge des Milans noch nie sah, den das Hochwild noch nie betrat, und den der Löwe noch
nie beschritt".
[80] So e.g. Bobzin (1974: 357).
[81] Perhaps with an inceptive nuance ("and he began bringing the hidden things to light")?
Cf. Waltke and O'Connor § 31.2 *c*.
[82] Vulgate: *produxit*, LXX: ἔδειξεν, Peshitta: ܐܦܩ; see König *ad loc*. Perhaps the verb
should be revocalized as a short imperfect?

"The grass dried up, the bloom withered, for the breath of YHWH blew upon it; indeed the people are grass. The grass dried up, the bloom withered, but the word of God will remain forever."

This is a "particular and representative case" according to Joüon and Muraoka.[83]

§ 2.5.2   *Proverbs Utilizing a Global/General Past Tense*

Consider the following proverbs:

45.   Many have been ruined by buying good pennyworths.

46.   More have repented of speech than of silence.

47.   Hot air warmed up many a cold reception.

In such examples an aspectually unmarked past tense refers to multiple occurrences in a summarizing way. We are calling such a use a "global" past tense (see § 2.1).

As noted above (§ 2.2), we encounter a considerable number of such statements in Ben Sira. They also occur in the Biblical literature:

48.   Pr 7.26

$$\text{כִּי־רַבִּים חֲלָלִים הִפִּילָה}$$

"for many are the slain she has laid low".

49.   Job 4.3

$$\text{יִסַּרְתָּ רַבִּים}$$

"You have instructed many."

In some examples the writer refers to his life in a summarizing way:

50.   Ps 88.10,14

$$\text{10 עֵינִי דָאֲבָה מִנִּי עֹנִי קְרָאתִיךָ יְהוָה בְּכָל־יוֹם שִׁטַּחְתִּי אֵלֶיךָ כַפָּי:}$$
$$\text{14 וַאֲנִי אֵלֶיךָ יְהוָה שִׁוַּעְתִּי וּבַבֹּקֶר תְּפִלָּתִי תְקַדְּמֶךָּ:}$$

---

[83] Joüon and Muraoka § 112 *d*. Likewise Ps 103.16 כִּי רוּחַ עָבְרָה־בּוֹ וְאֵינֶנּוּ ("for a wind passed through it and it was no more"), though in this case כִּי might be temporal/conditional rather than causal (Peshitta: ܟܕ; vs. Is 40.7 ܠܐ).

"My eye has become faint from affliction, I have called to you every day, O Yhwh, I have spread out my hands to you... And I have cried out to you, O Yhwh, and in the morning my prayer kept coming before you."

The phrase "every day" in v.10 indicates that we are dealing with multiple occurrences.[84]

51.   Ps 119.10-14

10 בְּכָל־לִבִּי דְרַשְׁתִּיךָ אַל־תַּשְׁגֵּנִי מִמִּצְוֺתֶיךָ׃

11 בְּלִבִּי צָפַנְתִּי אִמְרָתֶךָ לְמַעַן לֹא אֶחֱטָא־לָךְ׃

12 בָּרוּךְ אַתָּה יְהוָה לַמְּדֵנִי חֻקֶּיךָ׃

13 בִּשְׂפָתַי סִפַּרְתִּי כֹּל מִשְׁפְּטֵי־פִיךָ׃

14 בְּדֶרֶךְ עֵדְוֺתֶיךָ שַׂשְׂתִּי כְּעַל כָּל־הוֹן׃

"I have sought you with all of my heart; do not let me go astray from your commands. I have hidden your word in my heart in order that I might not sin against you... With my lips I have recounted all the judgments of your mouth. I have rejoiced in the way of your testimonies..."

52.   Ps 119.23

גַּם יָשְׁבוּ שָׂרִים בִּי נִדְבָּרוּ עַבְדְּךָ יָשִׂיחַ בְּחֻקֶּיךָ׃

"Even princes sat and spoke together against me; your servant meditates on your decrees."

This example is particularly interesting because the versions rendered some of the *qatals* with an imperfective past,[85] which suggests that this was understood as a reference to multiple events rather than a single one. It should also be noted that in this example we encounter *qatals* alongside a *yiqtol* form which appears to have a general present meaning. Such parallelism is sometimes taken as an indication that *qatal* should also be understood as a general present,[86] but this does not seem necessary in this example, nor in many others in which this parallelism occurs.[87]

53.   Qoh 7.28

אֲשֶׁר עוֹד־בִּקְשָׁה נַפְשִׁי וְלֹא מָצָאתִי

"which my mind sought again but I did not find."[88]

---

[84] Therefore they are not performative utterances (cf. § 4), as argued by Wagner (1997: 126).

[85] LXX: κατελάλουν, Peshitta: ܗܘܘ ܡܬܡܠܠܝܢ, ܗܘܘ ܪܢܐ, Vulgate: *loquebantur*.

[86] Cf. Buth (1986).

[87] Cf. e.g. examples 59, 63, 64, 68 and 82.

[88] Isaksson (1987: 91) argues for a present meaning, but see Schoors (1992: 175) and Herzberg *ad loc*.

We have already argued above (§ 2.4) for the existence of a "general past tense" in addition to a "general present". For example:

54.   Men were deceivers ever.

55.   Tall men had ever empty heads.

56.   Woman was constant never.

57.   Hunger never saw bad bread.

Such cases indicate that a situation has typically occurred (or never occurred) in the past. In agreement with a number of scholars (cf. § 2.1) I would view this as an extension of the global use of the past tense just discussed: Multiple occurrences are summarily stated, without expressing imperfective (habitual, iterative, etc.) aspect.[89]

In English I have encountered mostly examples which express what has "not ever," i.e. *never*, happened. In Biblical Hebrew:

58.   Pr 13.1

וְלֵץ לֹא־שָׁמַע גְּעָרָה

"But a mocker never listened to a rebuke."[90]

59.   Pr 30.15-16

15 לַעֲלוּקָה שְׁתֵּי בָנוֹת הַב הַב שָׁלוֹשׁ הֵנָּה לֹא תִשְׂבַּעְנָה אַרְבַּע לֹא־אָמְרוּ הוֹן: 16 שְׁאוֹל וְעֹצֶר רָחַם אֶרֶץ לֹא־שָׂבְעָה מַּיִם וְאֵשׁ לֹא־אָמְרָה הוֹן:

"The leech has two daughters (who say) 'Give, give.' Three things are never satisfied, four things have never said 'enough': Sheol, the barren womb, land which has never been satisfied with water, and fire, which has never said 'enough'."[91]

---

[89] The question arises whether there is any distinction between a global past tense and a general past. If there is a distinction, perhaps it lies in the fact that the examples of the "global" past simply refer to "many" cases but do not necessarily state that the situation is one that typically occurs, whereas the general past is more universal in scope and does express the typical nature of the situation described. A possible distinguishing test could be to transform an uncertain case as follows: In Pr 14.18 (example 64 below) "[Many] simpletons have inherited folly" sounds odd (somewhat akin to "Many dogs have four legs"), whereas "Simpletons have [ever] inherited folly" seems much more fitting.
[90] Also Pr 13.8.
[91] Similarly Job 3.16 (לֹא־רָאוּ), 18 (לֹא שָׁמְעוּ); 28.7-8 (example 43); Qoh 6.5 (לֹא רָאָה).

38

60. Ps 9.11

כִּי לֹא־עָזַבְתָּ דֹרְשֶׁיךָ יְהוָה

"For you have never abandoned those who seek you, O YHWH."[92]

61. Ps 103.10

לֹא כַחֲטָאֵינוּ עָשָׂה לָנוּ וְלֹא כַעֲוֹנֹתֵינוּ גָּמַל עָלֵינוּ:

"He has never done to us according to our sins, and he has never re-payed us according to our iniquities."

There are some possible examples which are phrased positively, however:

62. Pr 1.7

חָכְמָה וּמוּסָר אֱוִילִים בָּזוּ

"Fools have (ever/always) despised wisdom and discipline."

63. Pr 6.8

תָּכִין בַּקַּיִץ לַחְמָהּ אָגְרָה בַקָּצִיר מַאֲכָלָהּ:

We could be dealing with a contrast between a general present and a global/general past: "She prepares her food in summer, she gathered/has (ever) gathered her food in the harvest." It would also be possible to take the *yiqtol* as expressing the habitual-iterative past[93] in contrast to the sim-ple past: "She would prepare/used to prepare her food in summer, she gathered her food in the harvest."

64. Pr 14.18

נָחֲלוּ פְתָאיִם אִוֶּלֶת וַעֲרוּמִים יַכְתִּרוּ דָעַת:

"The simple have (ever/always) obtained folly as an inheritance, but the intelligent wear knowledge as a crown."

65. Pr 14.19

שַׁחוּ רָעִים לִפְנֵי טוֹבִים וּרְשָׁעִים עַל־שַׁעֲרֵי צַדִּיק:

"The evil have (ever/always) bowed down before the good, and the wicked at the gates of the righteous."

66. Pr 18.8

דִּבְרֵי נִרְגָּן כְּמִתְלַהֲמִים וְהֵם יָרְדוּ חַדְרֵי־בָטֶן:

---

[92] See Joüon and Muraoka § 112 *d*.
[93] The long form indicates that this is not a preterital *yiqtol* (*pace* G. R. Driver 1936:141).

"The words of a gossip are like tasty morsels; and they have (ever/always) gone down into the inner parts."[94]

67.   Pr 22.12

עֵינֵי יְהוָה נָצְרוּ דָעַת וַיְסַלֵּף דִּבְרֵי בֹגֵד:

"The eyes of YHWH preserved knowledge, and he overthrew the words of the deceiver."

It is debated whether דָעַת is an *abstractum pro concreto*[95] or simply "knowledge".[96] If the former is correct I would analyze this according to § 2.5.1, but if the latter is correct I would take it as a global/general past.

68.   Pr 30.21

תַּחַת שָׁלוֹשׁ רָגְזָה אֶרֶץ וְתַחַת אַרְבַּע לֹא־תוּכַל שְׂאֵת:

"Under three things the earth has (ever/always) trembled, and under four it cannot bear up."

69.   Qoh 1.14

רָאִיתִי אֶת־כָּל־הַמַּעֲשִׂים שֶׁנַּעֲשׂוּ תַּחַת הַשָּׁמֶשׁ

"I have seen everything which has been done under the sun..."[97]

70.   Jer 8.7

גַּם־חֲסִידָה בַשָּׁמַיִם יָדְעָה מוֹעֲדֶיהָ וְתֹר וְסִיס
וְעָגוּר שָׁמְרוּ אֶת־עֵת בֹּאָנָה וְעַמִּי לֹא יָדְעוּ אֵת מִשְׁפַּט יְהוָה:

"Even the stork in the sky knows her season, and dove, swallow and crane have kept the time of their migration; but my people do no know the ordinance of YHWH."

---

[94] Also Pr 26.22.

[95] So e.g. Delitzsch, Gemser, Ringgren.

[96] So e.g. NBG, NIV, Ehrlich, McKane, Meinhold.

[97] Schoors (1992: 96f.) argues that Qoheleth "considers the whole of world history, everything that has happened until today", *pace* Isaksson (1987: 69ff.), who argues for a general present meaning. We find a number of other cases of the *nifal* of עשׂה in Qoheleth, once with *yiqtol* (1.9 שֶׁיֵּעָשֶׂה) and once with the participle (4.1 אֲשֶׁר נַעֲשִׂים). The remaining cases utilize נַעֲשָׂה (1.9, 13; 2.17; 4.3; 8.9, 11, 14, 16, 17; 9.3, 6). Schoors questions the vocalization in several cases and suggests reading participles which express the general present (1992: 96f.). A textual decision is difficult here since the expression is attested in the book itself with both *qatal* and participle, and furthermore the witness of the versions is mixed. Given the difficulty in deciding between reading *qatal* or participle in the remaining cases we would simply suggest that Schoors' explanation for 1.14 may be applied to those instances which are viewed as perfects.

The question here is whether or not the verb שָׁמְרוּ is to be understood as a general present.[98] Though 4QJerᵃ reads an imperfect (cf. Peshitta: ܢܛܪܘ), the MT is supported by the LXX (ἐφύλαξαν) and Vulgate (*custodierunt*). This is capable of being explained as a general past: "They have (ever/always) kept their times."

§ 2.5.3 *Uncertain Examples*

Many alleged examples of the gnomic perfect are either best understood as past tenses or are simply too ambiguous to function as useful examples of a supposedly general present meaning of *qatal*.

71. Job 3.17

שָׁם רְשָׁעִים חָדְלוּ רֹגֶז וְשָׁם יָנוּחוּ יְגִיעֵי כֹחַ:

"There the wicked have ceased from raging."

This refers to those who have died and hence a past rendering of חָדְלוּ is understandable.

72. Ps 7.13

אִם־לֹא יָשׁוּב חַרְבּוֹ יִלְטוֹשׁ קַשְׁתּוֹ דָרַךְ וַיְכוֹנְנֶהָ:

"If he does not relent, he sharpens his sword. He has drawn his bow and prepared it."

Delitzsch comments: "Judgment is being gradually prepared, as the *fut.* implies; but, as the *perff.* imply, it is also on the other hand like a bow that is already strung against the sinner with the arrow pointed towards him, so that it can be executed at any moment".[99]

73. Ps 10.14

רָאִתָה כִּי־אַתָּה עָמָל וָכַעַס תַּבִּיט לָתֵת בְּיָדֶךָ עָלֶיךָ
יַעֲזֹב חֵלֶכָה יָתוֹם אַתָּה הָיִיתָ עוֹזֵר:

"You have seen, for you observe trouble and affliction, in order to place it in your hands. The unfortunate one commits himself to you; you are a helper to the orphan."

---

[98] The statives יָדְעָה and יָדְעוּ are excluded here, cf. § 2.5.
[99] Similar cases: Pss 11.2; 37.14.

There is no reason that רָאִתָה cannot be a past tense: "you have seen..."[100]

74.   Ps 37.23

מֵיהוָה מִצְעֲדֵי־גָבֶר כּוֹנָנוּ

"By YHWH have the steps of a man been established."

75.   Ps 88.6

וְהֵמָּה מִיָּדְךָ נִגְזָרוּ

"And they have been cut off from your hand."

As example 71, this also refers to the dead.

76.   Ps 119.21

גָּעַרְתָּ זֵדִים אֲרוּרִים הַשֹּׁגִים מִמִּצְוֹתֶיךָ׃

"You have rebuked the arrogant, accursed ones, who wander from your commandments."

גָּעַרְתָּ could be a preterite, a global/general past or simply a "perfect".

77.   Ps 119.30

דֶּרֶךְ־אֱמוּנָה בָחָרְתִּי מִשְׁפָּטֶיךָ שִׁוִּיתִי׃

"I have chosen the way of faithfulness, I have accounted your judgments suitable (?)."

78.   Job 33.3

וְדַעַת שְׂפָתַי בָּרוּר מִלֵּלוּ

"And my lips have spoken knowledge knowledge clearly."

Despite some textual and philological difficulties, מִלֵּלוּ can be understood as referring to the recent past.[101]

79.   Qoh 7.10

אַל־תֹּאמַר מֶה הָיָה שֶׁהַיָּמִים הָרִאשֹׁנִים הָיוּ טוֹבִים
מֵאֵלֶּה כִּי לֹא מֵחָכְמָה שָׁאַלְתָּ עַל־זֶה׃

"Do not say: Why were the first days better than these? For it is not from wisdom that you have asked about this."

---

[100] See e.g. Delitzsch, Craigie, Kraus.

[101] See e.g. Delitzsch. Bobzin (1974: 413f.) argues that מִלֵּלוּ is not a "Perf. der Gewohnheit" but rather a case of *Koinzidenzfall*. Cf. chapter 4.

42

שָׁאַלְתְּ is easily understood either as a past tense or as a future perfect (so Herzberg).[102]

The following examples are open to various interpretations:

80.　Ps 39.12

בְּתוֹכָחוֹת עַל־עָוֹן יִסַּרְתָּ אִישׁ וַתֶּמֶס כָּעָשׁ חֲמוּדוֹ

"You have instructed a man with rebukes for sin, and you have consumed his desired things like a moth."

König sees this as a global/general past ("Durch Züchtigungen für Vergehen hast du schon immer den Mann in die Schule genommen"), yet it could simply be continuing the preceding reference to the psalmist's own sufferings (vv. 9-11), albeit in less specific terms which allow for the transition to the general statement which follows (אַךְ הֶבֶל כָּל־אָדָם) "surely every man is fleeting").

81.　Ps 65.10, 12

10 פָּקַדְתָּ הָאָרֶץ וַתְּשֹׁקְקֶהָ רַבַּת תַּעְשְׁרֶנָּה פֶּלֶג אֱלֹהִים מָלֵא
מָיִם תָּכִין דְּגָנָם כִּי־כֵן תְּכִינֶהָ׃
12 עִטַּרְתָּ שְׁנַת טוֹבָתֶךָ וּמַעְגָּלֶיךָ יִרְעֲפוּן דָּשֶׁן׃

"You have visited the earth and watered it; you enrich it greatly. The river of God is full of water; you prepare their grain, for thus you prepare it... You have crowned the year of your goodness, and your tracks drip with fatness."

These verses are rather obscure and open to a variety of interpretations (cf. the versions). It would be possible to take them as references to some particular event[103] or as global/general past tenses.[104] It should be noted that Dahood interprets these as "precative" perfects.[105]

82.　Ps 103.12-13

12 כִּרְחֹק מִזְרָח מִמַּעֲרָב הִרְחִיק מִמֶּנּוּ אֶת־פְּשָׁעֵינוּ׃
13 כְּרַחֵם אָב עַל־בָּנִים רִחַם יְהוָה עַל־יְרֵאָיו׃

"He has distanced our sins from us as far as the east is from the west. YHWH has shown compassion to those who fear him as a father shows compassion to his children."

---

[102] It is taken as a general present by e.g. Isaksson (1987: 89); cf. the Peshitta's ܐܢܬ ܫܐܠܬ.

[103] Cf. e.g. Kraus.

[104] Cf. König.

[105] See our concluding chapter (§ 5).

These could be interpreted either as "perfects" or as global/general pasts (§ 2.5.2).

In some alleged gnomics in the prophetic literature the prophet uses past tenses when condemning the sins of the people.[106] That the prophet is referring to sins which *have been* committed is not at all problematic, and hence a general present rendering is unnecessary. Similarly, in Job 24.2-11 we find some *qatals* and *wayyiqtols* which can be understood as referring to the past behavior of wicked people. Although these are interspersed with *yiqtols* that seem to refer to the general present, I think that the past tenses can be understood in terms of any of the categories discussed so far.[107]

§ 2.5.4   *Proverbs Utilizing Relative Past Tenses*

In our introductory chapter we discussed the difference between "absolute" and "relative" tense (§ 1.2). The examples which we have examined so far are open to either analysis. There are some proverbs, however, that appear to be analyzable only in terms of relative tense. For example:

83.   He who pleased everybody died before he was born.

84.   He hath liv'd ill, that knows not how to die well.

85.   He who never made a mistake never made anything.

86.   He who has seen the land of the Christians has wasted his days.

These proverbs appear to be describing a *type* of person, rather than a particular individual. It is for this reason that I would not analyze them as the report of an experience or observation (§ 2.5.1). Moreover, these do not seem to be analogous to the global/general past tenses discussed above (§ 2.5.2). It seems unlikely to me that the verb expresses a past relative to the speaker's actual moment in time (S), and hence it would seem that in these examples the verb expresses a past tense relative to some other reference point (R).[108]

In Biblical Hebrew we find similar examples of proverbs that appear to refer to a type of person. If our analysis of the English examples is

---

[106] E.g. Is 5.12; Hos 8.12; Am 5.12, 14; Mic 6.12; Zeph 3.7.

[107] For some possible solutions see e.g. Groß (1976: 138f.), Bobzin (1974: 325ff.), Birkeland (1935: 20), König (*ad loc.*). On the interchange between *qatal* and *yiqtol*, see example 52 above.

[108] Cf. Bache (1995: 221), Dempsey (1989: 26ff.).

correct, and if these Hebrew examples are to be understood in an analogous fashion, then this would be one indication that *qatal* is marked as a relative past tense, not an absolute tense.[109]

Such examples occur in both main and subordinate clauses:

87.　Pr 3.13

אַשְׁרֵי אָדָם מָצָא חָכְמָה

"Blessed is the man who has found wisdom."

88.　Pr 8.35

כִּי מֹצְאִי מָצָא חַיִּים וַיָּפֶק רָצוֹן מֵיהוָה:

"For the one who finds me has found life, and has received favor from YHWH."

89.　Pr 14.31

עֹשֵׁק־דָּל חֵרֵף עֹשֵׂהוּ וּמְכַבְּדוֹ חֹנֵן אֶבְיוֹן:

"He who oppresses a poor man has reproached his maker; but the one who honors him is kind to the needy."

90.　Pr 16.30

עֹצֶה עֵינָיו לַחְשֹׁב תַּהְפֻּכוֹת קֹרֵץ שְׂפָתָיו כִּלָּה רָעָה:

"He who closes his eyes, plotting perversity, he who presses his lips, has completed an evil thing."[110]

91.　Pr 17.5

לֹעֵג לָרָשׁ חֵרֵף עֹשֵׂהוּ

"He who mocks a poor man has reproached his maker."[111]

92.　Job 20.15

חַיִל בָּלַע וַיְקִאֶנּוּ מִבִּטְנוֹ יוֹרִשֶׁנּוּ אֵל:

---

[109] Cf. also § 3.4.1 and our concluding chapter (§ 5).

[110] Cf. *Einheitsübersetzung*, NBG, *Traduction œcuménique*, Segond, Scott, Hermisson (1968: 54). The view of e.g. McKane that לַחְשֹׁב is a finite verb form with a prefixed *lamedh* is untenable; see Muraoka (1985: 113ff., esp. p.121), Bergsträsser § 141 *i* note, Gesenius-Kautzsch-Cowley § 114 *i* n.1. It appears that the infinitive is to be taken not just with the first participle but with the second as well and that we are dealing with a case of ellipsis.

[111] Cf. Meinhold. Perhaps also the syntactically similar 27.16 (צָפֶן־רוּחַ צֹפְנֶיהָ), though this is very difficult both textually and lexically. See the commentaries.

Pronominal suffixes with *nun energicum* do not occur with *wayyiqtol*, so it appears necessary to emend to וִיקִאֶנּוּ.[112] There appear to be two possibilities here: With Dhorme and Clines we could take v.15a as an asyndetic relative clause with the verb functioning as a relative past ("The wealth which he has swallowed, he will vomit up"), or we could be dealing with a conditional statement with *weyiqtol* introducing the apodosis[113] ("If he has swallowed wealth, he will vomit it...").

93. Pr 13.24

חוֹשֵׂךְ שִׁבְטוֹ שׂוֹנֵא בְנוֹ וְאֹהֲבוֹ שִׁחֲרוֹ מוּסָר:

"He who withholds his rod hates his son; but he who loves his son sought him early (?) with discipline."

94. Ps 1.1

אַשְׁרֵי־הָאִישׁ אֲשֶׁר לֹא הָלַךְ בַּעֲצַת רְשָׁעִים וּבְדֶרֶךְ חַטָּאִים
לֹא עָמָד וּבְמוֹשַׁב לֵצִים לֹא יָשָׁב:

"Blessed is the man who has never walked in the counsel of the wicked, and has never stood in the path of sinners, and has never sat in the seat of scoffers."[114]

95. Ps 24.4

נְקִי כַפַּיִם וּבַר־לֵבָב אֲשֶׁר לֹא־נָשָׂא לַשָּׁוְא נַפְשִׁי וְלֹא נִשְׁבַּע לְמִרְמָה:

"...who has never lifted up his soul to a vain thing, and has never sworn deceitfully."

96. Ps 15.3-5

3 לֹא־רָגַל עַל־לְשֹׁנוֹ לֹא־עָשָׂה לְרֵעֵהוּ רָעָה וְחֶרְפָּה לֹא־נָשָׂא
עַל־קְרֹבוֹ: 4 נִבְזֶה בְּעֵינָיו נִמְאָס וְאֶת־יִרְאֵי יְהוָה יְכַבֵּד
נִשְׁבַּע לְהָרַע וְלֹא יָמִר: 5 כַּסְפּוֹ לֹא־נָתַן בְּנֶשֶׁךְ
וְשֹׁחַד עַל־נָקִי לֹא לָקָח עֹשֵׂה־אֵלֶּה לֹא יִמּוֹט לְעוֹלָם:

"(who) has never slandered with his tongue; who has never done harm to his neighbor, nor taken up a reproach against his fellow; who disdains a despicable one, but honors those who fear YHWH; who has sworn to (his) hurt and would not change; who has never given out his money at interest, and has never accepted a bribe against the innocent..."

---

[112] Muraoka (1975: 64).

[113] Cf. Kelly (1920: 4).

[114] Delitzsch: "The *perff.* in ver. 1 describe what he all along has never done".

46

97.　Ps 40.5

אַשְׁרֵי הַגֶּבֶר אֲשֶׁר־שָׂם יְהוָה מִבְטַחוֹ
וְלֹא־פָנָה אֶל־רְהָבִים וְשָׂטֵי כָזָב:

"Blessed is the man who has made[115] YHWH his trust; who has never turned to the proud and to those who go after false things."

98.　Ps 119.2-3

2 אַשְׁרֵי נֹצְרֵי עֵדֹתָיו בְּכָל־לֵב יִדְרְשׁוּהוּ:
3 אַף לֹא־פָעֲלוּ עַוְלָה בִּדְרָכָיו הָלָכוּ:

"Blessed are they who keep his testimonies and seek him with all their heart; who moreover have never done unrighteousness and have (ever/always) walked in his ways."

§ 2.6 Conclusion

It is unlikely that the preceding discussion has addressed every possible example of a "gnomic perfect" which could be cited. A reason for this is that translations and commentators often resort to what Groß calls "die Flucht ins Präsens."[116] That is to say, if the use of verb tenses in a given passage is felt to be unusual or difficult, one can conveniently solve the problem by translating with present tenses, since they are broad enough to cover the present (general or actual), future or past ("historical present"). Hence there are no doubt other passages in which a present tense translation "works" and which could have been examined here.[117] Nonetheless, by focusing primarily on the examples cited in the grammatical literature I believe that the most important ones have been addressed and that it has been shown that in a good many cases *qatal* does not require a general present interpretation but should be understood as a past tense. Admittedly, some uncertain cases remain. The main point which we have attempted to make here is that there is a much greater variety of past tense usage in "gnomic" or "proverbial" statements than is sometimes supposed. The results of our investigation can, I believe, be fruitfully applied to more extensive passages. This cannot be done exhaustively here but is rather a task for more specialized exegetical studies to pursue. However, we will illustrate how this might be done with the following example.

---

[115] שָׂם could be a participle, but the parallelism indicates a perfect.

[116] Groß (1976: 4).

[117] A present tense translation could indeed be the best one in a given case in any particular language (cf. n.50). What one must be on one's guard against, however, is the temptation to impose the structure of the target language upon the source language (in this case, Hebrew).

99. Ps 14.1-3, 5

1 לַמְנַצֵּחַ לְדָוִד אָמַר נָבָל בְּלִבּוֹ אֵין אֱלֹהִים הִשְׁחִיתוּ
הִתְעִיבוּ עֲלִילָה אֵין עֹשֵׂה־טוֹב: 2 יְהוָה מִשָּׁמַיִם הִשְׁקִיף
עַל־בְּנֵי־אָדָם לִרְאוֹת הֲיֵשׁ מַשְׂכִּיל דֹּרֵשׁ אֶת־אֱלֹהִים:
3 הַכֹּל סָר יַחְדָּו נֶאֱלָחוּ אֵין עֹשֵׂה־טוֹב אֵין גַּם־אֶחָד וגו׳
5 שָׁם פָּחֲדוּ פָחַד כִּי־אֱלֹהִים בְּדוֹר צַדִּיק:

"The fool has said in his heart: 'There is no God.' They have acted
corruptly, they have performed vile deeds, there is no one who does good.
YHWH looked down from heaven upon the sons of man to see whether
there is anyone who acts wisely, who seeks God. All of them have turned
aside, together they have become corrupt. There is no one who does
good, there is no even one... There they feared greatly, for God was in
the generation of the righteous."

אָמַר in v.1a is open to a number of interpretations. It is highly doubtful
that the psalmist had a particular "fool" in mind, and hence this would not
appear to be similar to the examples in § 2.5.1 above. It seems that this is
to be understood as a relative past tense which describes a type of person
(§ 2.5.4). It would be possible to understand it as a global/general past (§
2.5.2): "The fool has (ever/always) said in his heart..." Alternatively, it
could be understood as the English "perfect" by referring to a past event
with perhaps a focus on its continuing consequences.[118] In v.1b and 3 the
poet switches to the plural and treats mankind as a totality; the verbs are
thus global past tenses that summarize all of history.[119] Since the poet is
viewing mankind as a whole, he is able to picture God "looking" upon
them as a totality; the verb הִשְׁקִיף could thus be understood either as
preterital or as a "perfect".[120] V.4 is not only syntactically uncertain but
also textually difficult, and is excluded here. In v.5 פָּחֲדוּ could be interpreted in a stative sense (cf. Brown-Driver-Briggs s.v.), though it could
also be interpreted in a manner similar to the verbs in vv.1b and 3.

---

[118] Similarly Ps 10.6, 11 אָמַר בְּלִבּוֹ.

[119] This is also the case in Psalm 90, where König argues that the tense forms indicate that
"das Auge des Dichters wesentlich auf die Vergangenheit gerichtet war". This explains
e.g. the shortened prefix conjugation in v.3 תָּשֵׁב (cf. Müller 1984: 271). Thus in v.10 the
verbs are past tenses by which the poet refers to the preceding generations in a global way
(cf. Birkeland 1935: 20; Groß 1976: 137).

[120] Similarly Ps 102.20 כִּי־הִשְׁקִיף מִמְּרוֹם קָדְשׁוֹ יְהוָה מִשָּׁמַיִם אֶל־אֶרֶץ הִבִּיט
and Ps 33.13-14

13 מִשָּׁמַיִם הִבִּיט יְהוָה רָאָה אֶת־כָּל־בְּנֵי הָאָדָם:
14 מִמְּכוֹן־שִׁבְתּוֹ הִשְׁגִּיחַ אֶל כָּל־יֹשְׁבֵי הָאָרֶץ:

It remains to be seen whether the categories discussed above will prove sufficient in every instance. Hence it is important to remember that while our study is primarily synchronic in approach, the diachronic factor should not be completely forgotten. The fact that the diachronic origin of *qatal* is from a "stative" verbal form makes it plausible to suppose that it could have been used for the general present in an earlier phase of Hebrew.[121] This question cannot be pursued here, as we are excluding archaic Hebrew texts from this study (§ 1.4, n.52). In any event, such a supposition does not appear to be a necessary to explain the data examined in this chapter.

---

[121] Cf. the views of G. R. Driver *et al.* (n.18 above) and compare Rowton (1962: 298f.).

APPENDIX I:
PAST TENSE PROVERBS

After 40 years the Bedouin took revenge and said, "I have been quick about it!"

They said "our bread is bigger than your bread", and we said, "Give us some!"

When I saw you I knew half of you; when we spoke I knew everything.

As soon as she was tired of harvesting she said, "My sickle is dull."

They asked the frog, "Why don't you speak up?" The frog said, "My mouth is full of water!"

When they started to shoe the Sultan's horse, the beetle stretched out its leg.

Seeing his friend being disemboweled, he asked, "Will you give me some for my cat?"

One man sold his son because of need, another bought him on credit.

The hedgehog put her hand on her children and smiled, "You are all prickly!"

I taught him to swim and he drowned me.

I put a date in his mouth and he poked me in the eye with a stick.

I told her, "I divorce you!" She said, "Come to bed!"

When I saw the mirage I threw away my water; now I have no water and no mirage.

The mason was guilty and they hanged the saddler.

I gave him the plague; he gave me pneumonia.

We coveted their sheep; they stole our camels.

To buy a winepress he sold his vineyard.

Looking for his son, his son was sitting on his shoulders.

We taught them to pray, and they got to the mosque ahead of us.

I went to Damascus to get rid of my worries. Damascus was full of worries.

Too much water drowned the miller.

The mountain has brought forth a mouse.

The owl thought her own birds fairest.

Acorns were good till bread was found.

For the want of a nail, the shoe was lost, for want of a shoe etc.

I planted an If in the valley of It Was and there grew I Would It Were.

Now that the pumpkin is large and round it has forgotten its past.
He promised mountains and gave molehills.
Great cry but little wool, as the devil said when he sheared his hogs.
The hare was outrun by the tortoise.
Adam ate the apple, and our teeth still ache.
In Adam's fall we sinned all.
By perseverance the snail reached the ark.
Samson was a strong man, yet he could not pay money before he had it.
God created serpents, rabbits, and Armenians!
God made man to lay up barley for asses.
After God created man God repented.
For the birds that cannot soar God has provided low branches.
When God made the Sudan he laughed.
God has omitted women from his mercy.
God made dirt, so dirt can't hurt.
Many have been ruined by buying good pennyworths.
More have repented of speech than of silence.
Bacchus has drowned more men than Neptune.
Wine has drowned more men than the sea.
Hot air thawed out many a cold reception.
Tall men had ever empty heads.
Men were deceivers ever.
Long jesting was never good.
Woman was constant never.
No tree has ever reached the sky.
Dew never filled an empty well.
Nothing good ever came out of the sea.
A wild goose never laid a tame egg.
Never a duck was hatched by a drake.
Never had ill workman good tools.
Never went out an ass, and came home a horse.
A muffled cat was never a good mouser.
A cracked pot never fell off the hook.
Pride never left his master without a fall.
Hunger never saw bad bread.
A man's hat in hand never did him any harm.
Cap in hand never did anyone any harm.
Fair words never hurt the tongue.
"Almost" never killed a fly.
Almsgiving never made any man poor, nor robbery rich, nor property
    wise.
A long nose never spoiled a handsome face.
Never a prophet was valued in his native country.
Borrowed garments never fit well.

He who pleased everybody died before he was born.

The man who has drunk once from the springs of Africa will drink from them again.

He hath liv'd ill, that knows not how to die well.

He who has seen the land of the Christians has wasted his days.

He who never made a mistake never made anything.

Rome was not built in a day.

What camel ever saw its own hump?

Who has seen tomorrow?

A rascal grown rich has lost all his kindred.

As you have brewed, so shall you drink.

Rain was not created solely to make mud.

Dirhams have sown discord among Moslems.

When I lent, I was a friend; when I asked, I was unkind.[122]

---

[122] These examples are primarily from Lunde (1984), Strauss (1994), Mieder-Kingsbury-Harder (1992).

§ 3. The Prophetic Perfect

§ 3.1 Previous Discussion

Unlike the gnomic and performative perfects, the so-called "prophetic perfect"[1] has a long history of discussion, beginning with the medieval Jewish grammarians. Abraham Ibn Ezra drew attention to the prophets' use of the past tense (עבר) in place of the future (עתיד) "for a decision has already been made that it be so".[2] According to David Qimchi, "the event of action is imminent beyond any doubt in the mind of the speaker or writer and is already regarded as accomplished".[3] Similar ideas were extensively expanded and developed in the treatments of later grammarians. Ewald wrote that *qatal* can be used

> Von handlungen die zwar der wirklichkeit nach weder vergangen noch gegenwärtig sind, die aber der wille oder die lebendige einbildung des redenden schon sogutals vollendet betrachtet, also als ganz unbedingt und gewiß sezt; wo man in neuern sprachen wenigstens das dringendere, bestimmtere präsens statt des futurum gebraucht. So wenn jemand seine willensmeinung kurz erklärt als den beschluß der seele der in ihm fest steht, also besonders oft in aussprüchen Gottes dessen wille der that gleich ist... Die phantasie ferner des dichters und propheten erschauet oft die zukunft schon als ihr klar vorliegend und erlebt...[4]

---

[1] In addition to the term "prophetic perfect," one also encounters the terms "perfect of confidence" or "perfect of certainty" (e.g. Gesenius-Kautzsch-Cowley § 106 *n*, Davidson § 41, Revell 1989: 5f., Waltke and O'Connor § 30.5.1 *e*). Some appear to use the terms synonymously (e.g. Driver § 14, Williams § 165; cf. Delitzsch *ad* Job 19.27), whereas others seem to distinguish between them (e.g. Davidson § 41; cf. Fenton 1973: 37). The precise distinction, however, is far from clear. Buttenwieser (1969: 19), for example, speaks of *qatals* used for "an action that is conceived of as sure to happen (the so-called prophetic perfect), or thought of as inevitable (the perfect of certitude)." If there is a difference between "inevitable" ("perfect of certitude") and "sure to happen" ("prophetic perfect") it is a very subtle one indeed, and hence I will simply use the term "prophetic perfect" in this chapter.

[2] ספר צחות) בעבור שכבר נגזרה גזירא נזירא להיות כן, 44a); see Bacher (1882: 127) for more references.

[3] Chomsky (1952: § 77 *b*).

[4] Ewald § 135 *c*.

And in the standard grammar of Gesenius-Kautzsch-Cowley we read that *qatal* is used

> to express facts which are undoubtedly imminent, and, therefore, in the imagination of the speaker, already accomplished (*perfectum confiden-tiae*)... This use of the perfect occurs most frequently in prophetic language (*perfectum propheticum*). The prophet so transports himself in imagination into the future that he describes the future event as if it had been already seen or heard by him.[5]

Driver expressed a number of similar ideas:

> The perfect is employed to indicate actions, the accomplishment of which lies indeed in the future, but is regarded as dependent upon such an unalterable determination of will that it may be spoken of as having already taken place.[6]

> But the most special and remarkable use of the tense, though little more than an extension of the last idiom, is as the *prophetic perfect*: its abrupt appearance in this capacity imparts to descriptions of the future a forcible and expressive touch of reality, and reproduces vividly the certainty with which the occurrence of a yet future event is contemplated by the speaker... But the pf. is also found ... where, in a description of the future, it is desired to give variety to the scene, or to confer particular emphasis upon individual isolated traits in it.[7]

Such ideas can be found in more recent discussions of the prophetic perfect,[8] but there are also some newer suggestions which should be mentioned. Several scholars attribute the prophetic perfect to perfective aspect.[9] From a diachronic perspective, Blau argues that the use of *qatal* for the "prophetic future" in poetry has its origin in the use of *qatal* for wishes and requests (בקשות, איחולים), which use is itself perhaps due to the speaker's emotion causing him to represent the requested matter "as if it had already been granted".[10] Blake understands *qatal* to have both present and past tense functions, and argues that the prophetic perfect is "to be

---

[5] Gesenius-Kautzsch-Cowley § 106 *n.*
[6] Driver § 13.
[7] Driver § 14.
[8] Cf. e.g. Dempsey (1988: 230), Revell (1989: 5f.), Hughes (1993: 134), Hendel (1996: 167), Bombeck (1997: 76).
[9] Waltke and O'Connor § 30.5.1 *e*, Hendel (1996: 167), Tropper (1998: 183f.), Gentry (1998: 19). So also Gibson § 59 *b*, though his understanding of "aspect" would be more accurately called *Aktionsart* (cf. § 4.1, n.7 on the views of Rundgren *et al.*).
[10] ייתכן, כי מתוך התרגשות מציגים את הדבר המבוקש כאילו הוא כבר ניתן (Blau 1972: 113). On the "precative perfect" see our concluding chapter (§ 5).

regarded as use of the present for the future";[11] a somewhat similar explanation is proposed by Andersen, who attributes this use to an originally progressive present value of the verb form.[12] Zuber denies the existence of the prophetic perfect as a grammatical category and instead argues that it is a matter of literary *Gattung* rather than grammar.[13] Likewise, Müller argues, "Das Phänomen gehört dann in die Formgeschichte, nicht in die Grammatik."[14] In this connection it is worth drawing attention to the grammar of Joüon and Muraoka, where it is stated that the prophetic perfect "is not a special grammatical perfect, but a rhetorical device."[15] Waltke and O'Connor state that "with an *accidental perfective* a speaker vividly and dramatically represents a future situation both as complete and as independent"[16] and Gibson claims that the prophetic perfect "may be regarded as injecting a note of permanency into the prediction."[17] Somewhat ironically, the only article devoted to the subject does not relate this use to the semantics of *qatal* but simply attempts to establish criteria by which an example may legitimately be considered "prophetic".[18]

It is evident that a wide variety of factors are appealed to in order to explain the prophetic perfect. Some scholars take an essentially pragmatic approach to the prophetic perfect, that is, it is not explained in terms of semantics or syntax but rather in terms of rhetoric or genre. Other explanations appeal to stylistic features such as "vividness", "expressiveness", "variety" or "emphasis" in describing a scene, though it is not clear to me whether such descriptions are intended as strictly pragmatic or involve semantics in some respect.[19] Other scholars attempt more explicitly to relate the prophetic perfect to the meaning of *qatal*, whether in terms of aspect, tense, mood[20] or some other semantic parameter. Diachronic factors are occasionally mentioned in support of such semantic explanations. Generally speaking it may be said that most of the

---

[11] Blake (1951: 17).

[12] T. Andersen (2000: 54f.).

[13] Zuber (1986: 173f.).

[14] Müller (1983: 51 n.109). See also *idem* (1984b: 122 n.97): "es ist ein literarisches, kein grammatisches Phänomen und erklärt sich am ehesten religionspsychologisch."

[15] Joüon and Muraoka § 111 *h*; similarly Van der Merwe-Naudé-Kroeze (1999: 146) and Dempsey (1988: 230). In fact, Dempsey goes somewhat further and argues that Joüon's distinction between the "parfait prophétique" (1923: § 112 *h*) and other present-future uses of *qatal* (1923: § 112 *g*) is a false one and that the same rhetoric is involved in all of these cases.

[16] Waltke and O'Connor § 30.5.1 *e*; the idea that *qatal* expresses an "independent" action is taken from Michel (1960).

[17] Gibson § 59.

[18] Klein (1990).

[19] As with the use of the ubiquitous term "emphasis" by Hebraists in general, such frequently-used descriptions are rarely defined with precision (cf. Muraoka 1985: 1).

[20] The notions of "confidence" or "certainty" frequently associated with the prophetic perfect would in fact be most properly described as relating to epistemic modality (cf. Garr 1998: xliiiff. and Gianto 1998: 194).

explanations offered combine a number of these various factors. Thus, for example, Waltke and O'Connor refer both to the semantic value of the verb form ("complete and independent") and to stylistic issues ("vividly and dramatically represents a future situation").

§ 3.2 Post-Biblical Hebrew

The prophetic perfect does not appear to be attested in the extant Hebrew text of Ben Sira,[21] Qumran Hebrew,[22] or Mishnaic Hebrew.[23]

§ 3.3 Comparative Semitics

There appear to be some analogies to the Hebrew prophetic perfect in other Semitic languages. A handful of examples are cited from Ugaritic[24] and Ethiopic.[25] There are two alleged examples in Biblical Aramaic: Dan 5.28 ("... ton royaume sera divisé (פְּרִיסַת) ... et sera donné (וִיהִיבַת) aux Mèdes et aux Perses")[26] and 7.27 ("the kingdom ... will be given (יְהִיבַת) to the people of the holy ones of the Most High").[27] There are a number of examples of the perfect in Classical Arabic which appear to be analogous to the Hebrew "prophetic perfect".[28]

---

[21] The one alleged example (48.11 אֲשֶׁר רָאָךְ וּמֵת) is very difficult; see Van Peursen (1999: 65f.).

[22] De Vries (1964-65: 412), Kesterson (1984: 41), Thorion-Vardi (1985); cf. Kutscher (1959: 272f.).

[23] Segal (1927: § 306; 1936: § 216), Hendel (1996: 158); cf. Sharvit (1980), Azar (1995: 1ff.), Pérez Fernández (1997: 118).

[24] Tropper (2000: 716f.)

[25] Dillmann-Bezold § 88, Chaine § 203.

[26] Dammron § 20 c.

[27] See e.g. Kautzsch § 72, Strack § 13 a, Rosenthal § 179, Charles. Others understand it to be a future perfect (e.g. Marti, Goldingay), and Collins even translates it as a simple past: "were given". Dan 6.6 is probably a *futurum exactum* (so e.g. Kautzsch § 71, Strack § 13 a, Marti), not a prophetic perfect. See further Rogland (2003: 424ff.). On some alleged prophetic perfects in the Deir 'Alla texts, see above, p. 20 n.25.

[28] See especially Aartun (1963: 88ff.) and Reuschel (1996: 211ff.). Comparison with Akkadian is complicated by the fact that Hebrew *qatal*, which is diacronically related to the Akkadian stative, has undergone a process of fientification, unlike its Akkadian counterpart. It is thus open to question whether the more valuable comparison would be with the diachronically unrelated *iprus* or *iptaras*, given the fact that these generally function as past tenses. Nevertheless, G. R. Driver (1936: 116) provides a few examples of the Akkadian stative with an allegedly future meaning. On Egyptian cf. Agam (1982).

§ 3.4 Textual Studies

In the following textual studies we will observe Klein's criteria for determining whether an example is "prophetic" or not.[29] Namely: 1. The example must be textually sound.[30] 2. The example must be indicative.[31] 3. The perfect must clearly have a future meaning. This third criterion is, as Klein notes, the most difficult one to satisfy, since many examples which are considered prophetic by some scholars are interpreted by others as past (see § 3.4.6; cf. § 1.1).[32]

---

[29] See Klein (1990: 48). The examples considered here are drawn not only from the grammatical literature but also from our own close reading of the prophetic corpus (cf. above, p. 14 n.74).

[30] Textually problematic: Gen 30.13; Is 8.8; 11.8 (see Gray, Wildberger); 17.11; 21.1 (בָּא could be a perfect or a participle), 2, 14; 24.14; 25.8; 28.2 (1QIs^a וְהִנִּיחַ) 30.5, 32; 34.5; 47.9; 49.17; 51.11; Jer 25.14; 31.5, 33; 50.31; 51.2, 44, 56; Ezek 7.14; 24.14; Hos 5.5; 10.5, 7 (נִדְמֶה a participle, not a perfect as claimed by Davidson § 41 b), 15 (see Borbone 1987: 97 n.235); 12.12; 13.9; 14.9 (cf. Borbone 1987: 79); Joel 2.2 (בָּא is probably a participle and not a perfect, pace e.g. Keil); Mic 6.13; Nah 1.10, 12; Hab 1.11; Zeph 2.2, 14; 3.18; Zech 9.15 (see e.g. Lamarche 1961: 48, Otzen 1964: 244f., Saebø 1969: 59f., 198ff.); 13.9.

[31] Hence e.g. interrogatives are excluded: Gen 18.12; Nu 23.10; Ju 9.9, 11; Hab 1.2; Zech 4.10. Note also that possible temporal or conditional statements are excluded (cf. p. 10 n.53), as the tense usage in such statements requires a separate treatment: Lev 26.44; 1 Sam 2.16; Is 30.19; Hos 12.12.

[32] Various indications of a future meaning are mentioned in the literature, the most important being context (Gibson § 59, Hendel 1996: 167). The grammarians also mention the use of particles such as הִנֵּה (Ewald § 135 c, J. A. Hughes 1970: 21), כִּי or לָכֵן (Driver § 14 β, Davidson § 41 rem. 1, Gibson § 59 rem. 1), word order (Ewald § 135 c: "übrigens aber muss das perf. selbst immer nachdrücklich vorne im saze stehen, oder durch den sinn des ganzen sazes als erst künftig möglich vonselbst klar seyn") and the interchange of qatal with yiqtols and weqatals (Gesenius-Kautzsch-Cowley § 106 n, Driver § 14, Davidson § 41 rem. 1, Bauer 1910: 35, Buttenwieser 1969: 21, Klein 1990: 48, 59f.; but contrast Bergsträsser § 6 h: "das prophetische Futurum, das jedoch nur verhältnismäßig selten anzunehmen ist und zwar dann, wenn in einem Abschnitt zur Darstellung zukünftiger Ereignisse in lebhafter Vergegenwärtigung durchgehend Perf. (und Imperf. cons.) verwendet ist"). Most cases involve a combination of these various factors. It should be mentioned in passing that scholars will occasionally explain examples of the prophetic perfect as vaticinia ex eventu, but such an explanation will be avoided here: If a passage is a description of events written after they occurred then qatal has a past referent and maintains its normal deictic function, and such cases are consequently not of interest to the present study. Cases in which it appears that a prophet is speaking of an actual historical event rather than a future one are discussed with other examples in which a future meaning is uncertain (§ 3.4.6). Note further that we are excluding stative verbs from the present study (§ 1.4), and hence the following alleged examples are excluded here: Ju 15.3 (נְקֵיתִי); Is 11.9 (מָלְאָה); 13.10 (חָשַׁךְ); 47.14 (הָיוּ); 50.11 (הָיְתָה); Jer 20.11 (בֹּשׁוּ); 31.9 (הָיִיתִי); Zeph 2.15 (הָיְתָה; cf. Irsigler 1977: 282 n.177); Zech 10.6 (רִחַמְתִּים).

58

§ 3.4.1   Relative Past

In our introductory chapter we discussed the difference between "absolute" and "relative" tense (§ 1.2), and we have already seen some examples of the latter in our examination of the gnomic perfect (§ 2.5.4). Another use of *qatal* as a relative past which has been noted in the standard grammars is its use for the expression of the future perfect.[33]   In such cases an event is viewed as past from a future reference point (R) rather than from the moment of speaking (S), thus: E<R. Some alleged examples of prophetic perfects in subordinate clauses can be understood in this way. As noted by Driver, in such cases the verb often follows כִּי, which could be functioning causally or, perhaps, as a temporal particle ("when").[34]

1.   Is 24.18-19

18 וְהָיָה הַנָּס מִקּוֹל הַפַּחַד יִפֹּל אֶל־הַפַּחַת וְהָעוֹלֶה מִתּוֹךְ הַפַּחַת
יִלָּכֵד בַּפָּח כִּי־אֲרֻבּוֹת מִמָּרוֹם נִפְתָּחוּ וַיִּרְעֲשׁוּ מוֹסְדֵי אָרֶץ:
19 רֹעָה הִתְרֹעֲעָה הָאָרֶץ פּוֹר הִתְפּוֹרְרָה אֶרֶץ מוֹט הִתְמוֹטְטָה אָרֶץ:

"And it will happen that whoever flees at the sound of terror will fall into the pit, and the one who climbs out of the pit will be captured in the snare, for the lattices of heaven will have been opened/when the lattices of heaven have been opened,[35] and the foundations of the earth shaken, the earth utterly broken, the earth split apart, the earth shaken."

2.   Is 32.10

יָמִים עַל־שָׁנָה תִּרְגַּזְנָה בֹּטְחוֹת כִּי כָּלָה בָצִיר אֹסֶף בְּלִי יָבוֹא:

"In little more than a year you will shudder, o careless ones, for the vintage will have failed/when the vintage has failed; the harvest will not come."

3.   Is 35.6

אָז יְדַלֵּג כָּאַיָּל פִּסֵּחַ וְתָרֹן לְשׁוֹן אִלֵּם כִּי־נִבְקְעוּ בַמִּדְבָּר
מַיִם וּנְחָלִים בָּעֲרָבָה:

"Then the lame one will leap like a deer, and the tongue of the dumb one will cry out, for waters will have broken forth in the desert/when waters have broken forth, and streams in the dry land."

---

[33] See e.g. Joüon and Muraoka § 112 *i*, Gibson § 59 *a*.
[34] Driver § 17.
[35] Cf. Gray *ad loc.*

4.   Is 43.20

תְּכַבְּדֵ֨נִי֙ חַיַּ֣ת הַשָּׂדֶ֔ה תַּנִּ֖ים וּבְנ֣וֹת יַֽעֲנָ֑ה כִּֽי־נָתַ֤תִּי בַמִּדְבָּ֨ר
מַ֜יִם נְהָר֣וֹת בִּֽישִׁימֹ֗ן לְהַשְׁק֛וֹת עַמִּ֖י בְחִירִֽי׃

"The beasts of the field will honor me, the jackals and ostriches, for I will have put water in the desert[36]/when I have put water in the desert."

In the following example כִּי is not functioning causally or temporally but rather introduces an object clause:

5.   Is 41.20

לְמַ֧עַן יִרְא֣וּ וְיֵדְע֗וּ וְיָשִׂ֤ימוּ וְיַשְׂכִּ֨ילוּ֙ יַחְדָּ֔ו כִּ֥י יַד־יְהוָ֖ה
עָ֣שְׂתָה זֹּ֑את וּקְד֥וֹשׁ יִשְׂרָאֵ֖ל בְּרָאָֽהּ׃

"So that together they may see and know and consider and understand that the hand of the Lord has done this/will have done this, the holy one of Israel created this."[37]

§ 3.4.2   Examples Involving Quoted Speech

Some alleged examples of the prophetic perfect involve quoted speech (e.g. laments), and in a number of such cases there are clear temporal indications that the speech will take place at a future time. For example:

6.   Zeph 1.10-11

10 וְהָיָה֩ בַיּ֨וֹם הַה֜וּא נְאֻם־יְהוָ֗ה ק֤וֹל צְעָקָה֙ מִשַּׁ֣עַר הַדָּגִ֔ים וִֽילָלָ֖ה
מִן־הַמִּשְׁנֶ֑ה וְשֶׁ֥בֶר גָּד֖וֹל מֵהַגְּבָעֽוֹת׃ 11 הֵילִ֨ילוּ֙ יֹשְׁבֵ֣י הַמַּכְתֵּ֔שׁ
כִּ֤י נִדְמָה֙ כָּל־עַ֣ם כְּנַ֔עַן נִכְרְת֖וּ כָּל־נְטִ֥ילֵי כָֽסֶף׃

"And there will be in that day—oracle of Yhwh—a sound of crying from the Fish Gate and a wailing from the Second Quarter and a great crashing from the hills: 'Wail, O inhabitants of the Mortar, for all of the merchants have been destroyed, all those laden with silver have been cut off!'"

The phrase וְהָיָה בַיּוֹם הַהוּא indicates that the following words will be uttered at a future time, and hence the event (E) described by the verbs נִדְמָה and נִכְרְתוּ is past in relation to this point.[38] Once it is recognized that v.11 is quoted speech, it becomes clear that we are not really dealing with a future meaning of the verb form. When we attempt to analyze this

---

[36] Dempsey (1988: 76, 85).
[37] Dempsey (1988: 44, 51).
[38] Cf. Joüon and Muraoka § 112 *h* n. 2.

60

in terms of Reichenbachian tense analysis, it must be noted that these examples involving quoted speech require us to distinguish between two different speaker times (S), namely that of the narrator or text itself and that of the speaker being quoted (indicated here with the symbols "S^{text}" and "S^{quote}", respectively). The destruction is future from the temporal perspective of the narrator or the text:

$$S^{text} < E$$

This is grammatically irrelevant, however, since the event (E) is not being described in relation to S^{text} but rather in relation to the temporal perspective of the speaker being quoted (S^{quote}), which is a future point in time:

$$E < S^{quote}$$

Since the speaker's time (S) in an absolute tense system can often be analyzed as the reference point (R) in a relative tense system,[39] we could apply a similar distinction to R (i.e. R^{text} and R^{quote}) and analyze this example in terms of relative tense:

$$E < R^{quote}$$

Further examples:

7.　Is 14.4ff.

4 וְנָשָׂאתָ הַמָּשָׁל הַזֶּה עַל־מֶלֶךְ בָּבֶל וְאָמָרְתָּ אֵיךְ שָׁבַת נֹגֵשׂ שָׁבְתָה מַדְהֵבָה: וגו'

"And you will lift up this proverb over the king of Babylon, and you will say: 'How the oppressor has ceased, boisterous behavior ceased...'"

8.　Is 21.12

אָמַר שֹׁמֵר אָתָה בֹקֶר וְגַם־לָיְלָה וגו'

"The watchman said: 'Morning has come, and also night...'"

9.　Is 26.1ff.

בַּיּוֹם הַהוּא יוּשַׁר הַשִּׁיר־הַזֶּה בְּאֶרֶץ יְהוּדָה עִיר עָז־לָנוּ וגו'

"In that day this song will be sung in the land of Judah: 'We have a strong city...'"

---

[39] See § 1.2.

10.   Ezek 26.17f.

וְנָשְׂאוּ עָלַיִךְ קִינָה וְאָמְרוּ לָךְ אֵיךְ אָבַדְתְּ נוֹשֶׁבֶת מִיַּמִּים וגו'

"And they will lift up this lament over you and they will say to you:
'How you have perished, O one inhabited from the seas (?)...'"

11.   Amos 8.3

וְהֵילִילוּ שִׁירוֹת הֵיכָל בַּיּוֹם הַהוּא נְאֻם אֲדֹנָי יְהוִה רַב
הַפֶּגֶר בְּכָל־מָקוֹם הִשְׁלִיךְ הָס:

"And the singing women of the palace (?) shall wail on that day–
oracle of my Lord YHWH: 'He/one has thrown so many corpses every-
where! Hush!'"[40]

In some cases it is not explicitly stated that the quoted speech will occur
at a future point in time, but it nevertheless appears possible to understand
such examples in a similar fashion:

12.   Ezek 19.1ff.

1 וְאַתָּה שָׂא קִינָה אֶל־נְשִׂיאֵי יִשְׂרָאֵל: 2 וְאָמַרְתָּ מָה אִמְּךָ
לְבִיָּא בֵּין אֲרָיוֹת רָבָצָה בְּתוֹךְ כְּפִרִים רִבְּתָה גוּרֶיהָ: וגו'

"And you, lift up a lament over the princes of Israel, and say: 'What a
lioness your mother was amongst the lions. She rested among the lions
and raised her cubs...'"

13.   Ezek 28.12ff.

12 בֶּן־אָדָם שָׂא קִינָה עַל־מֶלֶךְ צוֹר וְאָמַרְתָּ לוֹ כֹּה
אָמַר אֲדֹנָי יְהוִה אַתָּה חוֹתֵם תָּכְנִית מָלֵא חָכְמָה וּכְלִיל יֹפִי:
13 בְּעֵדֶן גַּן־אֱלֹהִים הָיִיתָ וגו'

"Son of man, take up this lament over the king of Tyre and say to him:
'Thus has the Lord YHWH spoken: You were the seal of measurement,
full of wisdom and perfect in beauty. You were in Eden, the garden of
God...'"

14.   Amos 5.1-2

1 שִׁמְעוּ אֶת־הַדָּבָר הַזֶּה אֲשֶׁר אָנֹכִי נֹשֵׂא עֲלֵיכֶם קִינָה בֵּית יִשְׂרָאֵל:
2 נָפְלָה לֹא־תוֹסִיף קוּם בְּתוּלַת יִשְׂרָאֵל נִטְּשָׁה עַל־אַדְמָתָהּ
אֵין מְקִימָהּ:

---

[40] Cf. e.g. Paul. There is considerable debate over a number of textual and exegetical issues in this verse, but this does not affect the basic point at hand.

"Hear this word which I am taking up concerning you; a lament, O house of Israel: 'She has fallen, Virgin Israel will not rise again; she has been forsaken on the ground, there is no one to lift her up.'"

15.   Nah 2.1

הִנֵּה עַל־הֶהָרִים רַגְלֵי מְבַשֵּׂר מַשְׁמִיעַ שָׁלוֹם חָגִּי יְהוּדָה חַגַּיִךְ
שַׁלְּמִי נְדָרָיִךְ כִּי לֹא יוֹסִיף עוֹד לַעֲבָר־בָּךְ בְּלִיַּעַל כֻּלֹּה נִכְרָת׃

"Behold, on the hills the feet of a herald, one who proclaims peace: 'Celebrate your feasts, O Judah, fulfill your vows, for the wicked one shall never pass through you again, he has been entirely cut off.'"[41]

The following example is especially noteworthy:

16.   Ezek 27.2ff.

2 וְאַתָּה בֶן־אָדָם שָׂא עַל־צֹר קִינָה׃ 3 וְאָמַרְתָּ לְצוֹר
הַיֹּשֶׁבֶת עַל־מְבוֹאֹת יָם רֹכֶלֶת הָעַמִּים אֶל־אִיִּים רַבִּים
כֹּה אָמַר אֲדֹנָי יְהוִה צוֹר אַתְּ אָמַרְתְּ אֲנִי כְּלִילַת יֹפִי׃
4 בְּלֵב יַמִּים גְּבוּלָיִךְ בֹּנַיִךְ כָּלְלוּ יָפְיֵךְ׃ וגו'

"And you, son of man, take up a lament over Tyre, and say to Tyre, who dwells at the entrances of the sea, merchant of the peoples (traveling) to many coastlands, thus has the Lord YHWH spoken: 'Tyre, you have said "I am perfect in beauty." Your borders are in the heart of the seas, your builders perfected your beauty...'"

Cf. examples 12 and 13. This example is remarkable in that we encounter past tenses consistently throughout this chapter, except in vv.27-32 where we find *yiqtols* and *weqatals*. I would suggest the following explanation for this: In vv.2-26 we have quoted speech that will take place in the future (absolute tense: E<S^{quote}; relative tense: E<R^{quote}). In v.27 we have a switch from the quoted speech to the temporal perspective of the narrator/text (S^{text}), from which perspective these events are still future (absolute: S^{text}<E; relative: R^{text}<E). Verse 32 again refers to a future lament (וְנָשְׂאוּ אֵלַיִךְ בְּנִיהֶם קִינָה וְקוֹנְנוּ עָלָיִךְ), and hence the rest of the chapter is to be understood as quoted speech (absolute: E<S^{quote}; relative: E<R^{quote}).

§ 3.4.3   Past Decisions

---

[41] Is 52.10 is perhaps to be interpreted similarly (cf. vv.8f.).

As we saw above (§ 3.1), the prophetic perfect is sometimes attributed at least in part to a past decree or decision. According to Revell, for example, with the "perfect of certainty" *qatal* is used "to present an event which has not occurred at the time of speaking, but which is known, or believed, to have been initiated by a decision made in the past".[42] A certain ambiguity in this description becomes apparent when we attempt to analyze it in Reichenbachian terms. On the one hand, it includes elements of a future tense since the verb refers to an event "which has not occurred at the time of speaking":

$$absolute: \text{S<E} \qquad relative: \text{R<E}$$

On the other hand, Revell also claims that this has been "initiated by a decision made in the past":

$$absolute: \text{E<S} \qquad relative: \text{E<R}$$

The ambiguity here concerns the nature of the event (E) to which the verb refers: Does it refer to some sort of mental activity such as a decision or rather to some other type of event occurring in the external world? If E in fact refers to decision made in the past then we are simply dealing with a past tense, regardless of whether or not other (future) events will result from this decision. In other words, the verb can be fully analyzed in deictic terms and there is no need to appeal to notions of "certainty", "confidence", etc. It is therefore important to determine the nature of E in certain cases. Possible examples:

17.   Is 34.2

הֶחֱרִימָם נְתָנָם לַטָּבַח

"He has laid the ban upon them, delivered them to the slaughter."[43]

This need not indicate physical destruction but could refer to a decision which YHWH has made to destroy them.

18.   Is 35.2

כְּבוֹד הַלְּבָנוֹן נִתַּן־לָהּ הֲדַר הַכַּרְמֶל וְהַשָּׁרוֹן

"The glory of Lebanon has been given to it, the splendor of Carmel and Sharon."[44]

---

[42] Revell (1989: 5f.); for similar opinions see § 3.1.

[43] Cf. Delitzsch, Kissane, Auvray, Wildberger, RSV, NBG, *Einheitsübersetzung*.

[44] Cf. Auvray, Procksch.

64

19. Jer 25.31

הָרְשָׁעִים נְתָנָם לַחֶרֶב נְאֻם־יְהוָה

"The wicked–he has delivered them to the sword. Oracle of YHWH."

For more possible examples see § 3.4.6 below.

§ 3.4.4   Narration of Events Which Occurred in a Vision

A number of scholars have noted that the prophetic perfect sometimes alternates with *yiqtols* and inverted *weqatals* (*weqataltis*).[45] Driver explains the phenomenon in this manner:

> Sometimes the perfect appears thus only for a single word; sometimes, as though nothing more than an ordinary series of past historical events were being described, it extends over many verses in succession: continually the series of perfects is interspersed with the simple future forms, as the prophet shifts his point of view, at one moment contemplating the events he is describing from the *real standpoint* of the present, at another moment looking back upon them as accomplished and done, and so viewing them from an *ideal position* in the future.[46]

Davidson likewise explains the shift between the prophetic perfect and future *yiqtol* or *weqatal* as "the prophet abandoning his ideal position and returning to the actual, and so falling into the ordinary *fut.* tenses".[47] As Goldfajn points out, the idea of "real" and "ideal" standpoints appears to correspond to "reference time" (R) in Reichenbach's method of analysis.[48] We can therefore analyze Driver's view as follows:

future tenses ("real" standpoint)
absolute:[49] $S=R^{real}<E$
relative: $R^{real}<E$

prophetic perfect ("ideal" standpoint)
absolute: $S<E<R^{ideal}$
relative: $E<R^{ideal}$

---

[45] See n.32.

[46] Driver § 14.

[47] Davidson § 41 rem. 1.

[48] Goldfajn (1998: 50, 55).

[49] Since absolute tenses require the speaker's time (S), all three points are necessary in this case (cf. § 1.2).

There is much to commend this attempt to explain the alternation of tenses, yet I will argue below (§ 3.4.4.3) that such cases of the prophetic perfect are better explained not in terms of the reference point (R) but rather in terms of the nature of the event (E) referred to. Some preliminary considerations are necessary by way of introduction to my thesis.

§ 3.4.4.1 Deixis and Events in Dreams

Consider the following example:

20.   Gen 37.7

וְהִנֵּה אֲנַחְנוּ מְאַלְּמִים אֲלֻמִּים בְּתוֹךְ הַשָּׂדֶה וְהִנֵּה קָמָה
אֲלֻמָּתִי וְגַם־נִצָּבָה וְהִנֵּה תְסֻבֶּינָה אֲלֻמֹּתֵיכֶם וַתִּשְׁתַּחֲוֶיןָ לַאֲלֻמָּתִי׃

"And behold, we were filling sheaves in the field, and behold, my sheaf arose and even stood upright, and behold your sheaves kept circling around and they bowed to my sheaf."

Joseph relates the events of his dream using a number of past tense forms (e.g קָמָה, נִצָּבָה, וַתִּשְׁתַּחֲוֶיןָ), which in itself is not particularly striking.[50] What deserves attention, however, is the reaction of his brothers in v.8: הֲמָלֹךְ תִּמְלֹךְ עָלֵינוּ "Will you really rule over us?" It appears that this dream, which Joseph related in the past tense, was understood by the brothers as having a future significance. The only way to account for this, it seems to me, is as follows: Joseph utilizes past tenses since he is narrating events which occurred *in a dream*, and this dream itself lies in Joseph's past. We are still dealing with temporal deixis:

absolute past: E<S   *relative past*: E<R

Joseph's brothers, on the other hand, are referring to the (future) realization of what is symbolically depicted in the dream. In deictic terms:

absolute future: S<E   *relative future*: R<E

It thus appears necessary to distinguish between events which occur in a dream (designated here as E^{dream}) and those which occur in the "real" or

---

[50] Cf. e.g. Fleischman (1989: 14ff.). Without a context, various temporal interpretations of *hinneh* plus the participle would be possible. Verse 6 establishes the context as past, however, and hence מְאַלְּמִים is readily understood as a progressive past (cf. § 1.4). תְסֻבֶּינָה is perhaps best interpreted as an iterative past.

"external" world (designated here as E^{real}).[51] In terms of temporal deixis, the past tense forms used to refer either to E^{dream} or E^{real} are to be analyzed in precisely the same way:

$$\begin{array}{ll} \textit{absolute past:} & \textit{relative past:} \\ E^{dream}{<}S & E^{dream}{<}R \\ E^{real}{<}S & E^{real}{<}R \end{array}$$

Yet it is the recognition of this distinction which allows us to explain the different temporal referents in Genesis 37: Joseph is referring to E^{dream}, and consequently employs past tenses, whereas his brothers are referring to E^{real}, and therefore use the future tense:

$$\begin{array}{l} \text{past tenses (Joseph)} \\ \textit{absolute}: E^{dream}{<}S \\ \textit{relative}: E^{dream}{<}R \end{array}$$

$$\begin{array}{l} \text{future tenses (brothers)} \\ \textit{absolute}: S{<}E^{real} \\ \textit{relative}: R{<}E^{real} \end{array}$$

A number of examples provide further illustration of this phenomenon:

21.   Gen 37.9

הִנֵּה חָלַמְתִּי חֲלוֹם עוֹד

וְהִנֵּה הַשֶּׁמֶשׁ וְהַיָּרֵחַ וְאַחַד עָשָׂר כּוֹכָבִים מִשְׁתַּחֲוִים לִי:

"Behold, I dreamed another dream, and behold, the sun and the moon and eleven stars were bowing down to me."

Compare Jacob's reaction in v.10:

הֲבוֹא נָבוֹא אֲנִי וְאִמְּךָ וְאַחֶיךָ לְהִשְׁתַּחֲוֹת לְךָ אָרְצָה:

"Will your mother and brothers and I really come to bow down to you?"

22.   Gen 40.9-11

9 וַיְסַפֵּר שַׂר־הַמַּשְׁקִים אֶת־חֲלֹמוֹ לְיוֹסֵף וַיֹּאמֶר לוֹ בַּחֲלוֹמִי

וְהִנֵּה־גֶפֶן לְפָנָי: 10 וּבַגֶּפֶן שְׁלֹשָׁה שָׂרִיגִם וְהִיא כְפֹרַחַת עָלְתָה נִצָּהּ

הִבְשִׁילוּ אַשְׁכְּלֹתֶיהָ עֲנָבִים: 11 וְכוֹס פַּרְעֹה בְּיָדִי וָאֶקַּח אֶת־הָעֲנָבִים

---

[51] Cf. Lindblom (1962: 122f.). This terminology is potentially problematic, and it would probably be more accurate to speak of "a *cognitive model* of the real world" (Creason 1995: 4 n.5).

וַיְסַפֵּר שַׂר־הַמַּשְׁקִים אֶת־חֲלֹמוֹ לְיוֹסֵף וַיֹּאמֶר לוֹ בַּחֲלוֹמִי וְהִנֵּה־גֶפֶן לְפָנָי:

וַאֶשְׁחַט אֹתָם אֶל־כּוֹס פַּרְעֹה וָאֶתֵּן אֶת־הַכּוֹס עַל־כַּף פַּרְעֹה:

"And the cupbearer related his dream to Joseph, and he said: 'In my dream, behold, a vine was before me, and on the vine there were three branches. And when it budded, its blossom came up and its grape clusters ripened into grapes. And the cup of Pharoah was in my hand, and I took the grapes and I squeezed them into Pharoah's cup and I put the cup into Pharoah's hand.'"

Joseph then interprets the dream in vv.12-13, using future tenses:

12 וַיֹּאמֶר לוֹ יוֹסֵף זֶה פִּתְרֹנוֹ שְׁלֹשֶׁת הַשָּׂרִגִים שְׁלֹשֶׁת יָמִים הֵם:

13 בְּעוֹד שְׁלֹשֶׁת יָמִים יִשָּׂא פַרְעֹה אֶת־רֹאשֶׁךָ וַהֲשִׁיבְךָ עַל־כַּנֶּךָ וְנָתַתָּ כוֹס־פַּרְעֹה בְּיָדוֹ כַּמִּשְׁפָּט הָרִאשׁוֹן אֲשֶׁר הָיִיתָ מַשְׁקֵהוּ:

"And Joseph said to him: 'This is the explanation of the three branches: They are three days. In three more days Pharaoh will lift up your head and restore you to your position, and you will put Pharaoh's cup in his hand as your earlier custom, when you were his cupbearer.'"

23. Gen 41.17-24

17 וַיְדַבֵּר פַּרְעֹה אֶל־יוֹסֵף בַּחֲלֹמִי הִנְנִי עֹמֵד עַל־שְׂפַת הַיְאֹר:

18 וְהִנֵּה מִן־הַיְאֹר עֹלֹת שֶׁבַע פָּרוֹת בְּרִיאוֹת בָּשָׂר וִיפֹת תֹּאַר וַתִּרְעֶינָה בָּאָחוּ: וגו'

"And Pharaoh said to Joseph: 'In my dream, behold, I was standing on the bank of the Nile. And behold, seven fat cows were coming up from the Nile and they were beautiful in appearance, and they grazed among the reeds...'"

Pharaoh recounts his dreams using a number of past tenses (cf. vv.1-7), but in vv.25-31 Joseph uses future tenses in explaining the meaning of the dreams.[52]

Similar examples can be found in Biblical Aramaic:

24. Dan 2.31-35

31 אַנְתְּ מַלְכָּא חָזֵה הֲוַיְתָ וַאֲלוּ צְלֵם חַד שַׂגִּיא צַלְמָא דִּכֵּן רַב וְזִיוֵהּ יַתִּיר קָאֵם לְקָבְלָךְ וְרֵוֵהּ דְּחִיל: 32 הוּא צַלְמָא רֵאשֵׁהּ דִּי־דְהַב טָב חֲדוֹהִי וּדְרָעוֹהִי דִּי כְסַף מְעוֹהִי וְיַרְכָתֵהּ דִּי נְחָשׁ:

33 שָׁקוֹהִי דִּי פַרְזֶל רַגְלוֹהִי מִנְּהֵין דִּי פַרְזֶל וּמִנְּהֵין דִּי חֲסַף:

34 חָזֵה הֲוַיְתָ עַד דִּי הִתְגְּזֶרֶת אֶבֶן דִּי־לָא בִידַיִן וּמְחָת לְצַלְמָא עַל־רַגְלוֹהִי דִּי פַרְזְלָא וְחַסְפָּא וְהַדֵּקֶת הִמּוֹן: 35 בֵּאדַיִן דָּקוּ כַחֲדָה

---

[52] Compare also the dream recounted in Ju 7.13 with v.14.

פַּרְזְלָא חַסְפָּא נְחָשָׁא כַּסְפָּא וְדַהֲבָא וַהֲווֹ כְּעוּר מִן־אִדְּרֵי־קַיִט וּנְשָׂא
הִמּוֹן רוּחָא וְכָל־אֲתַר לָא־הִשְׁתְּכַח לְהוֹן וְאַבְנָא דִּי־מְחָת לְצַלְמָא
הֲוָת לְטוּר רַב וּמְלָת כָּל־אַרְעָא:

"You, O king, were watching, and behold, there was a great image…
(v.34) While you were watching a rock was cut out, but not by hands, and
it smashed the image…"

The king's dream is narrated with past tenses,[53] but then is explained in
vv.36-45 using future tenses.

25. Dan 4.7-15

7 וְחֶזְוֵי רֵאשִׁי עַל־מִשְׁכְּבִי חָזֵה הֲוֵית וַאֲלוּ אִילָן בְּגוֹא אַרְעָא וְרוּמֵהּ
שַׂגִּיא: 8 רְבָה אִילָנָא וּתְקִף וְרוּמֵהּ יִמְטֵא לִשְׁמַיָּא וַחֲזוֹתֵהּ לְסוֹף
כָּל־אַרְעָא: 9 עָפְיֵהּ שַׁפִּיר וְאִנְבֵּהּ שַׂגִּיא וּמָזוֹן לְכֹלָּא־בֵהּ תְּחֹתוֹהִי
תַּטְלֵל חֵיוַת בָּרָא וּבְעַנְפוֹהִי יְדוּרָן צִפֲּרֵי שְׁמַיָּא וּמִנֵּהּ יִתְּזִין
כָּל־בִּשְׂרָא: 10 חָזֵה הֲוֵית בְּחֶזְוֵי רֵאשִׁי עַל־מִשְׁכְּבִי וַאֲלוּ עִיר וְקַדִּישׁ
מִן־שְׁמַיָּא נָחִת: 11 קָרֵא בְחַיִל וְכֵן אָמַר גֹּדּוּ אִילָנָא וְקַצִּצוּ עַנְפוֹהִי
אַתַּרוּ עָפְיֵהּ וּבַדַּרוּ אִנְבֵּהּ תְּנֻד חֵיוְתָא מִן־תַּחְתּוֹהִי וְצִפֲּרַיָּא
מִן־עַנְפוֹהִי: 12 בְּרַם עִקַּר שָׁרְשׁוֹהִי בְּאַרְעָא שְׁבֻקוּ וּבֶאֱסוּר דִּי־פַרְזֶל
וּנְחָשׁ בְּדִתְאָא דִּי בָרָא וּבְטַל שְׁמַיָּא יִצְטַבַּע וְעִם־חֵיוְתָא חֲלָקֵהּ
בַּעֲשַׂב אַרְעָא: 13 לִבְבֵהּ מִן־אֲנָשָׁא יְשַׁנּוֹן וּלְבַב חֵיוָה יִתְיְהִב לֵהּ
וְשִׁבְעָה עִדָּנִין יַחְלְפוּן עֲלוֹהִי: 14 בִּגְזֵרַת עִירִין פִּתְגָמָא וּמֵאמַר
קַדִּישִׁין שְׁאֵלְתָא עַד־דִּבְרַת דִּי יִנְדְּעוּן חַיַּיָּא דִּי־שַׁלִּיט עִלָּאָה
בְּמַלְכוּת אֲנָשָׁא וּלְמַן־דִּי יִצְבֵּא יִתְּנִנַּהּ וּשְׁפַל אֲנָשִׁים יְקִים עֲלַהּ:
15 דְּנָה חֶלְמָא חֲזֵית אֲנָה מַלְכָּא נְבוּכַדְנֶצַּר וְאַנְתְּ בֵּלְטְשַׁאצַּר פִּשְׁרֵא
אֱמַר כָּל־קֳבֵל דִּי כָּל־חַכִּימֵי מַלְכוּתִי לָא־יָכְלִין פִּשְׁרָא לְהוֹדָעֻתַנִי
וְאַנְתְּ כָּהֵל דִּי רוּחַ־אֱלָהִין קַדִּישִׁין בָּךְ:

---

[53] The tense system in the Aramaic of Daniel has, admittedly, been the subject of debate,
and cannot be discussed in detail here. We think that it can be safely argued, *pace* Rosén
(1961: 185ff.), that the perfect does in fact function as a narrative past tense here, as it
does in other Aramaic corpora (cf. Muraoka and Porten § 51 *a*, Cook 1998: 376, Bezer
1976-77, Bauer and Leander § 79). The chief difficulty in Daniel relates to the rather frequent use of the imperfect and participle as simple preterites (see e.g. Joüon 1941, Blau
1987: 6ff., Bombeck 1996, Rogland 2003: 427ff.; for additional discussion of the preterital
prefix conjugation in Old Aramaic see Muraoka 1998 and Muraoka and Rogland 1998,
and the literature cited there). Although this is indeed a peculiar phenomenon that requires
further investigation, I do not think it a sufficient basis for rejecting a tense-based understanding of the perfect in Biblical Aramaic.

"And as for the visions of my head as I was upon my bed: I was watching, and behold, there was a tree in the earth and its height was great. The tree grew and became strong..."

The king relates his dream using past tenses, yet Daniel uses future tenses when he interprets it in vv.17ff.

26. Dan 7.2-16

2 חָזֵה הֲוֵית בְּחֶזְוִי עִם־לֵילְיָא וַאֲרוּ אַרְבַּע רוּחֵי שְׁמַיָּא מְגִיחָן
לְיַמָּא רַבָּא: 3 וְאַרְבַּע חֵיוָן רַבְרְבָן סָלְקָן מִן־יַמָּא שָׁנְיָן דָּא מִן־דָּא:
4 קַדְמָיְתָא כְאַרְיֵה וְגַפִּין דִּי־נְשַׁר לַהּ חָזֵה הֲוֵית עַד דִּי־מְרִיטוּ
גַפַּיהּ וּנְטִילַת מִן־אַרְעָא וְעַל־רַגְלַיִן כֶּאֱנָשׁ הֳקִימַת וּלְבַב אֱנָשׁ יְהִיב
לַהּ: 5 וַאֲרוּ חֵיוָה אָחֳרִי תִנְיָנָה דָּמְיָה לְדֹב וְלִשְׂטַר־חַד הֳקִמַת וּתְלָת
עִלְעִין בְּפֻמַּהּ בֵּין שִׁנַּהּ וְכֵן אָמְרִין לַהּ קוּמִי אֲכֻלִי בְּשַׂר שַׂגִּיא:
6 בָּאתַר דְּנָה חָזֵה הֲוֵית וַאֲרוּ אָחֳרִי כִּנְמַר וְלַהּ גַּפִּין אַרְבַּע
דִּי־עוֹף עַל־גַּבַּהּ וְאַרְבְּעָה רֵאשִׁין לְחֵיוְתָא וְשָׁלְטָן יְהִיב לַהּ:
7 בָּאתַר דְּנָה חָזֵה הֲוֵית בְּחֶזְוֵי לֵילְיָא וַאֲרוּ חֵיוָה רְבִיעָאָה דְּחִילָה
וְאֵימְתָנִי וְתַקִּיפָא יַתִּירָא וְשִׁנַּיִן דִּי־פַרְזֶל לַהּ רַבְרְבָן אָכְלָה וּמַדֱּקָה
וּשְׁאָרָא בְּרַגְלַהּ רָפְסָה וְהִיא מְשַׁנְּיָה מִן־כָּל־חֵיוָתָא דִּי קָדָמַיהּ
וְקַרְנַיִן עֲשַׂר לַהּ: 8 מִשְׂתַּכַּל הֲוֵית בְּקַרְנַיָּא וַאֲלוּ קֶרֶן אָחֳרִי זְעֵירָה
סִלְקָת בֵּינֵיהֵן וּתְלָת מִן־קַרְנַיָּא קַדְמָיָתָא אֶתְעֲקַרָה מִן־קֳדָמַהּ
וַאֲלוּ עַיְנִין כְּעַיְנֵי אֲנָשָׁא בְּקַרְנָא־דָא וּפֻם מְמַלִּל רַבְרְבָן:
9 חָזֵה הֲוֵית עַד דִּי כָרְסָוָן רְמִיו וְעַתִּיק יוֹמִין יְתִב לְבוּשֵׁהּ
כִּתְלַג חִוָּר וּשְׂעַר רֵאשֵׁהּ כַּעֲמַר נְקֵא כָּרְסְיֵהּ שְׁבִיבִין דִּי־נוּר
גַּלְגִּלּוֹהִי נוּר דָּלִק: 10 נְהַר דִּי־נוּר נָגֵד וְנָפֵק מִן־קֳדָמוֹהִי אֶלֶף
אַלְפִין יְשַׁמְּשׁוּנֵּהּ וְרִבּוֹ רִבְבָן קָדָמוֹהִי יְקוּמוּן דִּינָא יְתִב
וְסִפְרִין פְּתִיחוּ: 11 חָזֵה הֲוֵית בֵּאדַיִן מִן־קָל מִלַּיָּא רַבְרְבָתָא דִּי
קַרְנָא מְמַלֱּלָה חָזֵה הֲוֵית עַד דִּי קְטִילַת חֵיוְתָא וְהוּבַד גִּשְׁמַהּ
וִיהִיבַת לִיקֵדַת אֶשָּׁא: 12 וּשְׁאָר חֵיוָתָא הֶעְדִּיו שָׁלְטָנְהוֹן וְאַרְכָה
בְחַיִּין יְהִיבַת לְהוֹן עַד־זְמַן וְעִדָּן: 13 חָזֵה הֲוֵית בְּחֶזְוֵי לֵילְיָא וַאֲרוּ
עִם־עֲנָנֵי שְׁמַיָּא כְּבַר אֱנָשׁ אָתֵה הֲוָה וְעַד־עַתִּיק יוֹמַיָּא מְטָה
וּקְדָמוֹהִי הַקְרְבוּהִי: 14 וְלֵהּ יְהִיב שָׁלְטָן וִיקָר וּמַלְכוּ וְכֹל עַמְמַיָּא
אֻמַיָּא וְלִשָּׁנַיָּא לֵהּ יִפְלְחוּן שָׁלְטָנֵהּ שָׁלְטָן עָלַם דִּי־לָא יֶעְדֵּה
וּמַלְכוּתֵהּ דִּי־לָא תִתְחַבַּל: 15 אֶתְכְּרִיַּת רוּחִי אֲנָה דָנִיֵּאל
בְּגוֹא נִדְנֶה וְחֶזְוֵי רֵאשִׁי יְבַהֲלֻנַּנִי: 16 קִרְבֵת עַל־חַד מִן־קָאֲמַיָּא
וְיַצִּיבָא אֶבְעֵא־מִנֵּהּ עַל־כָּל־דְּנָה וַאֲמַר־לִי וּפְשַׁר מִלַּיָּא יְהוֹדְעִנַּנִי:

"I was watching in my vision at night, and behold, the four winds of heaven were stirring up the great sea. And four great beasts came up out of the sea..."

Compare the future tenses used in the explanation of the dream (vv.17ff.).

§ 3.4.4.2 Deixis and Events in Visions

Consider now the following example:

27. Dan 8.2-12

2 וָאֶרְאֶה בֶּחָזוֹן וַיְהִי בִּרְאֹתִי וַאֲנִי בְּשׁוּשַׁן הַבִּירָה אֲשֶׁר בְּעֵילָם
הַמְּדִינָה וָאֶרְאֶה בֶּחָזוֹן וַאֲנִי הָיִיתִי עַל־אוּבַל אוּלָי: 3 וָאֶשָּׂא עֵינַי
וָאֶרְאֶה וְהִנֵּה אַיִל אֶחָד עֹמֵד לִפְנֵי הָאֻבָל וְלוֹ קְרָנָיִם וְהַקְּרָנַיִם
גְּבֹהוֹת וְהָאַחַת גְּבֹהָה מִן־הַשֵּׁנִית וְהַגְּבֹהָה עֹלָה בָּאַחֲרֹנָה:
4 רָאִיתִי אֶת־הָאַיִל מְנַגֵּחַ יָמָּה וְצָפוֹנָה וָנֶגְבָּה וְכָל־חַיּוֹת לֹא־יַעַמְדוּ
לְפָנָיו וְאֵין מַצִּיל מִיָּדוֹ וְעָשָׂה כִרְצֹנוֹ וְהִגְדִּיל: 5 וַאֲנִי הָיִיתִי מֵבִין
וְהִנֵּה צְפִיר־הָעִזִּים בָּא מִן־הַמַּעֲרָב עַל־פְּנֵי כָל־הָאָרֶץ וְאֵין נוֹגֵעַ
בָּאָרֶץ וְהַצָּפִיר קֶרֶן חָזוּת בֵּין עֵינָיו: 6 וַיָּבֹא עַד־הָאַיִל בַּעַל
הַקְּרָנַיִם אֲשֶׁר רָאִיתִי עֹמֵד לִפְנֵי הָאֻבָל וַיָּרָץ אֵלָיו בַּחֲמַת כֹּחוֹ:
7 וּרְאִיתִיו מַגִּיעַ אֵצֶל הָאַיִל וַיִּתְמַרְמַר אֵלָיו וַיַּךְ אֶת־הָאַיִל
וַיְשַׁבֵּר אֶת־שְׁתֵּי קְרָנָיו וְלֹא־הָיָה כֹחַ בָּאַיִל לַעֲמֹד לְפָנָיו
וַיַּשְׁלִיכֵהוּ אַרְצָה וַיִּרְמְסֵהוּ וְלֹא־הָיָה מַצִּיל לָאַיִל מִיָּדוֹ:
8 וּצְפִיר הָעִזִּים הִגְדִּיל עַד־מְאֹד וּכְעָצְמוֹ נִשְׁבְּרָה הַקֶּרֶן
הַגְּדוֹלָה וַתַּעֲלֶנָה חָזוּת אַרְבַּע תַּחְתֶּיהָ לְאַרְבַּע רוּחוֹת הַשָּׁמָיִם:
9 וּמִן־הָאַחַת מֵהֶם יָצָא קֶרֶן־אַחַת מִצְּעִירָה וַתִּגְדַּל־יֶתֶר אֶל־הַנֶּגֶב
וְאֶל־הַמִּזְרָח וְאֶל־הַצֶּבִי: 10 וַתִּגְדַּל עַד־צְבָא הַשָּׁמָיִם וַתַּפֵּל אַרְצָה
מִן־הַצָּבָא וּמִן־הַכּוֹכָבִים וַתִּרְמְסֵם: 11 וְעַד שַׂר־הַצָּבָא הִגְדִּיל וּמִמֶּנּוּ
הוּרַם הַתָּמִיד וְהֻשְׁלַךְ מְכוֹן מִקְדָּשׁוֹ: 12 וְצָבָא תִּנָּתֵן עַל־הַתָּמִיד
בְּפָשַׁע וְתַשְׁלֵךְ אֱמֶת אַרְצָה וְעָשְׂתָה וְהִצְלִיחָה:

"I looked in my vision, and when I looked I was in Susa the capital, which is in the province of Elam, and I looked in the vision and I was at the river Ulai. And I lifted up my eyes and looked and behold, there was a ram standing beside the river..."

Daniel narrates the events of his vision using a number of past tense forms, yet in vv.17ff. Gabriel explains that the events described are yet to take place, much like the examples of dreams discussed above. Therefore, just as we found it necessary to distinguish E^{dream} and E^{real}, it also appears necessary here to distinguish between E^{vision} and E^{real}. Daniel's use of past tenses reflects the time of the vision, whereas Gabriel's future tenses refer to the future realization of the events that are symbolically announced in the vision:

past tenses (Daniel)
absolute: $E^{vision} < S$
relative: $E^{vision} < R$

future tenses (Gabriel)
absolute: $S < E^{real}$
relative: $R < E^{real}$

Compare Gen 37.7 (example 20):

past tenses (Joseph)
absolute: $E^{dream} < S$
relative: $E^{dream} < R$

future tenses (brothers)
absolute: $S < E^{real}$
relative: $R < E^{real}$

§ 3.4.4.3   The "Prophetic Perfect"

We have discussed the preceding examples at some length in order to lay the groundwork for our thesis regarding the prophetic perfect, namely that in many cases we are dealing with a similar phenomenon of past tenses that refer to events which occurred in a vision (E^{vision}) or in a dream (E^{dream}).[54] Thus, rather than expressing notions of e.g. "certainty", "immi-

---

[54] The possible effect of visionary experience on tense usage is mentioned by e.g. Rainey (1988: 35f.) and Dempsey (1988: 130f.), although they do not develop the idea as we have done so here. A similar explanation has been proposed for some cases of the aorist in NT Greek (e.g. Rev 19.17ff.; 20.1ff.; 21.1ff.); see Mussies (1971: 340) and Fanning (1990: 274 n.163). In his study of future-referring perfects in Classical Arabic, Aartun (1963: 88f.) also draws attention to a prophecy in which the prophetess explicitly claims to have *seen* something (*ra'aitu sulḥafā... fa-daḥalat-i -l-ḥadiqata* "Ich habe eine Schildkröte gesehen ... dann kam sie in den Garten..."). Note that in the preceding discussion we have treated dreams and visions separately because of the terms explicitly used in the examples cited. In fact, it might be artificial to draw too sharp a distinction between the two, as indicated by the fact that some of the Aramaic examples above are not only called "dreams" (חֶלְמָא) but also "visions" (חֶזְוָא; Dan 4.6f.; 7.15) as well as by the parallel expressions one finds in e.g. Nu 12.6 (מַרְאָה, חֲלוֹם) and Joel 3.1 (חֶזְיֹנוֹת, חֲלֹמוֹת). Our concern here is not to establish any sort of typology of prophetic revelation (contrast e.g.

nence" or "vividness" often attributed to the prophetic perfect, they are simply to be understood as past tenses which refer to E^vision; it is the vision itself that lies in the prophet's past. If this analysis is correct, then it is the non-past forms that are often interspersed with the past tenses which require explanation.[55]

We will illustrate this proposal with two examples.

28. Is 22.1-14

1 מַשָּׂא גֵּיא חִזָּיוֹן מַה־לָּךְ אֵפוֹא כִּי־עָלִית כֻּלָּךְ לַגַּגּוֹת:
2 תְּשֻׁאוֹת מְלֵאָה עִיר הוֹמִיָּה קִרְיָה עַלִּיזָה חֲלָלַיִךְ לֹא חַלְלֵי־חֶרֶב
וְלֹא מֵתֵי מִלְחָמָה: 3 כָּל־קְצִינַיִךְ נָדְדוּ־יַחַד מִקֶּשֶׁת אֻסָּרוּ
כָּל־נִמְצָאַיִךְ אֻסְּרוּ יַחְדָּו מֵרָחוֹק בָּרָחוּ: 4 עַל־כֵּן אָמַרְתִּי שְׁעוּ מִנִּי
אֲמָרֵר בַּבֶּכִי אַל־תָּאִיצוּ לְנַחֲמֵנִי עַל־שֹׁד בַּת־עַמִּי: 5 כִּי יוֹם
מְהוּמָה וּמְבוּסָה וּמְבוּכָה לַאדֹנָי יְהוִה צְבָאוֹת בְּגֵיא חִזָּיוֹן
מְקַרְקַר קִר וְשׁוֹעַ אֶל־הָהָר: 6 וְעֵילָם נָשָׂא אַשְׁפָּה בְּרֶכֶב אָדָם
פָּרָשִׁים וְקִיר עֵרָה מָגֵן: 7 וַיְהִי מִבְחַר־עֲמָקַיִךְ מָלְאוּ רָכֶב וְהַפָּרָשִׁים
שֹׁת שָׁתוּ הַשָּׁעְרָה: 8 וַיְגַל אֵת מָסַךְ יְהוּדָה וַתַּבֵּט בַּיּוֹם הַהוּא
אֶל־נֶשֶׁק בֵּית הַיָּעַר: 9 וְאֵת בְּקִיעֵי עִיר־דָּוִד רְאִיתֶם כִּי־רָבּוּ
וַתְּקַבְּצוּ אֶת־מֵי הַבְּרֵכָה הַתַּחְתּוֹנָה: 10 וְאֶת־בָּתֵּי יְרוּשָׁלִַם סְפַרְתֶּם
וַתִּתְצוּ הַבָּתִּים לְבַצֵּר הַחוֹמָה: 11 וּמִקְוָה עֲשִׂיתֶם בֵּין הַחֹמֹתַיִם לְמֵי
הַבְּרֵכָה הַיְשָׁנָה וְלֹא הִבַּטְתֶּם אֶל־עֹשֶׂיהָ וְיֹצְרָהּ מֵרָחוֹק לֹא רְאִיתֶם:
12 וַיִּקְרָא אֲדֹנָי יְהוִה צְבָאוֹת בַּיּוֹם הַהוּא לִבְכִי וּלְמִסְפֵּד וּלְקָרְחָה
וְלַחֲגֹר שָׂק: 13 וְהִנֵּה שָׂשׂוֹן וְשִׂמְחָה הָרֹג בָּקָר וְשָׁחֹט צֹאן
אָכֹל בָּשָׂר וְשָׁתוֹת יַיִן אָכוֹל וְשָׁתוֹ כִּי מָחָר נָמוּת:
14 וְנִגְלָה בְאָזְנָי יְהוָה צְבָאוֹת אִם־יְכֻפַּר הֶעָוֹן הַזֶּה לָכֶם עַד־תְּמֻתוּן
אָמַר אֲדֹנָי יְהוִה צְבָאוֹת:

Lindblom 1962: 122ff.) but simply to draw attention to the different types of events (E) to which one can refer. For convenience I will only refer to E^vision in the following.

[55] One might object to our thesis on the grounds that in many alleged examples of the prophetic perfect, unlike examples 20-27 above, there are no explicit indications that the events described took place in a vision or dream. However, I think it can plausibly be argued that this is simply a convention of the prophetic genre that does not always need to be stated explicitly. Note, for example, that the superscriptions of some prophetic books contain the noun חָזוֹן "vision" (Is 1.1; Obad 1; Nah 1.1) or the verb חָזָה (Am 1.1; Mic 1.1; Hab 1.1). Cf. Maimonides' *Guide of the Perplexed* (II § 46): "Some of [the actions performed by a prophet] are set forth in the books of prophecy without qualification. For since it is known that all these things occur in a vision of prophecy, Scripture in the re-counting of all details of the parable may dispense with reiterating that they happened in a vision of prophecy."

"An oracle: the valley of vision. What troubles you then, that all of you have gone up to the housetops? O clamorous city, exultant town, full of noise, your slain were not slain of the sword, nor dead from war. All your chiefs fled together, they were captured without a bow..."

In this passage we are dealing almost exclusively with past tense forms. Gray argues that a number of these are prophetic since, in his opinion, v.5 is a prediction of a coming day of YHWH. However, it should be noted that the other references to "that day" in this section (vv.8, 12) occur with past tense forms. Consequently, it seems more probable that the verbless clause of v.5 has a past referent: "for the Lord, YHWH Almighty, *had* a day of tumult, trampling and confusion". If one takes the whole passage as referring to catastrophic events which the prophet has seen in a vision (E[vision]) then the only form requiring explanation is v.14 וְנִגְלָה.[56] This could be understood as an iterative past[57] or perhaps as a conjunctive *weqatal*.

29. Is 8.23-9.6

8:23 כִּי לֹא מוּעָף לַאֲשֶׁר מוּצָק לָהּ כָּעֵת הָרִאשׁוֹן הֵקַל אַרְצָה זְבֻלוּן
וְאַרְצָה נַפְתָּלִי וְהָאַחֲרוֹן הִכְבִּיד דֶּרֶךְ הַיָּם עֵבֶר הַיַּרְדֵּן גְּלִיל הַגּוֹיִם:
9:1 הָעָם הַהֹלְכִים בַּחֹשֶׁךְ רָאוּ אוֹר גָּדוֹל יֹשְׁבֵי בְּאֶרֶץ צַלְמָוֶת
אוֹר נָגַהּ עֲלֵיהֶם: 2 הִרְבִּיתָ הַגּוֹי לוֹ הִגְדַּלְתָּ הַשִּׂמְחָה שָׂמְחוּ לְפָנֶיךָ
כְּשִׂמְחַת בַּקָּצִיר כַּאֲשֶׁר יָגִילוּ בְּחַלְּקָם שָׁלָל: 3 כִּי אֶת־עֹל סֻבֳּלוֹ וְאֵת
מַטֵּה שִׁכְמוֹ שֵׁבֶט הַנֹּגֵשׂ בּוֹ הַחִתֹּתָ כְּיוֹם מִדְיָן: 4 כִּי כָל־סְאוֹן סֹאֵן
בְּרַעַשׁ וְשִׂמְלָה מְגוֹלָלָה בְדָמִים וְהָיְתָה לִשְׂרֵפָה מַאֲכֹלֶת אֵשׁ:
5 כִּי־יֶלֶד יֻלַּד־לָנוּ בֵּן נִתַּן־לָנוּ וַתְּהִי הַמִּשְׂרָה עַל־שִׁכְמוֹ וַיִּקְרָא שְׁמוֹ
פֶּלֶא יוֹעֵץ אֵל גִּבּוֹר אֲבִיעַד שַׂר־שָׁלוֹם: 6 לְמַרְבֵּה הַמִּשְׂרָה וּלְשָׁלוֹם
אֵין־קֵץ עַל־כִּסֵּא דָוִד וְעַל־מַמְלַכְתּוֹ לְהָכִין אֹתָהּ וּלְסַעֲדָהּ בְּמִשְׁפָּט
וּבִצְדָקָה מֵעַתָּה וְעַד־עוֹלָם קִנְאַת יְהוָה צְבָאוֹת תַּעֲשֶׂה־זֹּאת:

"For there is no more gloom to the one who was in anguish. In the former times he humbled the land of Zebulun and the land of Naphtali, but in later times he honored the route of the sea, across the Jordan, Galilee of the gentiles. The people walking in darkness saw a great light; a light has dawned upon those living in a land of deepest darkness..."

---

[56] Ehrlich revocalises this as a first person plural imperfect (וְנִגְלֶה) and connects it to the preceding quote (v.13): "Essen und Trinken! denn morgen sind wir tot oder gehen in die Verbannung". The *yiqtol* forms in v. 4 and v. 13 occur in quoted speech and do not establish a non-past setting for the visionary events being narrated.

[57] See König § 367 *h* and his commentary *ad loc.* ("da enthüllte sich immer wieder in meinen Ohren").

This passage is frequently cited as a classic example of the prophetic perfect. As in the preceding example, we encounter mostly past tense forms here. According to our proposal, these are to be understood as a narration of events that occurred in a vision which the prophet had (E^{vision}). There are only a few non-past forms which require discussion. In 9.2 the verb יָגִילוּ does not indicate a future setting,[58] since this is a general statement which occurs in a comparison: "They rejoiced before you as with joy at the harvest, as men rejoice when dividing the plunder". As such it does not affect the temporal setting of the past narration. A number of translations take וְהָיְתָה in 9.4 as future (Vulgate: *erit*), yet it could also be an inverted *weqatal* indicating an iterative past or a conjunctive *weqatal* (LXX: ἐγενήθησαν; perhaps the Peshitta's ܘܗܘܐ). In 9.6 תַּעֲשֶׂה clearly seems to refer to the future (cf. the versions).

The future reference in v.6 calls for further comment. It would appear that we are dealing here with a switch from narrating the events as they occurred in the prophet's vision (E^{vision}) to referring to the future realization of the events that are announced in the vision (E^{real}). We have seen in the examples above that different speakers refer to E in different ways, but what is interesting in this case is that it is the same speaker who switches from E^{vision} to E^{real}. However, this phenomenon occurs even in some of the examples above. For example, in Dan 8.22 (example 27) Gabriel explains

וְהַנִּשְׁבֶּרֶת וַתַּעֲמֹדְנָה אַרְבַּע תַּחְתֶּיהָ
אַרְבַּע מַלְכֻיוֹת מִגּוֹי יַעֲמֹדְנָה וְלֹא בְכֹחוֹ

"And as for the broken (horn), in whose place four (horns) arose: Four kingdoms will arise from the nation, but not by his power."

Similarly, in Dan 7.14 (example 26) we find וְלֵהּ יְהִיב שָׁלְטָן וִיקָר וּמַלְכוּ "and to him was given dominion and glory and kingdom", followed by

וְכֹל עַמְמַיָּא אֻמַיָּא וְלִשָּׁנַיָּא לֵהּ יִפְלְחוּן
שָׁלְטָנֵהּ שָׁלְטָן עָלַם דִּי־לָא יֶעְדֵּה וּמַלְכוּתֵהּ דִּי־לָא תִתְחַבַּל:

"...and all peoples, nations, and tongues will serve him, his dominion is an eternal dominion which will not pass away, and his kingdom is one which will not be destroyed."

---

[58] *Pace* Klein (1990: 53).

It appears that Daniel is no longer referring to E^{vision} but rather to E^{real}, and thus switches from past to future tenses.[59] Consequently, the switch from E^{vision} in Is 8.23-9.5 to E^{real} in 9.6 should not necessarily be considered strange. We will have occasion to return to this subject later in connection with several examples. For the moment, however, it should be added that, as far as I can see, it simply appears to be the speaker's choice whether to refer to E^{vision} or to E^{real}. In other words, I have not been able to determine any reason why Daniel should have chosen to refer to E^{vision} instead of E^{real}, nor why he should have begun by referring to E^{vision} and then shifted to E^{real}. Consequently, our thesis concerning the prophetic perfect should only be understood as explaining the tense usage itself and not the speaker's choice which determines the use of the tenses. An answer to this latter question requires a separate study.

As we mentioned above (§ 3.4.4), Driver's explanation of the prophetic perfect relates to a shift between "real" and "ideal" reference points (R), rather than a difference in the nature of the event (E) referred to, as argued here. There are two reasons why I think that Driver's explanation is to be rejected. Firstly, we find past tenses in many narrations of dreams and visions (e.g. Gen 28.12f.; Jer 25.15ff.; Zech 1-6 and frequently in Ezekiel) which do not have any future significance and consequently cannot be explained in terms of an "ideal" reference point. At the same time, the events described clearly did not occur in the external world (E^{real}). The only explanation for such cases is that the past tenses reflect the time of the vision (E^{vision}). Secondly, the distinction proposed here is able to account for cases in which one person describes visionary events that are occurring as he speaks, whereas another person can use future tenses to refer to the realization of what is symbolically portrayed in the vision:

30.   Jer 1.13ff.

13 וַיְהִי דְבַר־יְהוָה אֵלַי שֵׁנִית לֵאמֹר מָה אַתָּה רֹאֶה וָאֹמַר
סִיר נָפוּחַ אֲנִי רֹאֶה וּפָנָיו מִפְּנֵי צָפוֹנָה: 14 וַיֹּאמֶר יְהוָה אֵלָי
מִצָּפוֹן תִּפָּתַח הָרָעָה עַל כָּל־יֹשְׁבֵי הָאָרֶץ: וגו'

"And the word of YHWH came to me a second time, saying: 'What do you see?' And I said: 'I see a boiling pot, facing away from the north.' And YHWH said to me: 'From the north the disaster will be set loose upon all the inhabitants of the land...'"

---

[59] This interpretation could perhaps be disputed. It might be possible to understand v.14 as continuing the reference to E^{vision} and to interpret יִפְלְחוּן as either preterital (NBG: "alle volken, natiën en talen dienden hem", NIV: "men of every language worshipped him"; cf. n.53 above), modal (RSV: "that all peoples, nations and languages should serve him"), or prospective (i.e. future-in-the-past). However, a preterital interpretation of לָא יֶעְדֵּה and לָא תִתְחַבַּל seems unlikely.

31. Amos 7.8f.

וַיֹּאמֶר יְהוָה אֵלַי מָה־אַתָּה רֹאֶה עָמוֹס וָאֹמַר אֲנָךְ וַיֹּאמֶר אֲדֹנָי 8
הִנְנִי שָׂם אֲנָךְ בְּקֶרֶב עַמִּי יִשְׂרָאֵל לֹא־אוֹסִיף עוֹד עֲבוֹר לוֹ: 9 וְנָשַׁמּוּ
בָּמוֹת יִשְׂחָק וּמִקְדְּשֵׁי יִשְׂרָאֵל יֶחֱרָבוּ וְקַמְתִּי עַל־בֵּית יָרָבְעָם בֶּחָרֶב:

"And YHWH said to me: 'What do you see, Amos?' And I said: 'A
measuring line.' And the Lord said: 'I am going to set a measuring line in
the midst of my people Israel. I will not pass by them again. And the
high places of Isaac will be desolated, and the sanctuaries of Israel laid
waste, and I will rise up against the house of Jeroboam with the sword.'"

Driver's theory would be incapable of explaining the shift between the
present and future references since in these cases both R^{real} and R^{ideal}
would correspond to the speaker's actual point in time (S). The different
temporal references are adequately explained by observing our distinction
between E^{vision} and E^{real}.

§ 3.4.4.4 Examples

32. Is 9.10-20

וַיְשַׂגֵּב יְהוָה אֶת־צָרֵי רְצִין עָלָיו וְאֶת־אֹיְבָיו יְסַכְסֵךְ: 10
אֲרָם מִקֶּדֶם וּפְלִשְׁתִּים מֵאָחוֹר וַיֹּאכְלוּ אֶת־יִשְׂרָאֵל בְּכָל־פֶּה 11
בְּכָל־זֹאת לֹא־שָׁב אַפּוֹ וְעוֹד יָדוֹ נְטוּיָה:
וְהָעָם לֹא־שָׁב עַד־הַמַּכֵּהוּ וְאֶת־יְהוָה צְבָאוֹת לֹא דָרָשׁוּ: 12
וַיַּכְרֵת יְהוָה מִיִּשְׂרָאֵל רֹאשׁ וְזָנָב כִּפָּה וְאַגְמוֹן יוֹם אֶחָד: 13
זָקֵן וּנְשׂוּא־פָנִים הוּא הָרֹאשׁ וְנָבִיא מוֹרֶה־שֶּׁקֶר הוּא הַזָּנָב: 14
וַיִּהְיוּ מְאַשְּׁרֵי הָעָם־הַזֶּה מַתְעִים וּמְאֻשָּׁרָיו מְבֻלָּעִים: 15
עַל־כֵּן עַל־בַּחוּרָיו לֹא־יִשְׂמַח אֲדֹנָי וְאֶת־יְתֹמָיו וְאֶת־אַלְמְנֹתָיו 16
לֹא יְרַחֵם כִּי כֻלּוֹ חָנֵף וּמֵרַע וְכָל־פֶּה דֹּבֵר נְבָלָה
בְּכָל־זֹאת לֹא־שָׁב אַפּוֹ וְעוֹד יָדוֹ נְטוּיָה: 17 כִּי־בָעֲרָה כָאֵשׁ רִשְׁעָה
שָׁמִיר וָשַׁיִת תֹּאכֵל וַתִּצַּת בְּסִבְכֵי הַיַּעַר וַיִּתְאַבְּכוּ גֵּאוּת עָשָׁן:
בְּעֶבְרַת יְהוָה צְבָאוֹת נֶעְתַּם אָרֶץ וַיְהִי הָעָם 18
כְּמַאֲכֹלֶת אֵשׁ אִישׁ אֶל־אָחִיו לֹא יַחְמֹלוּ: 19 וַיִּגְזֹר עַל־יָמִין
וְרָעֵב וַיֹּאכַל עַל־שְׂמֹאול וְלֹא שָׂבֵעוּ אִישׁ בְּשַׂר־זְרֹעוֹ יֹאכֵלוּ:
מְנַשֶּׁה אֶת־אֶפְרַיִם וְאֶפְרַיִם אֶת־מְנַשֶּׁה יַחְדָּו הֵמָּה עַל־יְהוּדָה 20
בְּכָל־זֹאת לֹא־שָׁב אַפּוֹ וְעוֹד יָדוֹ נְטוּיָה:

"And YHWH exalted the foes of Rezin against him, and he kept spur-
ring on his enemies. Aram from the east and the Philistines from the
west, they devoured Israel with an open mouth…"

If one takes the entire section as referring to E^{vision} then it is the *yiqtols* in vv. 10, 16-19 which require explanation.[60] The *yiqtols* in vv.10, 17 and 19 are easily understood as iterative pasts, and a modal past is fitting in vv.16 and 18.[61] It seems most likely that v.19 וְרָעֵב is *waw* + adjectival stative.

33. Is 23.1-14

1 מַשָּׂא צֹר הֵילִילוּ אֳנִיּוֹת תַּרְשִׁישׁ כִּי־שֻׁדַּד מִבַּיִת מִבּוֹא מֵאֶרֶץ
כִּתִּים נִגְלָה־לָמוֹ: 2 דֹּמּוּ יֹשְׁבֵי אִי סֹחֵר צִידוֹן עֹבֵר יָם מִלְאוּךְ:
3 וּבְמַיִם רַבִּים זֶרַע שִׁחֹר קְצִיר יְאוֹר תְּבוּאָתָהּ וַתְּהִי סְחַר גּוֹיִם:
4 בּוֹשִׁי צִידוֹן כִּי־אָמַר יָם מָעוֹז הַיָּם לֵאמֹר לֹא־חַלְתִּי
וְלֹא־יָלַדְתִּי וְלֹא גִדַּלְתִּי בַּחוּרִים רוֹמַמְתִּי בְתוּלוֹת:
5 כַּאֲשֶׁר־שֵׁמַע לְמִצְרָיִם יָחִילוּ כְּשֵׁמַע צֹר:
6 עִבְרוּ תַּרְשִׁישָׁה הֵילִילוּ יֹשְׁבֵי אִי:
7 הֲזֹאת לָכֶם עַלִּיזָה מִימֵי־קֶדֶם קַדְמָתָהּ יֹבִלוּהָ רַגְלֶיהָ מֵרָחוֹק לָגוּר:
8 מִי יָעַץ זֹאת עַל־צֹר הַמַּעֲטִירָה אֲשֶׁר סֹחֲרֶיהָ שָׂרִים כִּנְעָנֶיהָ
נִכְבַּדֵּי־אָרֶץ: 9 יְהוָה צְבָאוֹת יְעָצָהּ לְחַלֵּל גְּאוֹן כָּל־צְבִי לְהָקֵל
כָּל־נִכְבַּדֵּי־אָרֶץ: 10 עִבְרִי אַרְצֵךְ כַּיְאֹר בַּת־תַּרְשִׁישׁ אֵין מֵזַח עוֹד:
11 יָדוֹ נָטָה עַל־הַיָּם הִרְגִּיז מַמְלָכוֹת יְהוָה צִוָּה אֶל־כְּנַעַן לַשְׁמִד
מָעֻזְנֶיהָ: 12 וַיֹּאמֶר לֹא־תוֹסִיפִי עוֹד לַעְלוֹז הַמְעֻשָּׁקָה בְּתוּלַת
בַּת־צִידוֹן כִּתִּים קוּמִי עֲבֹרִי גַּם־שָׁם לֹא־יָנוּחַ לָךְ: 13 הֵן אֶרֶץ
כַּשְׂדִּים זֶה הָעָם לֹא הָיָה אַשּׁוּר יְסָדָהּ לְצִיִּים הֵקִימוּ בַחוּנָיו עֹרְרוּ
אַרְמְנוֹתֶיהָ שָׂמָהּ לְמַפֵּלָה: 14 הֵילִילוּ אֳנִיּוֹת תַּרְשִׁישׁ כִּי שֻׁדַּד מָעֻזְּכֶן:

"Oracle of Tyre. Wail, you ships of Tarshish, for (Tyre) is destroyed, without house or harbor (?)…"

---

[60] The verb tenses in this example have occasioned a good deal of discussion (see especially Gray *ad loc.*), namely whether or not this refers to actual historical events, future events, or to a mixture of both. As stated above (n.32), we are assuming in this chapter that our examples are not merely *vaticinia ex eventu*. That being said, it should be pointed out that our proposal does not, in fact, *necessarily* conflict with an *ex eventu* interpretation, since it is quite possible for a prophet to have a vision of an event which is already past. Consequently one can agree with Delitzsch when he remarks that it is impossible to tell in this example how much of this prophecy had or had not already been fulfilled, and that it does not matter: "The prophet, from his ideal standing-place, had not only this or that behind him, but all that is expressed in this section by perfects and aorists [i.e. *wayyiqtols*]..." We would simply attribute this to E^{vision} rather than to an "ideal standing-place" (R^{ideal}; cf. § 3.4.4.3).

[61] Joosten (1999: 19f.) notes that modal past uses of *yiqtol* frequently occur with negation.

This passage contains references to Tyre's past prosperity,[62] yet we also find a number of verbs that refer to some sort of calamity which has befallen the city[63] and which can be understood as references to E[vision]. The imperfects in v.12 occur in quoted speech and do not affect this analysis. יְחִילוּ in v.5 is somewhat difficult, but it seems most likely that we are dealing with a temporal clause in which the verb that normally occurs with כאשר has been omitted:[64] "when the report (comes) to Egypt they will writhe..." A future meaning here does not seem problematic.

34.　Jer 14.1-6

1 אֲשֶׁר הָיָה דְבַר־יְהוָה אֶל־יִרְמְיָהוּ עַל־דִּבְרֵי הַבַּצָּרוֹת: 2 אָבְלָה
יְהוּדָה וּשְׁעָרֶיהָ אֻמְלְלוּ קָדְרוּ לָאָרֶץ וְצִוְחַת יְרוּשָׁלַ͏ִם עָלָתָה:
3 וְאַדִּרֵיהֶם שָׁלְחוּ צְעִירֵיהֶם לַמָּיִם בָּאוּ עַל־גֵּבִים לֹא־מָצְאוּ מַיִם
שָׁבוּ כְלֵיהֶם רֵיקָם בֹּשׁוּ וְהָכְלְמוּ וְחָפוּ רֹאשָׁם: 4 בַּעֲבוּר הָאֲדָמָה
חַתָּה כִּי לֹא־הָיָה גֶשֶׁם בָּאָרֶץ בֹּשׁוּ אִכָּרִים חָפוּ רֹאשָׁם:
5 כִּי גַם־אַיֶּלֶת בַּשָּׂדֶה יָלְדָה וְעָזוֹב כִּי לֹא־הָיָה דֶּשֶׁא: 6 וּפְרָאִים
עָמְדוּ עַל־שְׁפָיִם שָׁאֲפוּ רוּחַ כַּתַּנִּים כָּלוּ עֵינֵיהֶם כִּי־אֵין עֵשֶׂב:

"The word of YHWH which came to Jeremiah concerning the drought. Judah mourned for the land, her gates have languished, grown dark, and the cry of Jerusalem went up..."

V.1 could be taken to suggest that the past tenses of vv.2-6 are simply describing past events, but the words of the false prophets in vv. 13 and 15[65] as well as the threat of v.16[66] seem to indicate that the drought and destruction have not yet occurred. If we take vv.2-6 as references to E[vision] then the only forms requiring explanation are the *weqatals* of v.3. וְהָכְלְמוּ appears to meet the normal criteria for a conjunctive *weqatal*, namely it stands in parallelism to בֹּשׁוּ and is semantically related to it.[67]

---

[62] E.g. vv. 2, 3, 7 (יְבָלוּהָ an iterative past; see Driver § 30 and compare the Vulgate: *portabant*).

[63] E.g. vv. 1, 11, 14. A calamity is also suggested by the picture of the sea renouncing its relationship with Tyre in v.4. The problematic v.13 is perhaps also part of the visionary description, depending upon whether or not the pronominal suffixes (either some or all of them) refer to Tyre; see the commentaries.

[64] So e.g. Brown-Driver-Briggs 455b.

[65] וְרָעָב לֹא יִהְיֶה

[66] וְהָעָם ... יִהְיוּ מֻשְׁלָכִים בְּחֻצוֹת יְרוּשָׁלַ͏ִם מִפְּנֵי הָרָעָב

[67] Revell (1985: 279); for further discussion of conjunctive *weqatals* see e.g. Van Peursen (1999: 136ff.), Kim (1998), Van Keulen (1996: 162ff.), Longacre (1994: 68ff.), Spieckermann (1982: 120ff.), Johnson (1979), Rubinstein (1963).

וְחָפוּ could perhaps also be conjunctive, though it could also be an inverted *weqatal* expressing the iterative past.

35.   Jer 25.17-26

17 וָאֶקַּח אֶת־הַכּוֹס מִיַּד יְהוָה וָאַשְׁקֶה אֶת־כָּל־הַגּוֹיִם
אֲשֶׁר־שְׁלָחַנִי יְהוָה אֲלֵיהֶם: 18 וגו'
26 וְאֵת כָּל־מַלְכֵי הַצָּפוֹן הַקְּרֹבִים וְהָרְחֹקִים אִישׁ אֶל־אָחִיו
וְאֵת כָּל־הַמַּמְלְכוֹת הָאָרֶץ אֲשֶׁר עַל־פְּנֵי הָאֲדָמָה
וּמֶלֶךְ שֵׁשַׁךְ יִשְׁתֶּה אַחֲרֵיהֶם:

"And I took the cup from the hand of YHWH and I made all the nations to which YHWH sent me drink…"

In v.26 יִשְׁתֶּה appears to be a future-in-the-past, unless the prophet has switched to E^{real}.

36.   Joel 2.18-27

18 וַיְקַנֵּא יְהוָה לְאַרְצוֹ וַיַּחְמֹל עַל־עַמּוֹ: 19 וַיַּעַן יְהוָה וַיֹּאמֶר לְעַמּוֹ
הִנְנִי שֹׁלֵחַ לָכֶם אֶת־הַדָּגָן וְהַתִּירוֹשׁ וְהַיִּצְהָר וּשְׂבַעְתֶּם אֹתוֹ וְלֹא־אֶתֵּן
אֶתְכֶם עוֹד חֶרְפָּה בַּגּוֹיִם: 20 וְאֶת־הַצְּפוֹנִי אַרְחִיק מֵעֲלֵיכֶם וְהִדַּחְתִּיו
אֶל־אֶרֶץ צִיָּה וּשְׁמָמָה אֶת־פָּנָיו אֶל־הַיָּם הַקַּדְמֹנִי וְסֹפוֹ אֶל־הַיָּם
הָאַחֲרוֹן וְעָלָה בָאְשׁוֹ וְתַעַל צַחֲנָתוֹ כִּי הִגְדִּיל לַעֲשׂוֹת: 21 אַל־תִּירְאִי
אֲדָמָה גִּילִי וּשְׂמָחִי כִּי־הִגְדִּיל יְהוָה לַעֲשׂוֹת: 22 אַל־תִּירְאוּ
בַהֲמוֹת שָׂדַי כִּי דָשְׁאוּ נְאוֹת מִדְבָּר כִּי־עֵץ נָשָׂא פִרְיוֹ
תְּאֵנָה וָגֶפֶן נָתְנוּ חֵילָם: 23 וּבְנֵי צִיּוֹן גִּילוּ וְשִׂמְחוּ בַּיהוָה אֱלֹהֵיכֶם
כִּי־נָתַן לָכֶם אֶת־הַמּוֹרֶה לִצְדָקָה וַיּוֹרֶד לָכֶם גֶּשֶׁם מוֹרֶה וּמַלְקוֹשׁ
בָּרִאשׁוֹן: 24 וּמָלְאוּ הַגֳּרָנוֹת בָּר וְהֵשִׁיקוּ הַיְקָבִים תִּירוֹשׁ וְיִצְהָר:
25 וְשִׁלַּמְתִּי לָכֶם אֶת־הַשָּׁנִים אֲשֶׁר אָכַל הָאַרְבֶּה הַיֶּלֶק וְהֶחָסִיל
וְהַגָּזָם חֵילִי הַגָּדוֹל אֲשֶׁר שִׁלַּחְתִּי בָּכֶם: 26 וַאֲכַלְתֶּם אָכוֹל וְשָׂבוֹעַ
וְהִלַּלְתֶּם אֶת־שֵׁם יְהוָה אֱלֹהֵיכֶם אֲשֶׁר־עָשָׂה עִמָּכֶם לְהַפְלִיא
וְלֹא־יֵבֹשׁוּ עַמִּי לְעוֹלָם: 27 וִידַעְתֶּם כִּי בְקֶרֶב יִשְׂרָאֵל אָנִי
וַאֲנִי יְהוָה אֱלֹהֵיכֶם וְאֵין עוֹד וְלֹא־יֵבֹשׁוּ עַמִּי לְעוֹלָם:

"And YHWH was jealous for his land and spared his people. And YHWH answered and said to his people: 'Behold, I am going to send to you grain, new wine and oil…'"

An application of our theory to this passage explains a number of disputed verbs. Thus, for example, the *wayyiqtols* in vv.18-19 can be understood as referring to E^{vision}, rather than to future events or to an actual historical event.[68] In this vision the prophet hears YHWH promise blessing and deliverance for his people (vv.19b-20). I would argue that this promise ends with וְעָלָה בָאְשׁוֹ in v.20 and that with the following וְתַעַל צַחֲנָתוֹ the prophet is again referring to what he saw in his vision (E[vision]). Hence the short *yiqtol*, which has puzzled scholars,[69] can be understood as a preterite (perhaps to be revocalized as a *wayyiqtol*, as already suggested by Nowack). The prophet thus hears YHWH promise that the "Northerner" will be destroyed, and then he sees it take place in his vision. I think this favors taking YHWH as the subject of the following כִּי הִגְדִּיל לַעֲשׂוֹת (also E[vision]), as clearly is the case in v.21.[70] The *qatals* in vv.21-23 would also refer to E[vision], with vv. 24-27 being a prediction of additional blessings to come.

37. Nahum 2.2-12

2 עָלָה מֵפִיץ עַל־פָּנַיִךְ נָצוֹר מְצֻרָה צַפֵּה־דֶרֶךְ חַזֵּק מָתְנַיִם אַמֵּץ כֹּחַ מְאֹד: 3 כִּי שָׁב יְהוָה אֶת־גְּאוֹן יַעֲקֹב כִּגְאוֹן יִשְׂרָאֵל כִּי בְקָקוּם בֹּקְקִים וּזְמֹרֵיהֶם שִׁחֵתוּ: 4 מָגֵן גִּבֹּרֵיהוּ מְאָדָּם אַנְשֵׁי־חַיִל מְתֻלָּעִים בְּאֵשׁ־פְּלָדוֹת הָרֶכֶב בְּיוֹם הֲכִינוֹ וְהַבְּרֹשִׁים הָרְעָלוּ: 5 יִתְהוֹלְלוּ הָרֶכֶב יִשְׁתַּקְשְׁקוּן בָּרְחֹבוֹת מַרְאֵיהֶן כַּלַּפִּידִם כַּבְּרָקִים יְרוֹצֵצוּ: 6 יִזְכֹּר אַדִּירָיו יִכָּשְׁלוּ בַּהֲלִיכָתָם יְמַהֲרוּ חוֹמָתָהּ וְהֻכַן הַסֹּכֵךְ: 7 שַׁעֲרֵי הַנְּהָרוֹת נִפְתָּחוּ וְהַהֵיכָל נָמוֹג: 8 וְהֻצַּב גֻּלְּתָה הֹעֲלָתָה וְאַמְהֹתֶיהָ מְנַהֲגוֹת כְּקוֹל יוֹנִים מְתֹפְפֹת עַל־לִבְבֵהֶן: 9 וְנִינְוֵה כִבְרֵכַת־מַיִם מִימֵי הִיא וְהֵמָּה נָסִים עִמְדוּ עֲמֹדוּ וְאֵין מַפְנֶה: 10 בֹּזּוּ כֶסֶף בֹּזּוּ זָהָב וְאֵין קֵצֶה לַתְּכוּנָה כָּבֹד מִכֹּל כְּלִי חֶמְדָּה: 11 בּוּקָה וּמְבוּקָה וּמְבֻלָּקָה וְלֵב נָמֵס וּפִק בִּרְכַּיִם וְחַלְחָלָה בְּכָל־מָתְנַיִם וּפְנֵי כֻלָּם קִבְּצוּ פָארוּר: 12 אַיֵּה מְעוֹן אֲרָיוֹת וּמִרְעֶה הוּא לַכְּפִרִים אֲשֶׁר הָלַךְ אַרְיֵה לָבִיא שָׁם גּוּר אַרְיֵה וְאֵין מַחֲרִיד:

"The scatterer went up against you. 'Guard the stronghold, watch the road, gird your loins, gather your strength!'[71] …"

If one takes the past tense forms as referring to a vision which the prophet has had of the siege and conquest of Nineveh (E[vision])[72] then there are a

---

[68] For the former view see Ibn-Ezra, for the latter see e.g. Keil, Driver § 82 *obs.* and his commentary *ad loc.*

[69] Driver § 175 *obs.*: "extremely difficult"; cf. Qimron (1986-87: 157).

[70] So several commentators, though often with textual emendation (cf. BHS).

[71] Meier (1992: 34) notes that v.9 is "unmarked direct discourse": "the poet employs a speaking voice other than his own without clarifying to whom it belongs"; similarly Alonso-Schökel (1988: 154f.). This is also the case with the volitives in vv.2 and 10 (cf. Spronk).

number of non-past verb forms which require discussion.[72] נָסִים in v.9 is most likely a progressive past: "...and they were fleeing."[74] There is a great deal of debate over the subject of the verbs in vv.5-6, and this has led to a number of different interpretations and emendations. Some scholars take the subject to be the attacking army (v.6 יִזְכֹּר is thus either emended to a plural or else the commander of the army is taken as the subject) since, in their view, this is the subject of the preceding verses. On such a reading יִכָּשְׁלוּ does not refer to soldiers falling in battle or clumsily stumbling in their haste but simply to some sort of rushed movement.[75] Others take the subject to be the defending soldiers of Nineveh (either with emendation of יִזְכֹּר or taking the subject to be the king of Assyria). The meaning of יִזְכֹּר itself is also debated. Some take it in its common sense and simply infer that the king/commander, upon "remembering" that he has mighty soldiers, summons them to the battle. Others argue for different meanings of the verb.[76] Such attempts frequently involve repointing the *binyan*, but Blau has made a good case that the *qal* of זכר occurs with the meaning "to name, mention".[77] If we accept Blau's argument then it seems possible to explain the MT as follows: During the battle the king/commander "mentions" or "names" his mighty ones, i.e. calls for his best soldiers by name, and they in turn "fall" (either in a positive or a negative sense) as they rush to the battle. On such a

---

[72] The visionary nature of the pericope is mentioned by e.g. Robinson and Horst, Humbert (1928-29), Spronk. Some commentators take v.3 שִׁחֵתוּ and בֹקְקוּם as references to Assyria's past treatment of Judah rather than to a (presumably future) battle.

[73] נָמֵס (v.11) could be taken as a perfect (note the following קִבְּצוּ פָארוּר) or as a participle functioning as an adjectival attribute (so e.g. Keil: "melted heart"), but neither analysis affects our interpretation significantly. In v.3 שֹׁד could be taken as a perfect or as a participle, but again this does not seem to be too significant: Even if one takes it as a participle (so Humbert 1926: 276) as *futurum instans*, it should be noted that it does not refer to the destruction of Assyria but rather to future blessing for Israel, and hence is not necessarily part of the description of the visionary siege. The famous crux of v.8 (וְהֻצַּב) is so uncertain that it can hardly be allowed to play a major role in one's interpretation of the passage; see the exegetical literature.

[74] Or it could be part of the quoted speech which follows (cf. n.71 above), in which case it would be an actual present.

[75] So e.g. Roberts.

[76] "Befehl erhalten" (Elliger), "to command, assign, appoint" (Roberts), "manhaftig, sterk zijn" (Van der Woude; cf. Dahood *ad* Ps 20.8), "être convoqué" (Humbert 1928-29: 15, Koehler-Baumgartner *s.v.*), "to boast, show oneself off" (G. R. Driver 1967: 54).

[77] Blau (1961), following a suggestion of Barth (1894: § 78 *a*), mentions e.g. Jer 23.36; 26.9; 31.20; Ps 63.7; 77.4, and additional examples from post-Biblical Hebrew are cited by Berggrün (1957-58). Blau's suggestion is taken up in Koehler-Baumgartner but not applied to this verse. Similar ideas had already been proposed for Jer 23.36 by e.g. König (1922, *s.v.*) "im Munde führen", Gesenius-Buhl (*s.v.*) "erwähnen".

reading the verbs can be understood as iterative pasts: He *kept naming his mighty ones*, who *kept falling*.[78]

38. Zech 6.1-8

1 וָאָשֻׁב וָאֶשָּׂא עֵינַי וָאֶרְאֶה וְהִנֵּה אַרְבַּע מַרְכָּבוֹת יֹצְאוֹת
מִבֵּין שְׁנֵי הֶהָרִים וְהֶהָרִים הָרֵי נְחֹשֶׁת: 2 בַּמֶּרְכָּבָה הָרִאשֹׁנָה סוּסִים
אֲדֻמִּים וּבַמֶּרְכָּבָה הַשֵּׁנִית סוּסִים שְׁחֹרִים: 3 וּבַמֶּרְכָּבָה הַשְּׁלִשִׁית
סוּסִים לְבָנִים וּבַמֶּרְכָּבָה הָרְבִעִית סוּסִים בְּרֻדִּים אֲמֻצִּים:
4 וָאַעַן וָאֹמַר אֶל־הַמַּלְאָךְ הַדֹּבֵר בִּי מָה־אֵלֶּה אֲדֹנִי: 5 וַיַּעַן הַמַּלְאָךְ
וַיֹּאמֶר אֵלָי אֵלֶּה אַרְבַּע רֻחוֹת הַשָּׁמַיִם יוֹצְאוֹת מֵהִתְיַצֵּב עַל־אֲדוֹן
כָּל־הָאָרֶץ: 6 אֲשֶׁר־בָּהּ הַסּוּסִים הַשְּׁחֹרִים יֹצְאִים אֶל־אֶרֶץ צָפוֹן
וְהַלְּבָנִים יָצְאוּ אֶל־אַחֲרֵיהֶם וְהַבְּרֻדִּים יָצְאוּ אֶל־אֶרֶץ הַתֵּימָן:
7 וְהָאֲמֻצִּים יָצְאוּ וַיְבַקְשׁוּ לָלֶכֶת לְהִתְהַלֵּךְ בָּאָרֶץ וַיֹּאמֶר לְכוּ
הִתְהַלְּכוּ בָאָרֶץ וַתִּתְהַלַּכְנָה בָּאָרֶץ: 8 וַיַּזְעֵק אֹתִי וַיְדַבֵּר אֵלַי לֵאמֹר
רְאֵה הַיּוֹצְאִים אֶל־אֶרֶץ צָפוֹן הֵנִיחוּ אֶת־רוּחִי בְּאֶרֶץ צָפוֹן:

"And I turned and lifted my eyes and looked, and behold, four chariots were coming out from between the two hills…"

There are some clear indications that a visionary experience is being described here (e.g. v.1 וָאֶשָּׂא עֵינַי וָאֶרְאֶה וְהִנֵּה וגו'), and hence v.8 הֵנִיחוּ is to be understood not as a prophetic perfect[79] but rather as a reference to E^{vision}.

As we noted in Is 9.6 (example 29), the prophet can refer to E^{vision} and then switch to E^{real}. We find such switching in other examples.

39. Is 24.4-12

4 אָבְלָה נָבְלָה הָאָרֶץ אֻמְלְלָה נָבְלָה תֵּבֵל אֻמְלָלוּ מְרוֹם עַם־הָאָרֶץ:
5 וְהָאָרֶץ חָנְפָה תַּחַת יֹשְׁבֶיהָ כִּי־עָבְרוּ תוֹרֹת חָלְפוּ חֹק הֵפֵרוּ
בְּרִית עוֹלָם: 6 עַל־כֵּן אָלָה אָכְלָה אֶרֶץ וַיֶּאְשְׁמוּ יֹשְׁבֵי בָהּ עַל־כֵּן
חָרוּ יֹשְׁבֵי אֶרֶץ וְנִשְׁאַר אֱנוֹשׁ מִזְעָר: 7 אָבַל תִּירוֹשׁ אֻמְלְלָה־גָפֶן נֶאֶנְחוּ
כָּל־שִׂמְחֵי־לֵב: 8 שָׁבַת מְשׂוֹשׂ תֻּפִּים חָדַל שְׁאוֹן עַלִּיזִים שָׁבַת מְשׂוֹשׂ
כִּנּוֹר: 9 בַּשִּׁיר לֹא יִשְׁתּוּ־יָיִן יֵמַר שֵׁכָר לְשֹׁתָיו: 10 נִשְׁבְּרָה קִרְיַת־תֹּהוּ
סֻגַּר כָּל־בַּיִת מִבּוֹא: 11 צְוָחָה עַל־הַיַּיִן בַּחוּצוֹת עָרְבָה
כָּל־שִׂמְחָה גָּלָה מְשׂוֹשׂ הָאָרֶץ: 12 נִשְׁאַר בָּעִיר שַׁמָּה וּשְׁאִיָּה יֻכַּת־שָׁעַר:

---

[78] Or perhaps these are preterital *yiqtols* (*yaqtul), in which case the common meaning "to remember" is perfectly acceptable for יִזְכֹּר (an iterative "he kept remembering" seems very odd).

[79] So e.g. Van der Woude.

"The earth mourned, withered, the world languished, withered, the heights languished with the earth..."

The author uses future tenses in vv.1-3 but switches to past tenses in vv.4-12, and I would argue that these refer to E^{vision}. It does not seem likely that v.6 וְנִשְׁאַר indicates an iterative past, and hence I would take it as a conjunctive *weqatal*. The imperfects of v.9 can be understood in various ways, all of which appear to be compatible with the interpretation proposed here: They could be expressing a general present or future, thereby indicating the continuing results of the destruction which the prophet has seen, or, if they are also narrating events in the vision then לֹא יִשְׁתּוּ could easily be understood as expressing either repetition or modality in the past: "they would not drink wine".[80] It is more difficult to explain יֵמַר in this way; perhaps it is a preterital *yiqtol*: "the beer became bitter to those who drank it". It is also difficult to explain יֻכַּת in v.12 as an iterative past and perhaps this should also be understood as a preterite: "the gate was shattered to ruins".[81] Another possibility is that the author has switched from E^{vision} back to E^{real} and that the reference is to the future (note the future-referring *yiqtols* in vv.13f.): "the gate shall be crushed into ruins".

40.   Jer 46.3-12

3 עִרְכוּ מָגֵן וְצִנָּה וּגְשׁוּ לַמִּלְחָמָה: 4 אִסְרוּ הַסּוּסִים וַעֲלוּ הַפָּרָשִׁים וְהִתְיַצְּבוּ בְּכוֹבָעִים מִרְקוּ הָרְמָחִים לִבְשׁוּ הַסִּרְיֹנֹת: 5 מַדּוּעַ רָאִיתִי הֵמָּה חַתִּים נְסֹגִים אָחוֹר וְגִבּוֹרֵיהֶם יֻכַּתּוּ וּמָנוֹס נָסוּ וְלֹא הִפְנוּ מָגוֹר מִסָּבִיב נְאֻם־יְהוָה: 6 אַל־יָנוּס הַקַּל וְאַל־יִמָּלֵט הַגִּבּוֹר צָפוֹנָה עַל־יַד נְהַר־פְּרָת כָּשְׁלוּ וְנָפָלוּ: 7 מִי־זֶה כַּיְאֹר יַעֲלֶה כַּנְּהָרוֹת יִתְגָּעֲשׁוּ מֵימָיו: 8 מִצְרַיִם כַּיְאֹר יַעֲלֶה וְכַנְּהָרוֹת יִתְגֹּעֲשׁוּ מָיִם וַיֹּאמֶר אַעֲלֶה אֲכַסֶּה־אֶרֶץ אֹבִידָה עִיר וְיֹשְׁבֵי בָהּ: 9 עֲלוּ הַסּוּסִים וְהִתְהֹלְלוּ הָרֶכֶב וְיֵצְאוּ הַגִּבּוֹרִים כּוּשׁ וּפוּט תֹּפְשֵׂי מָגֵן וְלוּדִים תֹּפְשֵׂי דֹּרְכֵי קָשֶׁת: 10 וְהַיּוֹם הַהוּא לַאדֹנָי יְהוִה צְבָאוֹת יוֹם נְקָמָה לְהִנָּקֵם מִצָּרָיו וְאָכְלָה חֶרֶב וְשָׂבְעָה וְרָוְתָה מִדָּמָם כִּי זֶבַח לַאדֹנָי יְהוִה צְבָאוֹת בְּאֶרֶץ צָפוֹן אֶל־נְהַר־פְּרָת: 11 עֲלִי גִלְעָד וּקְחִי צֳרִי בְּתוּלַת בַּת־מִצְרָיִם לַשָּׁוְא הִרְבֵּית רְפֻאוֹת תְּעָלָה אֵין לָךְ: 12 שָׁמְעוּ גוֹיִם קְלוֹנֵךְ

---

[80] Joosten (1999: 22f.) points out that it is sometimes difficult to decide between these two notions; e.g. does Est 3.2 וּמָרְדֳּכַי לֹא יִכְרַע וְלֹא יִשְׁתַּחֲוֶה ("But Mordecai would not bow down or do obeisance") indicate repeated (non-)activity (i.e. he did not do it on repeated occasions) or modality (i.e. he was not willing to do it)?

[81] Cf. Delitzsch; Rudolph (1933: 11) calls it "das Impf. des begleitenden Umstands". Lindblom (1938: 19) rejects Rudolph's solution and instead reads a hofal perfect.

וְצֻוֹחָתֵךְ מָלְאָה הָאָרֶץ כִּי־גִבּוֹר בְּגִבּוֹר כָּשָׁלוּ יַחְדָּיו נָפְלוּ שְׁנֵיהֶם:

"'Prepare shield and great shield, and draw near for the battle! Harness the horses and mount, O horsemen; take your stand with your helmets, scour the spears, put on armor!' Why did I see them shattered, retreating? Their warriors kept being beaten, and they fled for refuge and did not turn around, and there was terror on every side—oracle of YHWH..."

As far as indicative verbal forms are concerned,[82] the past tenses in vv.5-6 which describe some sort of defeat experienced by Egypt can be understood as references to E^{vision}.[83] In v.5 נֹסִים and יֻכַּתּוּ are easily understood as progressive and iterative pasts, respectively. It seems most likely that v.6 וְנָפְלוּ is a conjunctive *weqatal* (cf. v.12 נָפְלוּ). The use of the negative אַל with a morphologically long *yiqtol* in v.6 (אַל־יָנוּס) is problematic[84] and any interpretation encounters difficulty here. Despite the long form, I take these *yiqtols* as jussives occurring in direct discourse, i.e. this is what was heard during the battle just described.[85] The *yiqtols* in vv.7-8a do not express an actual present (cf. p. 10 n.54) but rather a general present and do not significantly affect the temporal setting of the passage, though these verses could be taken to imply a situation prior to Egypt's defeat. וַיֹּאמֶר in v.8b with the following quotation (vv.8b-9) simply indicates Egypt's desire for conquest at some point in the past. In v.10 we finally encounter a clear indication that Egypt's defeat is still a future event (וְאָכְלָה ... וְשָׂבְעָה וְרָוְתָה); the prophet has thus shifted to E^{real}. However, the following command to seek healing (v.11) implies that Egypt has experienced some sort of calamity,[86] and this is confirmed by the past tenses in v.12 (נָפְלוּ, כָּשָׁלוּ, מָלְאָה, שָׁמְעוּ). Hence it appears

---

[82] The volitives in vv.3-4 and 9 are direct discourse and not very helpful for establishing a temporal setting. Cf. n.71 above.

[83] Note v.5 רָאִיתִי; on the visionary nature of the oracle cf. Jones, McKane, De Jong (1997).

[84] Cf. Joüon and Muraoka § 114 g n.1.

[85] Cf. n.82. Keil likewise takes these as jussives. A number of scholars take these as indicative futures or presents or as a modal expression of non-ability (e.g. De Jong 1978: 93, McKane, Holladay, König § 186 c, Gesenius-Kautzsch-Cowley § 107 p, Joüon and Muraoka § 114 k). If one rejects a jussive sense then perhaps they could be understood as indicating modality (non-ability) in the past: "the swift one could not flee, and the warrior could not escape" (cf. n.61). However, v.5 says that they *did* flee, and hence I prefer the jussive interpretation.

[86] This is true regardless of whether one takes the addressee to be Judah (so McKane, LXX) or Egypt (so Holladay and many commentators). Rudolph's suggestion that הִרְבֵּית is a prophetic perfect is unnecessary.

that we have shifted back to E^{vision}. Leaving the non-indicative verb forms aside, the passage can be analyzed as follows:

vv.5-6 E^{vision}
vv.7-9   uncertain (general present, past behavior)
v.10 E^{real}
v.12 E^{vision}

We have already seen instances of shifting between E^{vision} and E^{real}, yet this example is particularly interesting in that it involves more than one such shift. As admitted above (§ 3.4.4.3), I have not been able to determine why a speaker chooses to refer to E^{real} or E^{vision} or to shift from one to the other. This does not necessarily mean that we are dealing with a confusing or chaotic phenomenon, however. The similar terminology of the E^{vision} sections (note e.g. כשל and נפל in vv. 6 and 12) suggests that they are descriptions of the same visionary event. In my judgment, this minimizes any possible confusion that could arise from such shifting between different temporal perspectives.

41.   Jer 46.14-28

14 הַגִּידוּ בְמִצְרַיִם וְהַשְׁמִיעוּ בְמִגְדּוֹל וְהַשְׁמִיעוּ בְנֹף וּבְתַחְפַּנְחֵס אִמְרוּ
הִתְיַצֵּב וְהָכֵן לָךְ כִּי־אָכְלָה חֶרֶב סְבִיבֶיךָ: 15 מַדּוּעַ נִסְחַף אַבִּירֶיךָ
לֹא עָמַד כִּי יְהוָה הֲדָפוֹ: 16 הִרְבָּה כּוֹשֵׁל גַּם־נָפַל אִישׁ אֶל־רֵעֵהוּ
וַיֹּאמְרוּ קוּמָה וְנָשֻׁבָה אֶל־עַמֵּנוּ וְאֶל־אֶרֶץ מוֹלַדְתֵּנוּ מִפְּנֵי חֶרֶב הַיּוֹנָה:
17 קָרְאוּ שָׁם פַּרְעֹה מֶלֶךְ־מִצְרַיִם שָׁאוֹן הֶעֱבִיר הַמּוֹעֵד: 18 חַי־אָנִי
נְאֻם־הַמֶּלֶךְ יְהוָה צְבָאוֹת שְׁמוֹ כִּי כְּתָבוֹר בֶּהָרִים וּכְכַרְמֶל בַּיָּם יָבוֹא:
19 כְּלֵי גוֹלָה עֲשִׂי לָךְ יוֹשֶׁבֶת בַּת־מִצְרָיִם כִּי־נֹף לְשַׁמָּה תִהְיֶה
וְנִצְּתָה מֵאֵין יוֹשֵׁב: ס 20 עֶגְלָה יְפֵה־פִיָּה מִצְרָיִם קֶרֶץ מִצָּפוֹן בָּא בָא:
21 גַּם־שְׂכִרֶיהָ בְקִרְבָּהּ כְּעֶגְלֵי מַרְבֵּק כִּי־גַם־הֵמָּה הִפְנוּ נָסוּ יַחְדָּיו לֹא
עָמָדוּ כִּי יוֹם אֵידָם בָּא עֲלֵיהֶם עֵת פְּקֻדָּתָם: 22 קוֹלָהּ כַּנָּחָשׁ יֵלֵךְ
כִּי־בְחַיִל יֵלֵכוּ וּבְקַרְדֻּמּוֹת בָּאוּ לָהּ כְּחֹטְבֵי עֵצִים: 23 כָּרְתוּ יַעְרָהּ
נְאֻם־יְהוָה כִּי לֹא יֵחָקֵר כִּי רַבּוּ מֵאַרְבֶּה וְאֵין לָהֶם מִסְפָּר:
24 הֹבִישָׁה בַּת־מִצְרָיִם נִתְּנָה בְּיַד עַם־צָפוֹן: 25 אָמַר יְהוָה צְבָאוֹת
אֱלֹהֵי יִשְׂרָאֵל הִנְנִי פוֹקֵד אֶל־אָמוֹן מִנֹּא וְעַל־פַּרְעֹה וְעַל־מִצְרַיִם
וְעַל־אֱלֹהֶיהָ וְעַל־מְלָכֶיהָ וְעַל־פַּרְעֹה וְעַל הַבֹּטְחִים בּוֹ: 26 וּנְתַתִּים בְּיַד
מְבַקְשֵׁי נַפְשָׁם וּבְיַד נְבוּכַדְרֶאצַּר מֶלֶךְ־בָּבֶל וּבְיַד־עֲבָדָיו וְאַחֲרֵי־כֵן
תִּשְׁכֹּן כִּימֵי־קֶדֶם נְאֻם־יְהוָה: 27 וְאַתָּה אַל־תִּירָא עַבְדִּי יַעֲקֹב
וְאַל־תֵּחַת יִשְׂרָאֵל כִּי הִנְנִי מוֹשִׁעֲךָ מֵרָחוֹק וְאֶת־זַרְעֲךָ מֵאֶרֶץ שִׁבְיָם
וְשָׁב יַעֲקוֹב וְשָׁקַט וְשַׁאֲנַן וְאֵין מַחֲרִיד: 28 אַתָּה אַל־תִּירָא עַבְדִּי יַעֲקֹב

נְאֻם־יְהוָה כִּי אִתְּךָ אָנִי כִּי אֶעֱשֶׂה כָלָה בְּכָל־הַגּוֹיִם אֲשֶׁר הִדַּחְתִּיךָ
שָׁמָּה וְאֹתְךָ לֹא־אֶעֱשֶׂה כָלָה וְיִסַּרְתִּיךָ לַמִּשְׁפָּט וְנַקֵּה לֹא אֲנַקֶּךָ:

"Announce in Egypt, and proclaim in Migdol, and proclaim in Mem-
phis and Taphanhes, say: 'Take a stand and prepare yourselves, for the
sword has devoured all around you...'"

The main subject in this passage is some sort of judgment upon Egypt, yet
we find this referred to as a future as well as a past event. As in the preceding example, we appear to be dealing with multiple shifts between
E^{vision} (past tenses) and E^{real} (future tenses). The basic structure is: 14-17
E^{vision} [87] 18-20 E^{real} [88] 21-24 E^{vision} [89] 25-28 E^{real}.

There are some very difficult *yiqtols* in vv.22-23 which require discussion. Only a tentative solution to v.22 קוֹלָהּ כַּנָּחָשׁ יֵלֵךְ כִּי־בְחַיִל יֵלֵכוּ
can be proposed here. The first clause appears to be: "Her sound is as a
snake moving." But the significance is uncertain:[90] What sort of "movement" does the author have in mind? Does the pronominal suffix refer to
Egypt or to Egypt's enemies? Does the expression refer to some sort of
hissing sound (cf. LXX: ὄφεως συρίζοντος)? In connection with the picture of Egypt fleeing in v.21 I take "her sound" to refer to Egypt and
would suggest that the "sound" of the moving snake is simply silence: It
is trying to avoid being detected and captured. In any event, the verb in
this comparison is a general present which does not affect the past references of the surrounding verbs. The second clause is also difficult, since
the subject of the verb could be the Egyptian soldiers (as in v.21) or their
enemies (as in vv.22b, 23). With either interpretation it seems to me that
יֵלֵכוּ can be taken as an iterative past: Egypt's soldiers fled (v.21), trying
to avoid detection (v.22a), either because "they (viz. Egypt's enemies)

---

[87] On v.15 נִסְחַף and the proposed emendation to נָס חַף "why is Apis fleeing?" see
Snaith (1971: 19f.), De Jong (1978: 352 n.32). The MT of v.17 (קָרְאוּ) is intelligible,
though many emend the verb to an imperative and שָׁם to שֵׁם "name".

[88] Apart from the text-critical difficulties, v.20 קֶרֶץ מִצָּפוֹן בָּא בָא presents two inter-
related problems: Firstly, is בָּא a perfect or a participle? Compare the RSV's "has come
upon her" with the NIV's "is coming". Secondly, does this verse belong with vv.18-19 or
with vv.21ff.? The answer to this depends to a certain extent on one's analysis of בָּא: A
participle indicating the *futurum instans* would fit nicely with the future references of the
preceding verses, whereas a perfect would fit well with the past tenses of the following
verses. It does not actually make much of a difference to our interpretation as a whole if
one takes the section break after v.19 or v.20.

[89] V.21 בָּא could be either a perfect or a participle, but the surrounding past tenses suggest
a perfect. In v.23 Ehrlich and De Jong (1978: 111) claim that כָּרְתוּ is a Piel imperative
(Peshitta: ܩܨܨܘ), but this *binyan* is not attested for the verb.

[90] Cf. Snaith (1971: 21f.).

kept coming in strength/force" or "they (viz. the Egyptians) kept going in force" (i.e. they left the scene of battle "in bands/army divisions",[91] *en masse*). I do not think that this latter option does justice to the particle כִּי, however, and hence I prefer to take Egypt's enemies as the subject of the verb. כִּי לֹא יֵחָקֵר (v.23) has also proved difficult.[92] It could be that the woodcutters of v.22, in looking for a snake, have cut down a forest "because it is impenetrable". Some manuscripts read the verb as plural, however, and this would refer not to the forest but rather to the fact that the number of the trees or of the woodcutters "cannot be counted". With any of these options, however, the verb can be understood as a modal past: "which *could not* be penetrated" or "which *could not* be counted".[93]

Though a description of visionary events naturally involves visual description, there are also examples which involve auditory phenomena. Some examples involve both visual and auditory description.[94]

42. Jer 4.15-26

15 כִּי קוֹל מַגִּיד מִדָּן וּמַשְׁמִיעַ אָוֶן מֵהַר אֶפְרָיִם: 16 הַזְכִּירוּ לַגּוֹיִם הִנֵּה הַשְׁמִיעוּ עַל־יְרוּשָׁלַ‍ִם נֹצְרִים בָּאִים מֵאֶרֶץ הַמֶּרְחָק וַיִּתְּנוּ עַל־עָרֵי יְהוּדָה קוֹלָם: 17 כְּשֹׁמְרֵי שָׂדַי הָיוּ עָלֶיהָ מִסָּבִיב כִּי־אֹתִי מָרָתָה נְאֻם־יְהוָה: 18 דַּרְכֵּךְ וּמַעֲלָלַיִךְ עָשׂוֹ אֵלֶּה לָךְ זֹאת רָעָתֵךְ כִּי מָר כִּי נָגַע עַד־לִבֵּךְ: 19 מֵעַי מֵעַי אוֹחִילָה קִירוֹת לִבִּי הֹמֶה־לִּי לִבִּי לֹא אַחֲרִישׁ כִּי קוֹל שׁוֹפָר שָׁמַעַתְּ נַפְשִׁי תְּרוּעַת מִלְחָמָה: 20 שֶׁבֶר עַל־שֶׁבֶר נִקְרָא כִּי שֻׁדְּדָה כָּל־הָאָרֶץ פִּתְאֹם שֻׁדְּדוּ אֹהָלַי רֶגַע יְרִיעֹתָי: 21 עַד־מָתַי אֶרְאֶה־נֵּס אֶשְׁמְעָה קוֹל שׁוֹפָר: 22 כִּי אֱוִיל עַמִּי אוֹתִי לֹא יָדָעוּ בָּנִים סְכָלִים הֵמָּה וְלֹא נְבוֹנִים הֵמָּה חֲכָמִים הֵמָּה לְהָרַע וּלְהֵיטִיב לֹא יָדָעוּ: 23 רָאִיתִי אֶת־הָאָרֶץ וְהִנֵּה־תֹהוּ וָבֹהוּ וְאֶל־הַשָּׁמַיִם וְאֵין אוֹרָם: 24 רָאִיתִי הֶהָרִים וְהִנֵּה רֹעֲשִׁים וְכָל־הַגְּבָעוֹת הִתְקַלְקָלוּ: 25 רָאִיתִי וְהִנֵּה אֵין הָאָדָם וְכָל־עוֹף הַשָּׁמַיִם נָדָדוּ: 26 רָאִיתִי וְהִנֵּה הַכַּרְמֶל הַמִּדְבָּר וְכָל־עָרָיו נִתְּצוּ מִפְּנֵי יְהוָה מִפְּנֵי חֲרוֹן אַפּוֹ:

"For a voice is announcing from Dan, and is proclaiming trouble from Mount Ephraim: 'Declare to the nations "Behold!", proclaim against Jerusalem...'"

---

[91] Cf. Brown-Driver-Briggs 299a.
[92] See the discussion by Snaith (1971: 20).
[93] See n.61.
[94] Cf. Lindblom (1962: 135).

The references to what the prophet he has "seen" (רָאִיתִי) in vv.23-26, as well as the perfects in v.20, are easily understood as referring to E^{vision}.[95] Since we are dealing with a number of references to E^{vision} in this pericope, it seems to me that the descriptions of what the prophet "heard" (vv.15, 19) should also be understood in the same way; vv.16-18 are to be understood as quoted speech (so NIV, RSV; cf. § 3.4.2). It may be noted that some of the clear examples of E^{dream} and E^{vision} mentioned above also involved auditory phenomena.[96]

The occurrence of auditory description observed in example 42 is significant in that it provides an additional means by which references to E^{vision} may be identified. In the following case, for example, the description is primarily auditory rather than visual, but may nonetheless be understood as a reference to E^{vision}:

43.   Jer 3.21-25

21 קוֹל עַל־שְׁפָיִים נִשְׁמָע בְּכִי תַחֲנוּנֵי בְּנֵי יִשְׂרָאֵל כִּי הֶעֱוּוּ
אֶת־דַּרְכָּם שָׁכְחוּ אֶת־יְהֹוָה אֱלֹהֵיהֶם: 22 שׁוּבוּ בָּנִים שׁוֹבָבִים אֶרְפָּה
מְשׁוּבֹתֵיכֶם הִנְנוּ אָתָנוּ לָךְ כִּי אַתָּה יְהֹוָה אֱלֹהֵינוּ: 23 אָכֵן לַשֶּׁקֶר
מִגְּבָעוֹת הָמוֹן הָרִים אָכֵן בַּיהֹוָה אֱלֹהֵינוּ תְּשׁוּעַת יִשְׂרָאֵל: 24 וְהַבֹּשֶׁת
אָכְלָה אֶת־יְגִיעַ אֲבוֹתֵינוּ מִנְּעוּרֵינוּ אֶת־צֹאנָם וְאֶת־בְּקָרָם אֶת־בְּנֵיהֶם
וְאֶת־בְּנוֹתֵיהֶם: 25 נִשְׁכְּבָה בְּבָשְׁתֵּנוּ וּתְכַסֵּנוּ כְּלִמָּתֵנוּ
כִּי לַיהֹוָה אֱלֹהֵינוּ חָטָאנוּ אֲנַחְנוּ וַאֲבוֹתֵינוּ מִנְּעוּרֵינוּ וְעַד־הַיּוֹם הַזֶּה
וְלֹא שָׁמַעְנוּ בְּקוֹל יְהֹוָה אֱלֹהֵינוּ:

"A voice was heard on the heights, the weeping and pleading of the sons of Israel…"

The prophet is reporting a dialogue which he "heard" take place between YHWH and his repentant people. I do not think it likely that this refers to E^{real}, since the surrounding context indicates that YHWH's people have not yet repented (e.g. 3.13 אַךְ דְּעִי עֲוֺנֵךְ), and hence it seems preferable to take this as E^{vision}.

The preceding example is somewhat unique in consisting entirely of auditory description. It appears most often, however, that this is combined with visual description.[97] In the following examples we find not only both types of description, but also shifting between E^{vision} and E^{real}.

44.   Jer 48

1 לְמוֹאָב כֹּה־אָמַר יְהֹוָה צְבָאוֹת אֱלֹהֵי יִשְׂרָאֵל הוֹי אֶל־נְבוֹ

---

[95] Cf. Zimmerli (1982: 99ff.), Lindblom (1962: 127).

[96] See § 3.4.4.1, § 3.4.4.2; e.g. Gen 28.13; Dan 4.11; 7.8, 11; 8.13f.; Zech 1-6.

[97] Other possible examples in the book of Jeremiah: 4.29; 31.15ff.; cf. Zimmerli (1982).

כִּי שֻׁדְּדָה הַבִּישָׁה נִלְכְּדָה קִרְיָתַיִם הֹבִישָׁה הַמִּשְׂגָּב וָחָתָּה: 2 אֵין עוֹד
תְּהִלַּת מוֹאָב בְּחֶשְׁבּוֹן חָשְׁבוּ עָלֶיהָ רָעָה לְכוּ וְנַכְרִיתֶנָּה מִגּוֹי
גַּם־מַדְמֵן תִּדֹּמִּי אַחֲרַיִךְ תֵּלֶךְ חָרֶב: וגו'

"Concerning Moab. Thus has YHWH Almighty, the god of Israel, spoken: Woe to Nebo, for it has been destroyed, Kiriathaim has been put to shame, captured, the stronghold has been put to shame and shattered. The praise of Moab is no more, in Heshbon they have plotted evil against her: 'Come, and let's cut her off from being a nation!' You also will be silenced, O Madmen, the sword will pursue you…"

Only a very tentative analysis can be given of this extremely difficult chapter. We find Moab's destruction referred to as both a past and a future event, and I would suggest that some of the shifting in verb tenses is due to a switch between E^{vision} and E^{real}.[98] I would analyze the indicative verb forms in this chapter as follows:

vv.1-5 E^{vision} (v.1 וָחָתָּה conjunctive *weqatal*; v.2 quoted speech; v.5 יַעֲלֶה either an iterative past or perhaps to be understood as a quotation, cf. v.3 קוֹל צְעָקָה)

vv.7-14 E^{real} (vv.11 and 13 refer to Moab's past[99])

v.15 E^{vision} (text?)

v.16 E^{real} (a nominal clause, but קָרוֹב אֵיד־מוֹאָב לָבוֹא seems to indicate a situation prior to Moab's destruction).

vv.17-25 E^{vision} (v.21 בָא could perhaps be a participle, but we find past tenses in the preceding and following verses)

vv.26-39 E^{real} (an extremely difficult section[100])

---

[98] On the visionary character of this chapter, cf. Jones.

[99] On v.11 see Clark (1981).

[100] This section is textually problematic and is made even more difficult by the fact that a good deal of material which occurs here has been "re-used" from Is 15 and 16–a passage which itself is exegetically difficult (example 62 below; cf. Huwyler 1997: 180ff.). We are dealing with E^{real} in vv.26-31 and apparently with quoted speech (cf. § 3.4.2) in vv.32-33 (taking וְנֶאֶסְפָה as a conjunctive *weqatal*, cf. RSV's "gladness and joy have been taken away", similarly Holladay), thus explaining the past tenses; v.33 לֹא־יִדְרֹךְ is a general present. The text of v.34 is extremely problematic and it is not certain if it is part of the preceding quotation. Vv.35-36 are E^{real}. The last two verbs of v.36 (עָשָׂה אָבָדוּ) are uncertain, but the fact that the speaker refers to his intent to take up a lament in the first part of the verse makes it possible that we are again dealing with quoted speech (§ 3.4.2); this certainly seems to be the case in vv.37-39. The interpretation of v.39b וְהָיָה is open to question. It is possible that we are dealing either with a conjunctive *weqatal* here (LXX: καὶ ἐγένετο) or simply an error for ויהי (see Stipp 1991: 526f.).

90

vv.40-44 These verses seem to refer to E^{real}, but there is a difficulty presented by the perfects in v.41, which are taken by many to be prophetic. This interpretation is not without its own problems: It is difficult to take הַקְּרִיּוֹת as a proper name due to the definite article, and to take it as a plural noun creates an incongruence with the singular verbs. I would suggest that נִלְכְּדָה and נִתְפָּשָׂה are not to be parsed as *nifal* perfects but rather as *qal* cohortatives (compare v.2; repointing נִתְפָּשָׂה to נִתְפְּשָׂה) and that the verse is to be understood as direct discourse similar to what we observed above in Nah 2.2 and 9f. (example 37, cf. n.71).

vv.45-46 E^{vision} (v.45 נָסִים is a progressive past)

v.47 E^{real}

It is obvious that this chapter presents numerous challenges in regard to the analysis of the verb tenses. The distinction between E^{real} and E^{vision} can in some cases explain the shifting between past and future tenses. However, occasionally this shifting occurs so rapidly that this proposal – or any other explanation, for that matter – can seem somewhat forced.[101] We also find this rapid shifting in the following example:

45. Jer 50.2-51.58

2 הַגִּידוּ בַגּוֹיִם וְהַשְׁמִיעוּ וּשְׂאוּ־נֵס הַשְׁמִיעוּ אַל־תְּכַחֵדוּ אִמְרוּ
נִלְכְּדָה בָבֶל הֹבִישׁ בֵּל חַת מְרֹדָךְ הֹבִישׁוּ עֲצַבֶּיהָ חַתּוּ גִּלּוּלֶיהָ:
3 כִּי עָלָה עָלֶיהָ גּוֹי מִצָּפוֹן הוּא־יָשִׁית אֶת־אַרְצָהּ לְשַׁמָּה וְלֹא־יִהְיֶה
יוֹשֵׁב בָּהּ מֵאָדָם וְעַד־בְּהֵמָה נָדוּ הָלָכוּ: וגו'

"Declare among the nations and proclaim, and lift up a banner and proclaim—do not conceal. Say: 'Babylon has been captured, Bel has been put to shame, Merodach has been shattered, her images have been put to shame, her idols shattered. For a nation came up against her from the north; it would make her land a desolation and there would not be an inhabitant in it. Man and beast fled away, they went…'"

We encounter a large number of indicative forms referring to Babylon's future downfall (E^{real}), yet we also find this referred to as a past event. These can be understood as narrating the events which the prophet has seen in his vision (E^{vision}): 50.2-3 (analyzing the *yiqtols* in v.3 יָשִׁית, וְלֹא־יִהְיֶה as future-in-the-past), 22-25, 46; 51.8-10 (v.9 וְנִשָּׂא probably a

---

[101] Perhaps such rapid shifting is related to the more general issue of linguistic coherence (or the occasional lack thereof) in prophetic literature; cf. Andersen (1995).

conjunctive *weqatal*; v.10 הוֹצִיא probably a perfect and not an imperative[102]), 29-32 (v.31 יָרוּץ an iterative past), 41-43 (v.43 וְלֹא־, לֹא־יֵשֵׁב
יַעֲבֹר probably past modal, cf. n.61).

In most cases we are dealing with passages of some verses in length.
There are some much shorter passages which appear to narrate "past"
events and could be viewed as analogous to the examples examined
above, though their brevity makes it is difficult to be certain:

46. Is 10.28-31[103]

28 בָּא עַל־עַיַּת עָבַר בְּמִגְרוֹן לְמִכְמָשׂ יַפְקִיד כֵּלָיו:
29 עָבְרוּ מַעְבָּרָה גֶּבַע מָלוֹן לָנוּ חָרְדָה הָרָמָה גִּבְעַת שָׁאוּל נָסָה:
30 צַהֲלִי קוֹלֵךְ בַּת־גַּלִּים הַקְשִׁיבִי לַיְשָׁה עֲנִיָּה עֲנָתוֹת:
31 נָדְדָה מַדְמֵנָה יֹשְׁבֵי הַגֵּבִים הֵעִיזוּ:

"He came to Aiath, he passed through Migron, he would deposit his
equipment at Michmash (?). They crossed the pass, (saying) 'Geba is our
lodging.' Ramah trembled, Gibeah of Saul fled. Cry out, O Daughter of
Gallim, pay heed, O Laishah, to afflicted Anathoth. Madmenah fled, the
inhabitants of Gebim took refuge."

If this brief section refers to E[vision], then v.28 יַפְקִיד requires an explanation. Unless we posit an error in pointing, the long form indicates that
this is not a preterital *yiqtol*. An iterative past does not seem very fitting
(unless the idea that "he kept depositing his equipment" is intended to
suggest that the invader had an extremely large amount of supplies for the
campaign), and hence I tentatively analyze it as a future-in-the-past.

47. Mic 2.13

עָלָה הַפֹּרֵץ לִפְנֵיהֶם פָּרְצוּ וַיַּעֲבֹרוּ שַׁעַר וַיֵּצְאוּ בוֹ וַיַּעֲבֹר
מַלְכָּם לִפְנֵיהֶם וַיהוָה בְּרֹאשָׁם:

"The breaker went up before them, they broke through and crossed the
gate, and they went in it. And their king crossed before them, and
YHWH was at their head."

This could be narrating visionary events, but the brevity of this example
makes it difficult to be certain.

---

[102] So e.g. Holladay, McKane.

[103] Perhaps the pericope begins in v.27, if one accepts Gray's proposed emendation: עָלָה
מִפְּנֵי־שָׁמֶן "he hath gone up..."

Finally it may be noted that, even though we are not including "archaic" Hebrew texts in this study, it nevertheless appears that the following example is to be explained according to our theory:

48.   Num 24.17-19

17 אֶרְאֶנּוּ וְלֹא עַתָּה אֲשׁוּרֶנּוּ וְלֹא קָרוֹב דָּרַךְ כּוֹכָב
מִיַּעֲקֹב וְקָם שֵׁבֶט מִיִּשְׂרָאֵל וּמָחַץ פַּאֲתֵי מוֹאָב וְקַרְקַר כָּל־בְּנֵי־שֵׁת׃
18 וְהָיָה אֱדוֹם יְרֵשָׁה וְהָיָה יְרֵשָׁה שֵׂעִיר אֹיְבָיו וְיִשְׂרָאֵל עֹשֶׂה חָיִל׃
19 וְיֵרְדְּ מִיַּעֲקֹב וְהֶאֱבִיד שָׂרִיד מֵעִיר׃

"I see him, but not now; I regard him, but he is not near. A star went forth from Jacob, and a scepter rose up from Israel, and he smashed the temples of Moab and the head (?) of all the sons of Seth. And Edom became his possession, and his enemy Seir became his possession, and Israel was acting mightily. And he ruled from Jacob, and he destroyed the remant of the city."

V.17 דָּרַךְ is frequently cited as an example of the prophetic perfect, and the string of *weqatal* forms which follows it seems to support this interpretation. This assumes that the *weqatal* forms are inverted perfects (*weqataltí*),[104] yet I think that there are reasons to question this assumption. One should note that, even according to classical grammar, וְקָם meets the criteria established by Revell for the conjunctive *weqatal* (*weqatálti*): It denotes an action synonymous with and/or simultaneous to דָּרַךְ.[105] Furthermore, it is unlikely that the short *yiqtol* in v.19 (וְיֵרְדְּ) has a jussive meaning, and hence would seem to be a preterite. In light of these factors it does not seem unreasonable to read the rest of the *weqatal* forms as conjunctive perfects (*weqatálti*) which refer to what Balaam has seen in his vision (E[vision]).

§ 3.4.5   Rhetorical Uses

In a number of languages one encounters instances in which a tense form does not refer to its usual temporal sphere ("idiomatic tense mismatches", to use DeCaen's terminology).[106] With the so-called "historical present", for example, a present tense form is used to refer to a past event. One also finds past tense forms that refer to present or future events:

---

[104] Klein (1990: 50), Driver § 113 (1).

[105] Revell (1985: 279); see also the literature cited in n.67 above.

[106] DeCaen (1995: 9ff.), Laude-Cirtautas (1974); cf. Comrie (1985: 20f.).

49. *Ja pošel* (Russian)

"I am leaving" [literally "left"]

50. *Ojbaj, öltirdi! öltirdi!* (Kazakh)

"Help! She will kill me!" [literally "killed"]

Such "tense mismatches" occur in many languages which possess gram-maticalized tense. This indicates that the mere existence of such mis-matches is insufficient to prove that a language is "tenseless". Comrie argues that such cases "should simply be treated as exceptions":

> With these examples, one can readily present a rationalisation for the non-literal use of the past tense, as an indication of the imminence of the fu-ture situation - it is as if it were already present - but this rationalisation does not remove the discrepancy between the literal meaning of the utter-ance and the context to which it is applied. This is not to belittle such ra-tionalisations: they certainly form part of the explanation as to why this discrepancy is tolerated...[107]

Although we have argued that the alleged examples of prophetic perfects discussed in the preceding sections are in fact to be understood as past tenses, there are nonetheless some examples in which *qatal* appears to be used when speaking of a future event. In such cases we are dealing with a "conflict" between the past-deictic function of *qatal* and its actual use. It would be possible to take this as evidence that *qatal* is not semantically marked as a past tense, and this is precisely what many scholars have done (cf. § 1.1, § 3.1). However, it is just as possible that these are sim-ply exceptions or "idiomatic tense mismatches" such as occur in many other languages. In these cases a future event is exaggeratedly described as already past.[108] This is, as it were, the "traditional" understanding of the prophetic perfect, and it would appear that an explanation of these cases will lie primarily in the realm of rhetoric, as several Hebraists have already argued (§ 3.1). There is certainly a danger of too easily appealing to "rhetoric" as an explanation, given our extremely limited knowledge of ancient Hebrew rhetoric and the difficulty one would have in attempting to verify such an explanation. Nevertheless, in this case it would seem to be justified by the cross-linguistic evidence for similar "exaggerated" uses of past tenses. The common description of the prophetic perfect as referring to an event "as good as done" seems to provide a sufficient ra-tionale for this phenomenon, yet in the absence of native speakers it would be difficult to determine what the precise rhetorical effect was, whether "certainty", "imminence", "vividness" or the like. We will not

---

[107] Comrie (1985: 20f.).

[108] For this reason it is possible that one still might wish to translate such examples as past.

94

attempt to answer this question here but will simply list the examples in which the use of the past tense appears to be rhetorically motivated.

51. Nu 17.27

וַיֹּאמְרוּ בְּנֵי יִשְׂרָאֵל אֶל־מֹשֶׁה לֵאמֹר הֵן גָּוַעְנוּ אָבַדְנוּ כֻּלָּנוּ אָבָדְנוּ׃

"And the sons of Israel said to Moses: 'Behold, we have died, we have perished, all of us have perished!'"

52. Is 6.5

וָאֹמַר אוֹי־לִי כִּי־נִדְמֵיתִי

"And I said, 'Woe to me, for I have perished!'"

53. Jer 4.13

אוֹי לָנוּ כִּי שֻׁדָּדְנוּ

"Woe to us, for we have been destroyed!"

54. Jer 28.2

שָׁבַרְתִּי אֶת־עֹל מֶלֶךְ בָּבֶל׃

"I have broken the yoke of the king of Babylon."

Compare אֶשְׁבֹּר "I will break" in v.4 and v.11.

55. Jer 33.5

בָּאִים לְהִלָּחֵם אֶת־הַכַּשְׂדִּים וּלְמַלְאָם אֶת־פִּגְרֵי הָאָדָם אֲשֶׁר־הִכֵּיתִי בְאַפִּי וּבַחֲמָתִי וַאֲשֶׁר הִסְתַּרְתִּי פָנַי מֵהָעִיר הַזֹּאת עַל כָּל־רָעָתָם׃

"Men komt om de Chaldeeën te bestrijden, om ze te vullen met de li-jken der mensen die Ik in mijn toorn en mijn gramschap verslagen heb, en om al wier boosheid Ik mijn aangezicht voor deze stad verborgen heb" (NBG)."[109]

56. Ezek 21.9

יַעַן אֲשֶׁר־הִכְרַתִּי מִמֵּךְ צַדִּיק וְרָשָׁע לָכֵן תֵּצֵא חַרְבִּי מִתַּעְרָהּ אֶל־כָּל־בָּשָׂר מִנֶּגֶב צָפוֹן׃

"Because I have cut off from you the righteous and the wicked, therefore my sword will come out of its sheath against everything from south to north."

57. Zeph 3.15

הֵסִיר יְהוָה מִשְׁפָּטַיִךְ פִּנָּה אֹיְבֵךְ מֶלֶךְ יִשְׂרָאֵל יְהוָה

---

[109] Or could this possibly be a relative past (§ 3.4.1)?

בְּקִרְבֵּךְ לֹא־תִירְאִי רָע עוֹד׃

"YHWH has turned aside your punishments, turned your enemy; YHWH, the king of Israel, is in your midst: You will not fear evil again."

§ 3.4.6   Future Referent Uncertain

In a large number of cases it is unlikely, or at least debatable, that the verb has a future referent (cf. § 3.4).

58.   Gen 4.23

כִּי אִישׁ הָרַגְתִּי לְפִצְעִי וְיֶלֶד לְחַבֻּרָתִי

"For I have slain a man for wounding me, a youth for striking me."

According to Klein this is not to be interpreted as prophetic but rather as gnomic (cf. § 2).[110] In fact, there is no reason why this cannot simply refer to the past.

59.   Nu 32.19

כִּי בָאָה נַחֲלָתֵנוּ אֵלֵינוּ

"For our inheritance has come to us."

60.   Ju 4.14

וַתֹּאמֶר דְּבֹרָה אֶל־בָּרָק קוּם כִּי זֶה הַיּוֹם אֲשֶׁר נָתַן יְהוָה
אֶת־סִיסְרָא בְּיָדֶךָ הֲלֹא יְהוָה יָצָא לְפָנֶיךָ

"And Deborah said to Barak: 'Arise, for this is the day on which YHWH has placed Sisera into your hand. Has YHWH not gone out before you?"

The verb נָתַן could be understood to refer to a decision or decree of YHWH (§ 3.4.3) or, perhaps, as rhetorical (§ 3.4.5).[111] יָצָא could likewise be rhetorical, though it does not seem difficult to interpret it simply as a past tense.

---

[110] Klein (1990: 48); it is interpreted as prophetic by e.g. Bergsträsser and Böttcher.

[111] So elsewhere with this fairly common expression: Ju 7.14; 18.10; 1 Sam 14.10; Jer 32.24f., and possibly also with the verb ברך in Dt 15.6. In some instances the speaker is also the subject of the verb, and under such conditions it would be possible to understand it as performative (§ 4); cf. n.154 below.

61. Is 2.6-11[112]

6 כִּי נָטַשְׁתָּה עַמְּךָ בֵּית יַעֲקֹב כִּי מָלְאוּ מִקֶּדֶם וְעֹנְנִים
כַּפְּלִשְׁתִּים וּבְיַלְדֵי נָכְרִים יַשְׂפִּיקוּ: 7 וַתִּמָּלֵא אַרְצוֹ כֶּסֶף וְזָהָב וְאֵין
קֵצֶה לְאֹצְרֹתָיו וַתִּמָּלֵא אַרְצוֹ סוּסִים וְאֵין קֵצֶה לְמַרְכְּבֹתָיו:
8 וַתִּמָּלֵא אַרְצוֹ אֱלִילִים לְמַעֲשֵׂה יָדָיו יִשְׁתַּחֲווּ לַאֲשֶׁר עָשׂוּ אֶצְבְּעֹתָיו:
9 וַיִּשַּׁח אָדָם וַיִּשְׁפַּל־אִישׁ וְאַל־תִּשָּׂא לָהֶם:
10 בּוֹא בַצּוּר וְהִטָּמֵן בֶּעָפָר מִפְּנֵי פַּחַד יְהוָה וּמֵהֲדַר גְּאֹנוֹ:
11 עֵינֵי גַּבְהוּת אָדָם שָׁפֵל וְשַׁח רוּם אֲנָשִׁים
וְנִשְׂגַּב יְהוָה לְבַדּוֹ בַּיּוֹם הַהוּא:

"For you have uprooted your people, the house of Jacob…"

Many of the verbs in this section do not require a future interpretation but simply refer to the sinful behavior of the Israelites in the past (v.6 יַשְׂפִּיקוּ and v.8 יִשְׁתַּחֲווּ could be iterative pasts or preterital *yiqtols*). There are references to YHWH's judgment in vv.6, 9 and 11 which are open to various interpretations. It is possible that these refer to events which have actually occurred (cf. 1.5ff.) or are rhetorical uses of the past tense (§ 3.4.5).[113] However, one should compare the past tense references to humbling in vv.9 and 11 with v.17:

וְשַׁח גַּבְהוּת הָאָדָם וְשָׁפֵל רוּם אֲנָשִׁים וְנִשְׂגַּב יְהוָה לְבַדּוֹ בַּיּוֹם הַהוּא:

It is possible that the references to "humbling" in vv.9 and 11 are to be understood as visionary occurrences (E^{vision}), and hence the whole pericope could consist of the narration of visionary events. וְשַׁח (v.11) is semantically related to the preceding שָׁפֵל and hence meets the established criteria for a conjunctive *weqatal* (cf. n.67), but וְנִשְׂגַּב does not. Although it could nonetheless be conjunctive, it is also possible that the prophet has switched to E^{real}; one may compare the similar shift from E^{vision} to E^{real} in Is 9.6 (example 29).

62. Is 15-16

1 מַשָּׂא מוֹאָב כִּי בְּלֵיל שֻׁדַּד עָר מוֹאָב נִדְמָה כִּי
בְּלֵיל שֻׁדַּד קִיר־מוֹאָב נִדְמָה: וגו'

"Oracle of Moab. For in a night Ar of Moab was destroyed, ruined; for in a night Kir of Moab was destroyed, ruined…"

---

[112] Whether v.5 is to be taken with this pericope or the preceding one is not very important for the point at hand; see the exegetical literature.

[113] Likewise Jer 5.3ff. (contrast e.g. Keil and Driver § 14 *a*).

The prophet refers to destruction experienced by Moab using past tenses, yet he also threatens that "additional" punishments are to come (15.9 נוֹסָפוֹת). This threat presupposes a past calamity of some sort. It is difficult to be certain whether this previous destruction occurred in reality (E^real) or in the prophet's vision (E^vision).[114]

63.   Is 25.12

וּמִבְצַר מִשְׂגַּב חוֹמֹתֶיךָ הֵשַׁח הִשְׁפִּיל הִגִּיעַ לָאָרֶץ עַד־עָפָר:
"And the high fortifications of your walls he has humbled, laid low, and brought down to the earth, unto the dust."

Though considered prophetic by some,[115] this is taken as a type of relative past (§ 3.4.1) by e.g. Watts ("when the fortification ... he has laid low, has knocked down and has made them touch the earth"). It seems more likely to me, however, that this is simply another reference to YHWH's destruction of "the city" which was already mentioned in v.2 (כִּי שַׂמְתָּ מֵעִיר לַגָּל); cf. 24.10, 12 and 26.5a.

64.   Is 29.20

כִּי־אָפֵס עָרִיץ וְכָלָה לֵץ וְנִכְרְתוּ כָּל־שֹׁקְדֵי אָוֶן:
"For/when (?) the ruthless have come to an end, and mockers will be destroyed, and all those who watch for evil will be cut off."

This could be either a relative past tense (§ 3.4.1) or rhetorical (§ 3.4.5).

65.   Is 32.14

כִּי־אַרְמוֹן נֻטָּשׁ הֲמוֹן עִיר עֻזָּב עֹפֶל וָבַחַן הָיָה בְעַד
מְעָרוֹת עַד־עוֹלָם מְשׂוֹשׂ פְּרָאִים מִרְעֵה עֲדָרִים:
"For the fortress has been forsaken, the crowd of the city abandoned; stronghold and watchtower became caves forever, the delight of donkeys, a pasture for flocks."

In this example the qatals could be understood either as expressing a relative past (§ 3.4.1) or as rhetorical (§ 3.4.5).

66.   Is 42.16

וְהוֹלַכְתִּי עִוְרִים בְּדֶרֶךְ לֹא יָדָעוּ בִּנְתִיבוֹת

---

[114] Likewise in Is 5.13-14, 25, 27, 30 (compare 1.5 עַל מֶה תֻכּוּ עוֹד "why will you be smitten *again*") and Mic 1.9ff. (note v.15 עַד הַיֹּרֵשׁ אָבִיא לָךְ "I will again bring the dispossessor to you").

[115] E.g. Driver § 14, Mulder (1954: 35); cf. RSV.

לֹא־יָדְעוּ אַדְרִיכֵם אָשִׂים מַחְשָׁךְ לִפְנֵיהֶם לָאוֹר וּמַעֲקַשִּׁים
לְמִישׁוֹר אֵלֶּה הַדְּבָרִים עֲשִׂיתִם וְלֹא עֲזַבְתִּים:

"And I (will) lead the blind in a way they do not know, I (will) make
them go in paths they do not know, I (will) make the darkness before
them into light and the crooked things smooth. These are the things I
have done, and I have not abandoned them."

It is uncertain whether the *yiqtols* and *weqatals* in the verses preceding
v.16 indicate the future or the general present. If the former, the *qatals* in
v.16 are most likely rhetorical (§ 3.4.5), but if the latter then we are
probably dealing with a global reference to the way YHWH has typically
acted in the past (cf. § 2.5.2).[116]

67. Is 45.16

בּוֹשׁוּ וְגַם־נִכְלְמוּ כֻּלָּם יַחְדָּו הָלְכוּ בַכְּלִמָּה חָרָשֵׁי צִירִים:

"They are all ashamed and also disgraced, the makers of idols have
walked in disgrace together."

It is uncertain whether this verse refers to a future event.

68. Is 46.1-2

1 כָּרַע בֵּל קֹרֵס נְבוֹ הָיוּ עֲצַבֵּיהֶם לַחַיָּה וְלַבְּהֵמָה
נְשֻׂאֹתֵיכֶם עֲמוּסוֹת מַשָּׂא לַעֲיֵפָה: 2 קָרְסוּ כָרְעוּ יַחְדָּו לֹא יָכְלוּ
מַלֵּט מַשָּׂא וְנַפְשָׁם בַּשְּׁבִי הָלָכָה:

"Bel bowed down, Nebo was stooping; their idols were for beasts and
for cattle. Your loads are burdened, a burden for the weary. They
stooped, bowed down together; they were not able to save the burden, and
they themselves went into captivity."

If this does not refer to an actual past event, it could be either rhetorical (§
3.4.5) or E[vision] (§ 3.4.4).[117]

69. Jer 2.26

כְּבֹשֶׁת גַּנָּב כִּי יִמָּצֵא כֵּן הֹבִישׁוּ בֵּית יִשְׂרָאֵל הֵמָּה
מַלְכֵיהֶם שָׂרֵיהֶם וְכֹהֲנֵיהֶם וּנְבִיאֵיהֶם:

---

[116] It would appear that in v.17 נָסֹגוּ אָחוֹר is to be understood as an asyndetic relative
clause: "those who have turned aside" (Dempsey 1988: 69). It is possible that Is 44.23
likewise refers to past behavior (§ 2.5.2) rather than a future E.
[117] Interestingly, Dempsey (1988: 130f.) mentions the latter possibility, though she rejects
it for a rhetorical explanation.

"As the shame of a thief when he is caught, thus has the house of Israel been put to shame: they, their kings, their princes, their priests, and their prophets."

It is unclear whether this refers to an event in the future or in the past.

70. Jer 10.19-25

19 אוֹי לִי עַל־שִׁבְרִי נַחְלָה מַכָּתִי וַאֲנִי אָמַרְתִּי אַךְ זֶה חֳלִי וְאֶשָּׂאֶנּוּ׃
20 אָהֳלִי שֻׁדָּד וְכָל־מֵיתָרַי נִתָּקוּ בָּנַי יְצָאֻנִי וְאֵינָם אֵין־נֹטֶה עוֹד
אָהֳלִי וּמֵקִים יְרִיעוֹתָי׃ 21 כִּי נִבְעֲרוּ הָרֹעִים וְאֶת־יְהוָה לֹא דָרָשׁוּ
עַל־כֵּן לֹא הִשְׂכִּילוּ וְכָל־מַרְעִיתָם נָפוֹצָה׃ 22 קוֹל שְׁמוּעָה הִנֵּה
בָאָה וְרַעַשׁ גָּדוֹל מֵאֶרֶץ צָפוֹן לָשׂוּם אֶת־עָרֵי יְהוּדָה שְׁמָמָה מְעוֹן
תַּנִּים׃ 23 יָדַעְתִּי יְהוָה כִּי לֹא לָאָדָם דַּרְכּוֹ לֹא־לְאִישׁ הֹלֵךְ וְהָכִין
אֶת־צַעֲדוֹ׃ 24 יַסְּרֵנִי יְהוָה אַךְ־בְּמִשְׁפָּט אַל־בְּאַפְּךָ פֶּן־תַּמְעִטֵנִי׃
25 שְׁפֹךְ חֲמָתְךָ עַל־הַגּוֹיִם אֲשֶׁר לֹא־יְדָעוּךָ וְעַל מִשְׁפָּחוֹת אֲשֶׁר בְּשִׁמְךָ
לֹא קָרָאוּ כִּי־אָכְלוּ אֶת־יַעֲקֹב וַאֲכָלֻהוּ וַיְכַלֻּהוּ וְאֶת־נָוֵהוּ הֵשַׁמּוּ׃

"Woe to me because of my injury; my wound is grievous. But I said to myself..."

The past tenses could be understood according to § 3.4.2 or § 3.4.5.

71.   Jer 12.4-13

4 עַד־מָתַי תֶּאֱבַל הָאָרֶץ וְעֵשֶׂב כָּל־הַשָּׂדֶה יִיבָשׁ מֵרָעַת יֹשְׁבֵי־בָהּ
סָפְתָה בְהֵמוֹת וָעוֹף כִּי אָמְרוּ לֹא יִרְאֶה אֶת־אַחֲרִיתֵנוּ׃ 5 כִּי
אֶת־רַגְלִים רַצְתָּה וַיַּלְאוּךָ וְאֵיךְ תְּתַחֲרֶה אֶת־הַסּוּסִים וּבְאֶרֶץ שָׁלוֹם
אַתָּה בוֹטֵחַ וְאֵיךְ תַּעֲשֶׂה בִּגְאוֹן הַיַּרְדֵּן׃ 6 כִּי גַם־אַחֶיךָ וּבֵית־אָבִיךָ
גַּם־הֵמָּה בָּגְדוּ בָךְ גַּם־הֵמָּה קָרְאוּ אַחֲרֶיךָ מָלֵא אַל־תַּאֲמֵן בָּם
כִּי־יְדַבְּרוּ אֵלֶיךָ טוֹבוֹת׃ 7 עָזַבְתִּי אֶת־בֵּיתִי נָטַשְׁתִּי אֶת־נַחֲלָתִי נָתַתִּי
אֶת־יְדִדוּת נַפְשִׁי בְּכַף אֹיְבֶיהָ׃ 8 הָיְתָה־לִּי נַחֲלָתִי כְּאַרְיֵה בַיָּעַר נָתְנָה
עָלַי בְּקוֹלָהּ עַל־כֵּן שְׂנֵאתִיהָ׃ 9 הַעַיִט צָבוּעַ נַחֲלָתִי לִי הַעַיִט סָבִיב
עָלֶיהָ לְכוּ אִסְפוּ כָּל־חַיַּת הַשָּׂדֶה הֵתָיוּ לְאָכְלָה׃ 10 רֹעִים רַבִּים שִׁחֲתוּ
כַרְמִי בֹּסְסוּ אֶת־חֶלְקָתִי נָתְנוּ אֶת־חֶלְקַת חֶמְדָּתִי לְמִדְבַּר שְׁמָמָה׃
11 שָׂמָהּ לִשְׁמָמָה אָבְלָה עָלַי שְׁמֵמָה נָשַׁמָּה כָּל־הָאָרֶץ
כִּי אֵין אִישׁ שָׂם עַל־לֵב׃
12 עַל־כָּל־שְׁפָיִם בַּמִּדְבָּר בָּאוּ שֹׁדְדִים כִּי חֶרֶב לַיהוָה אֹכְלָה
מִקְצֵה־אֶרֶץ וְעַד־קְצֵה הָאָרֶץ אֵין שָׁלוֹם לְכָל־בָּשָׂר׃ 13 זָרְעוּ חִטִּים
וְקֹצִים קָצָרוּ נֶחְלוּ לֹא יוֹעִלוּ וּבֹשׁוּ מִתְּבוּאֹתֵיכֶם מֵחֲרוֹן אַף־יְהוָה׃

100

"How long will the land mourn, and the grass of every field wither? On account of the wickedness of those who inhabit it the beasts and birds have been swept away..."

It is uncertain whether this refers to an actual past event or rather to a visionary one (§ 3.4.4).[118]

72.   Jer 13.17-27

17 וְאִם לֹא תִשְׁמָעוּהָ בְּמִסְתָּרִים תִּבְכֶּה־נַפְשִׁי מִפְּנֵי גֵוָה
וְדָמֹעַ תִּדְמַע וְתֵרַד עֵינִי דִּמְעָה כִּי נִשְׁבָּה עֵדֶר יְהוָה: 18 אֱמֹר לַמֶּלֶךְ
וְלַגְּבִירָה הַשְׁפִּילוּ שֵׁבוּ כִּי יָרַד מַרְאֲשׁוֹתֵיכֶם עֲטֶרֶת תִּפְאַרְתְּכֶם:
19 עָרֵי הַנֶּגֶב סֻגְּרוּ וְאֵין פֹּתֵחַ הָגְלָת יְהוּדָה כֻּלָּהּ הָגְלָת שְׁלוֹמִים:
20 שְׂאוּ עֵינֵיכֶם וּרְאוּ הַבָּאִים מִצָּפוֹן אַיֵּה הָעֵדֶר נִתַּן־לָךְ צֹאן
תִּפְאַרְתֵּךְ: 21 מַה־תֹּאמְרִי כִּי־יִפְקֹד עָלַיִךְ וְאַתְּ לִמַּדְתְּ אֹתָם עָלַיִךְ
אַלֻּפִים לְרֹאשׁ הֲלוֹא חֲבָלִים יֹאחֱזוּךְ כְּמוֹ אֵשֶׁת לֵדָה: 22 וְכִי תֹאמְרִי
בִּלְבָבֵךְ מַדּוּעַ קְרָאֻנִי אֵלֶּה בְּרֹב עֲוֹנֵךְ נִגְלוּ שׁוּלַיִךְ נֶחְמְסוּ עֲקֵבָיִךְ:
23 הֲיַהֲפֹךְ כּוּשִׁי עוֹרוֹ וְנָמֵר חֲבַרְבֻּרֹתָיו גַּם־אַתֶּם תּוּכְלוּ לְהֵיטִיב לִמֻּדֵי
הָרֵעַ: 24 וַאֲפִיצֵם כְּקַשׁ־עוֹבֵר לְרוּחַ מִדְבָּר: 25 זֶה גוֹרָלֵךְ מְנָת־מִדַּיִךְ
מֵאִתִּי נְאֻם־יְהוָה אֲשֶׁר שָׁכַחַתְּ אוֹתִי וַתִּבְטְחִי בַּשָּׁקֶר: 26 וְגַם־אֲנִי
חָשַׂפְתִּי שׁוּלַיִךְ עַל־פָּנָיִךְ וְנִרְאָה קְלוֹנֵךְ: 27 נִאֻפַיִךְ וּמִצְהֲלוֹתַיִךְ
זִמַּת זְנוּתֵךְ עַל־גְּבָעוֹת בַּשָּׂדֶה רָאִיתִי שִׁקּוּצָיִךְ אוֹי לָךְ יְרוּשָׁלַם
לֹא תִטְהֲרִי אַחֲרֵי מָתַי עֹד:

"And if you will not listen, my soul will weep in secret because of (your) pride, and my eyes will weep and flow with tears because the flock of YHWH has gone into captivity..."

An analysis of the tense usage in this passage is difficult, since it is not entirely clear whether the judgments spoken of are actually past or still future. The latter seems to be suggested by v.16. Verse 17 כִּי נִשְׁבָּה עֵדֶר יְהוָה can be understood as a relative past according to § 3.4.1 above. The past tenses in the following verses could be rhetorical (§ 3.4.5), but they could perhaps refer to E^{vision} (§ 3.4.4) or could be understood as quoted speech (§ 3.4.2; note v.18 אֱמֹר).

73.   Jer 25.38

עָזַב כַּכְּפִיר סֻכּוֹ כִּי־הָיְתָה אַרְצָם לְשַׁמָּה מִפְּנֵי חֲרוֹן
הַיּוֹנָה וּמִפְּנֵי חֲרוֹן אַפּוֹ:

---

[118] Cf. e.g. Holladay, Rudolph.

"Like a lion, he has left his lair, for their land has become a desolation because of the wrath of oppression and because of his fierce anger."

This could be a rhetorical use of *qatal* (§ 3.4.5), but the verse is exegetically difficult (cf. e.g. McKane).

74.   Jer 31.11

כִּי־פָדָה יְהוָה אֶת־יַעֲקֹב וּגְאָלוֹ מִיַּד חָזָק מִמֶּנּוּ:

"For YHWH has redeemed Jacob and redeemed him from one stronger than he."

Several interpretations are possible for v.11 (וּגְאָלוֹ ,פָדָה). It could be a reference to an actual past event (cf. v.2), a relative past (§ 3.4.1; note כִּי), a decision (§ 3.4.3) or perhaps it is simply rhetorical (§ 3.4.5).

75.   Jer 31.25

כִּי הִרְוֵיתִי נֶפֶשׁ עֲיֵפָה וְכָל־נֶפֶשׁ דָּאֲבָה מִלֵּאתִי:

"For I have satisfied the weary soul and have filled every faint soul."

The temporal reference of הִרְוֵיתִי and מִלֵּאתִי is not entirely obvious. They could perhaps refer to the way in which YHWH has acted in the past (cf. § 2.5.2). However, there are similarities to the future events reported in vv.12, 14, which could suggest that the events of v.25 are also to be understood as future. If this is the case, it could be understood as a reference to E^{vision} (§ 3.4.4) or according to either § 3.4.1 or § 3.4.5.

76.   Jer 40.4

וְעַתָּה הִנֵּה פִתַּחְתִּיךָ הַיּוֹם מִן־הָאזִקִים אֲשֶׁר עַל־יָדֶךָ

"And now, behold, I have released (?) you this day from the chains on your hands."

פִתַּחְתִּיךָ could be understood as a "perfect" (past event with e.g. continuing relevance), a past decision (§ 3.4.3), rhetorical (§ 3.4.5) or as a performative perfect (see § 4).[119]

77.   Jer 47.3-7

2 כֹּה אָמַר יְהוָה הִנֵּה־מַיִם עֹלִים מִצָּפוֹן וְהָיוּ לְנַחַל שׁוֹטֵף וְיִשְׁטְפוּ אֶרֶץ וּמְלוֹאָהּ עִיר וְיֹשְׁבֵי בָהּ וְזָעֲקוּ הָאָדָם וְהֵילִל

---

[119] Such interpretations are also possible in: Is 41.10, 13ff.; 42.1; 43.3, 14; 44.22; 45.8; Jer 28.14; Ezek 3.25; 4.8; 29.5; 33.27; 39.4. Compare e.g. Wagner (1997: 296ff.) with Dempsey (1988: 230ff.). Cf. also n.154 below.

כָּל יוֹשֵׁב הָאָרֶץ: 3 מִקּוֹל שַׁעֲטַת פַּרְסוֹת אַבִּירָיו מֵרַעַשׁ לְרִכְבּוֹ
הֲמוֹן גַּלְגִּלָּיו לֹא־הִפְנוּ אָבוֹת אֶל־בָּנִים מֵרִפְיוֹן יָדָיִם: 4 עַל־הַיּוֹם
הַבָּא לִשְׁדוֹד אֶת־כָּל־פְּלִשְׁתִּים לְהַכְרִית לְצֹר וּלְצִידוֹן כֹּל שָׂרִיד
עֹזֵר כִּי־שֹׁדֵד יְהוָה אֶת־פְּלִשְׁתִּים שְׁאֵרִית אִי כַפְתּוֹר: 5 בָּאָה קָרְחָה
אֶל־עַזָּה נִדְמְתָה אַשְׁקְלוֹן שְׁאֵרִית עִמְקָם עַד־מָתַי תִּתְגּוֹדָדִי: 6 הוֹי
חֶרֶב לַיהוָה עַד־אָנָה לֹא תִשְׁקֹטִי הֵאָסְפִי אַל־תַּעְרֵךְ הֵרָגְעִי וָדֹמִּי:
7 אֵיךְ תִּשְׁקֹטִי וַיהוָה צִוָּה־לָהּ אֶל־אַשְׁקְלוֹן וְאֶל־חוֹף הַיָּם שָׁם יְעָדָהּ:

"Thus has YHWH spoken: Behold, waters are coming up out of the
north, and they will become a flooding torrent, and they will flood the
land and its fullness, the city and its dwellers, and they will cry and all the
dwellers of the land will wail. At the sound of the stamping of the hoofs
of his mighty ones, at the shaking of his chariots, the tumult of his wheels,
fathers did not turn back to their sons from limpness of hands…"

A number of interpretations seem to be possible here.[120] We could be
dealing with a description of visionary events in vv.3ff. (§ 3.4.4); the non-
predicative participle הַבָּא in v.4 is ambiguous as to time and the predicative participle שֹׁדֵד could possibly be a progressive past. The past tenses
in this passage could perhaps be understood as rhetorical as well (§ 3.4.5).
On the other hand, v.2 (וְהֵילִל, וְזָעֲקוּ) could indicate that v.3 is to be understood as quoted speech (§ 3.4.2), which could be continued in vv.5ff.

78. Jer 49.7-22

7 לֶאֱדוֹם כֹּה אָמַר יְהוָה צְבָאוֹת הַאֵין עוֹד חָכְמָה בְּתֵימָן
אָבְדָה עֵצָה מִבָּנִים נִסְרְחָה חָכְמָתָם: 8 נֻסוּ הָפְנוּ הֶעְמִיקוּ לָשֶׁבֶת יֹשְׁבֵי
דְדָן כִּי אֵיד עֵשָׂו הֵבֵאתִי עָלָיו עֵת פְּקַדְתִּיו: 9 אִם־בֹּצְרִים בָּאוּ לָךְ לֹא
יַשְׁאִרוּ עוֹלֵלוֹת אִם־גַּנָּבִים בַּלַּיְלָה הִשְׁחִיתוּ דַיָּם: 10 כִּי־אֲנִי חָשַׂפְתִּי
אֶת־עֵשָׂו גִּלֵּיתִי אֶת־מִסְתָּרָיו וְנֶחְבָּה לֹא יוּכָל שָׁדַד זַרְעוֹ וְאֶחָיו וּשְׁכֵנָיו
וְאֵינֶנּוּ: 11 עָזְבָה יְתֹמֶיךָ אֲנִי אֲחַיֶּה וְאַלְמְנֹתֶיךָ עָלַי תִּבְטָחוּ: 12 כִּי־כֹה
אָמַר יְהוָה הִנֵּה אֲשֶׁר־אֵין מִשְׁפָּטָם לִשְׁתּוֹת הַכּוֹס שָׁתוֹ יִשְׁתּוּ
וְאַתָּה הוּא נָקֹה תִנָּקֶה לֹא תִנָּקֶה כִּי שָׁתֹה תִשְׁתֶּה: 13 כִּי בִי נִשְׁבַּעְתִּי
נְאֻם־יְהוָה כִּי־לְשַׁמָּה לְחֶרְפָּה לְחֹרֶב וְלִקְלָלָה תִּהְיֶה בָצְרָה
וְכָל־עָרֶיהָ תִהְיֶינָה לְחָרְבוֹת עוֹלָם: 14 שְׁמוּעָה שָׁמַעְתִּי מֵאֵת יְהוָה
וְצִיר בַּגּוֹיִם שָׁלוּחַ הִתְקַבְּצוּ וּבֹאוּ עָלֶיהָ וְקוּמוּ לַמִּלְחָמָה:
15 כִּי־הִנֵּה קָטֹן נְתַתִּיךָ בַּגּוֹיִם בָּזוּי בָּאָדָם: 16 תִּפְלַצְתְּךָ הִשִּׁיא אֹתָךְ
זְדוֹן לִבֶּךָ שֹׁכְנִי בְּחַגְוֵי הַסֶּלַע תֹּפְשִׂי מְרוֹם גִּבְעָה כִּי־תַגְבִּיהַ

---

[120] Cf. Huwyler (1997: 141).

כַּנֶּשֶׁר קִנֶּךָ מִשָּׁם אוֹרִידְךָ נְאֻם־יְהוָה: 17 וְהָיְתָה אֱדוֹם לְשַׁמָּה
כֹּל עֹבֵר עָלֶיהָ יִשֹּׁם וְיִשְׁרֹק עַל־כָּל־מַכּוֹתֶהָ: 18 כְּמַהְפֵּכַת סְדֹם וַעֲמֹרָה
וּשְׁכֵנֶיהָ אָמַר יְהוָה לֹא־יֵשֵׁב שָׁם אִישׁ וְלֹא־יָגוּר בָּהּ בֶּן־אָדָם:
19 הִנֵּה כְּאַרְיֵה יַעֲלֶה מִגְּאוֹן הַיַּרְדֵּן אֶל־נְוֵה אֵיתָן כִּי־אַרְגִּיעָה
אֲרִיצֶנּוּ מֵעָלֶיהָ וּמִי בָחוּר אֵלֶיהָ אֶפְקֹד כִּי מִי כָמוֹנִי וּמִי יֹעִידֶנִּי
וּמִי־זֶה רֹעֶה אֲשֶׁר יַעֲמֹד לְפָנָי: 20 לָכֵן שִׁמְעוּ עֲצַת־יְהוָה אֲשֶׁר יָעַץ
אֶל־אֱדוֹם וּמַחְשְׁבוֹתָיו אֲשֶׁר חָשַׁב אֶל־יֹשְׁבֵי תֵימָן אִם־לֹא יִסְחָבוּם
צְעִירֵי הַצֹּאן אִם־לֹא יַשִּׁים עֲלֵיהֶם נְוֵהֶם: 21 מִקּוֹל נִפְלָם
רָעֲשָׁה הָאָרֶץ צְעָקָה בְּיַם־סוּף נִשְׁמַע קוֹלָהּ:
22 הִנֵּה כַּנֶּשֶׁר יַעֲלֶה וְיִדְאֶה וְיִפְרֹשׂ כְּנָפָיו עַל־בָּצְרָה
וְהָיָה לֵב גִּבּוֹרֵי אֱדוֹם בַּיּוֹם הַהוּא כְּלֵב אִשָּׁה מְצֵרָה:

I am inclined to take vv.8-10 as references to E^{vision} (§ 3.4.4), though other
interpretations are possible. One could also understand most of these
verbs as "perfects" which refer to a past event with continuing relevance,
e.g. v.10 "I have stripped Esau bare, I have uncovered his hiding places,
and he is not able to conceal himself" (RSV). In this case, it would seem
likely that v.10 שָׁדַד is a rhetorical use of *qatal* (see especially § 3.4.5,
examples 51, 52, 53). Vv.12-20 are easily understood as E^{real}.[121] It appears that we are dealing with rapid shifting between E^{vision} in v.21 and
E^{real} in v.22; this is admittedly somewhat peculiar, but cf. § 3.4.4.4, examples 44 and 45.

79.   Jer 50.15

הָרִיעוּ עָלֶיהָ סָבִיב נָתְנָה יָדָהּ נָפְלוּ אָשְׁיוֹתֶיהָ נֶהֶרְסוּ חוֹמוֹתֶיהָ וגו׳

"Raise a shout against her from round about: 'She has surrendered, her
towers have fallen, her walls have been overthrown…'"

This could be understood either as quoted speech (§ 3.4.2) or as exaggerated rhetoric (§ 3.4.5).

80.   Jer 51.14

נִשְׁבַּע יְהוָה צְבָאוֹת בְּנַפְשׁוֹ כִּי אִם־מִלֵּאתִיךְ אָדָם כַּיֶּלֶק
וְעָנוּ עָלַיִךְ הֵידָד:

"YHWH Almighty has sworn by himself: I will fill/have filled (?) you
with men as with locusts, and they will raise a shout of victory over you."

---

[121] On v.15 see the discussion of Obad 2 (example 89).

There is a great deal of debate whether מִלֵּאתִיךְ refers to a future or to a past event (see the exegetical literature).

81.   Ezek 14.4

לָכֵן דַּבֶּר־אוֹתָם וְאָמַרְתָּ אֲלֵיהֶם כֹּה־אָמַר אֲדֹנָי יהוה
אִישׁ אִישׁ מִבֵּית יִשְׂרָאֵל אֲשֶׁר יַעֲלֶה אֶת־גִּלּוּלָיו אֶל־לִבּוֹ וּמִכְשׁוֹל עֲוֹנוֹ
יָשִׂים נֹכַח פָּנָיו וּבָא אֶל־הַנָּבִיא אֲנִי יהוה נַעֲנֵיתִי לוֹ בָהּ בְּרֹב גִּלּוּלָיו:

"Therefore speak to them, and say to them, 'Thus has the Lord YHWH spoken: Any man from the house of Israel who puts his idols in his heart and sets the stumbling block of his iniquity before his face, and comes to the prophet—I YHWH have answered (?) him in it, in the multitude of his idols.'"

The lexical meaning of נַעֲנֵיתִי is too disputed for this to function as a useful example of the prophetic perfect.

82.   Hos 4.6

נִדְמוּ עַמִּי מִבְּלִי הַדָּעַת כִּי־אַתָּה הַדַּעַת מָאַסְתָּ וְאֶמְאָסְאךָ
מִכַּהֵן לִי וַתִּשְׁכַּח תּוֹרַת אֱלֹהֶיךָ אֶשְׁכַּח בָּנֶיךָ גַּם־אָנִי:

"My people have been destroyed from lack of knowledge..."

נִדְמוּ has proved extremely difficult not only as far as the tense is concerned but also in regard to its lexical meaning (cf. the versions). This could be a rhetorical use of *qatal* (§ 3.4.5; see especially examples 51, 52, 53) if it refers to judgment upon Israel. It is possible, however, that this refers to moral corruption instead,[122] and hence could be interpreted as past.

83.   Hos 8.8

נִבְלַע יִשְׂרָאֵל עַתָּה הָיוּ בַגּוֹיִם כִּכְלִי אֵין־חֵפֶץ בּוֹ:

"Israel has been swallowed up; now they are among the nations as a worthless vessel."

As Van Leeuwen points out, it is not at all certain whether this refers to a past judgment or to a future one.[123]

84.   Hos 9.7

בָּאוּ יְמֵי הַפְּקֻדָּה בָּאוּ יְמֵי הַשִׁלֻּם

---

[122] So Simson; disputed by Keil.
[123] For the former interpretation see e.g. Simson, Harper, Rudolph, Macintosh; for the latter see Rosenmüller *ad loc*.

"The days of requital have come, the days of retribution have come."

Although this is interpreted by some as a prophetic perfect,[124] it can easily be understood as the English perfect: the time of judgment or retribution "has come".[125]

85.   Hos 9.16

הֻכָּה אֶפְרַיִם שָׁרְשָׁם יָבֵשׁ פְּרִי בַלי־יַעֲשׂוּן גַּם כִּי
יֵלֵדוּן וְהֵמַתִּי מַחֲמַדֵּי בִטְנָם:

"Ephraim has been struck, their root has withered, they bear no fruit. Even if they bear children I will put to death the delights of their womb."

It is not certain whether הֻכָּה refers to a future punishment or to one that has already begun.

86.   Hos 10.11

וְאֶפְרַיִם עֶגְלָה מְלֻמָּדָה אֹהַבְתִּי לָדוּשׁ וַאֲנִי עָבַרְתִּי
עַל־טוּב צַוָּארָהּ אַרְכִּיב אֶפְרַיִם יַחֲרוֹשׁ יְהוּדָה יְשַׂדֶּד־לוֹ יַעֲקֹב:

"And Ephraim is a trained cow that loves to thresh. And I have passed over (?) the goodness of her neck; I will hitch Ephraim up, Judah will plow, Jacob will harrow for himself."

The meaning of this verse and of עָבַרְתִּי is too uncertain to function as a useful example.

87.   Hos 10.14

וְקָאם שָׁאוֹן בְּעַמֶּךָ וְכָל־מִבְצָרֶיךָ יוּשַּׁד כְּשֹׁד שַׁלְמַן
בֵּית אַרְבֵאל בְּיוֹם מִלְחָמָה אֵם עַל־בָּנִים רֻטָּשָׁה:

"And tumult shall arise among your people, and all your fortresses will be destroyed as Shalman destroyed Beth Arbel on the day of battle, mothers were dashed to pieces upon their sons."

The referent of this verse is uncertain, but is understood as past by several commentators.[126]

88.   Joel 2.10-11

10 לְפָנָיו רָגְזָה אֶרֶץ רָעֲשׁוּ שָׁמָיִם שֶׁמֶשׁ וְיָרֵחַ קָדָרוּ וְכוֹכָבִים

---

[124] E.g. Van Leeuwen, Wolff.

[125] So also Is 7.17; 13.9; Jer 50.27, 31; 51.13; Mic 7.4.

[126] E.g. Andersen and Freedman, Davies, Van Leeuwen; cf. Keil, Van Gelderen and Gispen.

אָסְפוּ נָגְהָם: 11 וַיהוָה נָתַן קוֹלוֹ לִפְנֵי חֵילוֹ כִּי רַב מְאֹד מַחֲנֵהוּ כִּי עָצוּם עֹשֵׂה דְבָרוֹ כִּי־גָדוֹל יוֹם־יְהוָה וְנוֹרָא מְאֹד וּמִי יְכִילֶנּוּ:

"Before him the earth shook, the heavens shook, sun and moon grew dark and the stars took away their light. And YHWH sounded his voice before his host, for his camp was very great..."

So also 4.15:

שֶׁמֶשׁ וְיָרֵחַ קָדָרוּ וְכוֹכָבִים אָסְפוּ נָגְהָם:

"Sun and moon grew dark, and the stars took away their light."

These can simply be understood as figurative descriptions of the precursors to God's judgment.

89.   Obad 2

הִנֵּה קָטֹן נְתַתִּיךָ בַּגּוֹיִם בָּזוּי אַתָּה מְאֹד:

"Behold, I have made you small among the nations; you are greatly despised."

Although some understand this to refer to a future judgment,[127] Raabe argues that it refers to "the insignificant and feeble status that Yahweh has given Edom among the nations. Accordingly, the perfect verb indicates a completed and present situation, completed and present not only from the speaker's perspective but also in historical reality."

90.   Obad 5-7

5 אִם־גַּנָּבִים בָּאוּ־לְךָ אִם־שׁוֹדְדֵי לַיְלָה אֵיךְ נִדְמֵיתָה הֲלוֹא יִגְנְבוּ דַּיָּם אִם־בֹּצְרִים בָּאוּ לָךְ הֲלוֹא יַשְׁאִירוּ עֹלֵלוֹת: 6 אֵיךְ נֶחְפְּשׂוּ עֵשָׂו נִבְעוּ מַצְפֻּנָיו: 7 עַד־הַגְּבוּל שִׁלְּחוּךָ כֹּל אַנְשֵׁי בְרִיתֶךָ הִשִּׁיאוּךָ יָכְלוּ לְךָ אַנְשֵׁי שְׁלֹמֶךָ לַחְמְךָ יָשִׂימוּ מָזוֹר תַּחְתֶּיךָ אֵין תְּבוּנָה בּוֹ:

These verses present a number of textual and grammatical difficulties.[128] In v.5 אֵיךְ נִדְמֵיתָה is textually suspect and has been emended by several scholars. I take this as a parenthetical interjection in the midst of the conditional statement[129] and thus understand v.5 אֵיךְ נִדְמֵיתָה to belong

---

[127] E.g. Wehrle (1980: 228), Bewer, Aalders.

[128] I exclude here the famous crux of v.7 (לַחְמְךָ יָשִׂימוּ מָזוֹר תַּחְתֶּיךָ אֵין תְּבוּנָה בּוֹ).

[129] So e.g. Keil, Raabe; cf. Wehrle (1980: 98).

with vv.6-7. This could be understood as quoted speech (§ 3.4.2),[130] a reference to E^vision (§ 3.4.4) or perhaps a rhetorical use of *qatal* (§ 3.4.5).

91.   Mic 7.8

אַל־תִּשְׂמְחִי אֹיַבְתִּי לִי כִּי נָפַלְתִּי קָמְתִּי כִּי־אֵשֵׁב בַּחֹשֶׁךְ יְהוָה אוֹר לִי:

"Do not rejoice at me, my enemy, for/when I have fallen, I have arisen/will arise (?), when I sit in darkness, YHWH is a light for me."

Though קָמְתִּי is interpreted as a prophetic perfect by some,[131] this is open to some question. In the first place, Hillers notes that the LXX has the copula *kai* plus the future, perhaps attesting to a different textual tradition. Moreover, other scholars understand this to be the apodosis of a conditional clause (e.g. Robinson-Horst). Finally, it should be pointed out that there is no reason why a past tense is not acceptable here: It could simply be a figurative expression indicating that the "fall" which God's people experienced was not fatal. All things considered, this example is simply too uncertain and should be excluded.

92.   Nahum 3.13

הִנֵּה עַמֵּךְ נָשִׁים בְּקִרְבֵּךְ לְאֹיְבַיִךְ פָּתוֹחַ נִפְתְּחוּ שַׁעֲרֵי אַרְצֵךְ אָכְלָה אֵשׁ בְּרִיחָיִךְ:

"Behold, your people are women in your midst, the gates of your land have been opened for your enemies, fire has devoured your bars."

Rather than referring to a future judgment upon Nineveh, this is more likely a figurative expression which simply indicates that Nineveh has no defense against God's impending judgement.

93.   Hab 2.16

שָׂבַעְתָּ קָלוֹן מִכָּבוֹד שְׁתֵה גַם־אַתָּה וְהֵעָרֵל תִּסּוֹב עָלֶיךָ כּוֹס יְמִין יְהוָה וְקִיקָלוֹן עַל־כְּבוֹדֶךָ:

"You have been satisfied with shame rather than honor; drink, yourself, and become as uncircumcised! The cup in YHWH's right hand will come around to you, and shame upon your glory."

The future translations of e.g. RSV and NIV appear to understand the verb שָׂבַעְתָּ as a reference to a future punishment. I am more inclined to agree with Humbert, however, who understands it to refer to sinful con-

---

[130] Wehrle (1980: 232f.) thinks it refers to a future event and that this is "eine bewußte künstlerische Gestaltung des Stoffes" (cf. § 3.4.5), but it should be noted that he calls it an "ironisches Leichenlied".

[131] E.g. Qimchi, McKane; cf. Andersen and Freedman.

duct in the past.[132] The *Pesher Habakuk* (1QpHab 11.12ff.) likewise understood it as a reference to sinful behavior:

פשרו על הכוהן אשר גבר קלונו מכבודו

כיא לוא מל את עורלת לבו וילך בדרכי הרויה

"Seine Deutung bezieht sich auf den Priester, dessen Schande größer war als seine Ehre. Denn er beschnitt die Vorhaut seines Herzens nicht und wandelte auf den Wegen der Völlerei" (Lohse).

94. Zeph 2.11

נוֹרָא יְהוָה עֲלֵיהֶם כִּי רָזָה אֵת כָּל־אֱלֹהֵי הָאָרֶץ

וְיִשְׁתַּחֲווּ־לוֹ אִישׁ מִמְּקוֹמוֹ כֹּל אִיֵּי הַגּוֹיִם׃

"YHWH is terrible against them, for he has (?) all the gods of the earth; all the shores of the nations will bow down to him, each one in its own place."

רָזָה is problematic in a number of respects. Some understand it to refer to future events,[133] while others render it with a present tense[134] or with a past (e.g. Seybold, R. Smith). Ryou particularly argues against the need to interpret it as future.[135] A great deal of difficulty is caused by the *hapax* רָזָה. Given the lexical uncertainty of this verb it is hard to say what it might be referring to. In light of these various difficulties it seems best to exclude this example.

95. Zech 1.16 (= 8.3)

שַׁבְתִּי לִירוּשָׁלַ͏ִם בְּרַחֲמִים בֵּיתִי יִבָּנֶה בָּהּ

It is not difficult to understand שַׁבְתִּי as past: "I have returned to Jerusalem with compassion; my house shall be built in it."[136]

96. Zech 2.10

הוֹי הוֹי וְנֻסוּ מֵאֶרֶץ צָפוֹן נְאֻם־יְהוָה כִּי כְּאַרְבַּע רוּחוֹת

הַשָּׁמַיִם פֵּרַשְׂתִּי אֶתְכֶם נְאֻם־יְהוָה׃

"...for I have spread you abroad as the four winds of the heavens..."

---

[132] Humbert (1944: 56), similarly Keil.
[133] E.g. Keller, J. Smith; cf. NIV. Renaud is uncertain whether to take it as a prophetic perfect or to read an imperfect due to haplography of the *yodh*.
[134] E.g. Vlaardingerbroek, Keil, Berlin.
[135] Ryou (1994: 41f.).
[136] See e.g. Meyers and Meyers, Smith, RSV.

Rather than interpreting this as a prophetic perfect (so e.g. Keil, Rudolph), I take פֵּרַשְׂתִּי as referring to God's judgment in the past[137] (most likely the exile).

97.   Zech 5.3-4

3 וַיֹּאמֶר אֵלַי זֹאת הָאָלָה הַיּוֹצֵאת עַל־פְּנֵי כָל־הָאָרֶץ כִּי כָל־הַגֹּנֵב מִזֶּה כָּמוֹהָ נִקָּה וְכָל־הַנִּשְׁבָּע מִזֶּה כָּמוֹהָ נִקָּה: 4 הוֹצֵאתִיהָ נְאֻם יְהוָה צְבָאוֹת וּבָאָה אֶל־בֵּית הַגַּנָּב וְאֶל־בֵּית הַנִּשְׁבָּע בִּשְׁמִי לַשָּׁקֶר וְלָנֶה בְּתוֹךְ בֵּיתוֹ וְכִלַּתּוּ וְאֶת־עֵצָיו וְאֶת־אֲבָנָיו:

Though v.3 נִקָּה and v.4 הוֹצֵאתִיהָ are taken as prophetic by some commentators, these verses are so uncertain syntactically and lexically that this can hardly function as a useful example (see the exegetical literature).

98.   Zech 7.13-14

13 וַיְהִי כַאֲשֶׁר־קָרָא וְלֹא שָׁמֵעוּ כֵּן יִקְרְאוּ וְלֹא אֶשְׁמָע אָמַר יְהוָה צְבָאוֹת: 14 וְאֵסָעֲרֵם עַל כָּל־הַגּוֹיִם אֲשֶׁר לֹא־יְדָעוּם וְהָאָרֶץ נָשַׁמָּה אַחֲרֵיהֶם מֵעֹבֵר וּמִשָּׁב וַיָּשִׂימוּ אֶרֶץ־חֶמְדָּה לְשַׁמָּה:

"And when he called they did not listen, so when they call I will not listen, said YHWH Almighty. And I scattered them with a stormwind upon all the nations who did not know them, and the land became a desolation behind them, without travelers, and they made their desirable land into a desolation."

Keil takes v.14 וְאֵסָעֲרֵם as a future tense continuing the threat of v.13b, and the following נָשַׁמָּה is thus understood to have a future reference: "the land will be waste" (LXX: ἀφανισθήσεται; Peshitta: ܬܚܪܒ). However, a number of scholars and BHS suggest reading a *wayyiqtol*: וָאֲסָעֲרֵם (Vulgate: *et dispersi*). Even if this emendation is not accepted, the verb is taken by many as either a simple or frequentative past, and hence נָשַׁמָּה is also understood as a past tense;[138] it should be noted that this is continued by a *wayyiqtol*. I would take the whole section from v.11 onwards as set in the past, except for the threat of v.13b. Whether וְאֵסָעֲרֵם is preterital or frequentative past is not entirely certain, but this seems to me insufficient reason for interpreting נָשַׁמָּה as future.

---

[137] So also Petersen, Meyers and Meyers; the latter draw attention to זֵרוּ in vv. 2 and 4.

[138] E.g. Petersen, Meyers and Meyers, R. Smith, Mitchell, RSV, NIV.

110

99. Zech 9.5

תֵּרֶא אַשְׁקְלוֹן וְתִירָא וְעַזָּה וְתָחִיל מְאֹד וְעֶקְרוֹן
כִּי־הֹבִישׁ מֶבָּטָהּ וְאָבַד מֶלֶךְ מֵעַזָּה וְאַשְׁקְלוֹן לֹא תֵשֵׁב:

"Let Ashkelon see and it will be afraid; and Gaza, and it will writhe
very much; and Ekron, for its expectation has been disappointed. And the
king will perish from Gaza, and Ashkelon will not be inhabited."

הֹבִישׁ could be understood as either a relative past (§ 3.4.1) or as a rhetorical use of *qatal* (§ 3.4.5).

100. Zech 9.8

כִּי עַתָּה רָאִיתִי בְעֵינָי

"For I have now seen with my eyes."

It hardly seems necessary to take this as having either a future or even a
present reference.[139] It simply indicates that God has seen and taken notice of the situation. Compare Jer 7.11: גַּם אָנֹכִי הִנֵּה רָאִיתִי.

101. Zech 9.11

גַּם־אַתְּ בְּדַם־בְּרִיתֵךְ שִׁלַּחְתִּי אֲסִירַיִךְ מִבּוֹר אֵין מַיִם בּוֹ:

"As for you also: By the blood of your covenant I have set free your
prisoners from a waterless pit."

The meaning of this verse is disputed. Many scholars understand it to
refer to a future event,[140] whilst others interpret it as having a past reference.[141] It also appears to be possible to interpret שִׁלַּחְתִּי as performative
(cf. § 4).[142]

102. Zech 9.13

כִּי־דָרַכְתִּי לִי יְהוּדָה קֶשֶׁת מִלֵּאתִי אֶפְרַיִם וְעוֹרַרְתִּי
בָנַיִךְ צִיּוֹן עַל־בָּנַיִךְ יָוָן וְשַׂמְתִּיךְ כְּחֶרֶב גִּבּוֹר:

"For I have drawn Judah as a bow, I have filled Ephraim (with ar-
rows?), and I will arouse your sons, O Zion, against your sons, O Greece,
and I will make you like the sword of a warrior."

---

[139] Future: Keil; Present: e.g. RSV, NIV, Smith, Meyers and Meyers, Rudolph.
[140] E.g. Keil, Smith; cf. RSV, NIV, Mitchell.
[141] So e.g. Petersen, Meyers and Meyers.
[142] According to Wagner (1997: 118 n.23), however, the first person in the *piel* stem is not
used performatively.

The verbs דָּרַכְתִּי and מִלֵּאתִי have been interpreted as future, present and past.[143] A past tense would indicate that God has already begun preparations for executing judgment upon his enemies.

103. Zech 10.3

עַל־הָרֹעִים חָרָה אַפִּי וְעַל־הָעַתּוּדִים אֶפְקוֹד כִּי־פָקַד יְהוָה צְבָאוֹת
אֶת־עֶדְרוֹ אֶת־בֵּית יְהוּדָה וְשָׂם אוֹתָם כְּסוּס הוֹדוֹ בַּמִּלְחָמָה:

"My anger is kindled against the shepherds, and I will punish the chiefs, for YHWH Almighty has visited (?) his flock, the house of Judah, and will make it as his majestic horse in the battle."

פָּקַד is clearly used in a favorable sense here, in contrast to אֶפְקוֹד. Nonetheless, the verb פקד has a fairly broad semantic range and it is not entirely certain which particular meaning is intended here (cf. Petersen): "to visit" (Keil), "to care for" (R. Smith), "to muster" (Petersen), or "to attend to" (Meyers and Meyers).[144] In any event, a future interpretation (so e.g. Keil) is not the only possible one. Meyers and Meyers, for instance, state: "The use of the perfect tense of the verb helps to affirm that Yahweh's actions on behalf of the people have already begun."

104. Zech 10.8

אֶשְׁרְקָה לָהֶם וַאֲקַבְּצֵם כִּי פְדִיתִים וְרָבוּ כְּמוֹ רָבוּ:

"I will whistle for them and I will gather them, for I have redeemed them, and they will become numerous as they were numerous."

פְדִיתִים could refer to a past event or to a past decision (§ 3.4.3).[145] Alternately, it could be a rhetorical use of *qatal* (§ 3.4.5) or a performative perfect (§ 4).

105. Zech 11.2-3

2 הֵילֵל בְּרוֹשׁ כִּי־נָפַל אֶרֶז אֲשֶׁר אַדִּרִים שֻׁדָּדוּ הֵילִילוּ
אַלּוֹנֵי בָשָׁן כִּי יָרַד יַעַר הַבָּצִיר: 3 קוֹל יִלְלַת הָרֹעִים כִּי
שֻׁדְּדָה אַדַּרְתָּם קוֹל שַׁאֲגַת כְּפִירִים כִּי שֻׁדַּד גְּאוֹן הַיַּרְדֵּן:

"Wail, O pine tree: 'The cedar has fallen…'/Wail, O pine tree, for the cedar has fallen…"

---

[143] Future: Mitchell, R. Smith; Present: Van der Woude; Past: Rudolph, Petersen, Meyers and Meyers.

[144] פָּקַדְתִּי in 1 Sam 15.2 is likewise uncertain.

[145] Cf. Smith, Meyers and Meyers, RSV.

This could be understood as quoted speech (§ 3.4.2), with כִּי possibly introducing the quotation. It could also be a rhetorical use of the past tenses (§ 3.4.5).

106. Malachi 2.2

אִם־לֹא תִשְׁמְעוּ וְאִם־לֹא תָשִׂימוּ עַל־לֵב לָתֵת כָּבוֹד
לִשְׁמִי אָמַר יְהוָה צְבָאוֹת וְשִׁלַּחְתִּי בָכֶם אֶת־הַמְּאֵרָה וְאָרוֹתִי
אֶת־בִּרְכוֹתֵיכֶם וְגַם אָרוֹתִיהָ כִּי אֵינְכֶם שָׂמִים עַל־לֵב:

"If you do not listen and if you do not lay it to heart to give honor to my name, said YHWH Almighty, I will send a curse against you, and I will curse your blessings, and I have even cursed (?) it, for you are not laying it to heart."

The interpretation of אָרוֹתִיהָ is disputed. Van der Woude interprets it as a prophetic perfect, whereas others interpret it simply as past[146] or as performative (§ 4).[147]

107. Malachi 2.9

וְגַם־אֲנִי נָתַתִּי אֶתְכֶם נִבְזִים וּשְׁפָלִים לְכָל־הָעָם כְּפִי אֲשֶׁר
אֵינְכֶם שֹׁמְרִים אֶת־דְּרָכַי וְנֹשְׂאִים פָּנִים בַּתּוֹרָה:

"And I also have made (?) you despised and humbled before all the people, as you are not keeping my ways and are showing partiality in instruction."

As with the preceding example, we find varied interpretations of נָתַתִּי: prophetic,[148] performative[149] and past.[150]

108. Dan 11.36

וְעָשָׂה כִרְצוֹנוֹ הַמֶּלֶךְ וְיִתְרוֹמֵם וְיִתְגַּדֵּל עַל־כָּל־אֵל וְעַל
אֵל אֵלִים יְדַבֵּר נִפְלָאוֹת וְהִצְלִיחַ עַד־כָּלָה זַעַם כִּי נֶחֱרָצָה נֶעֱשָׂתָה:

"And the king will act according to his pleasure. And he will exalt himself and magnify himself against every god, and he will speak astonishing things against the God of gods, and he will prosper until the wrath has been completed, for a decree has been made."

---

[146] So e.g. Petersen, Hill ("recent perfective"), Verhoeff ("Het perfectum is hier niet propheticum maar historicum"); cf. RSV.

[147] Cf. Wagner (1997: 127 n.32).

[148] E.g. Van der Woude.

[149] Hill ("instantaneous perfective", with reference to Waltke and O'Connor § 30.5.1 *d*); cf. Keil, Petersen, RSV, NBG.

[150] Cf. Verhoeff.

The RSV renders נֶעֱשָׂתָה[151] as a future ("what is determined shall be done"), yet the Peshitta's ܬܪ ܠܐ ܕܦܣܝܩܬܐ ܐܬܬܥܒܕܬ ("for a determination has been made") appears to understand this to refer to a past decision (cf. § 3.4.3).[152] כִּי נֶחֱרָצָה נֶעֱשָׂתָה thus does not refer to the future events indicated by the preceding verbs but rather to the fact that it has been decreed that these events will take place.

Finally, there are some passages in Isaiah in which the alternation of tenses is peculiar, but which do not seem to fit easily into the categories discussed above: Is 18.5; 19.6-8 (textually problematic in any event); 33.3ff.; 34.14-16. I have no solution to propose for these.

§ 3.5 Conclusion

We have attempted to demonstrate in this chapter that the examples of the "prophetic perfect" which are cited in the grammatical literature are not all to be understood as one use of *qatal* but rather as several distinct ones. In some instances (§ 3.4.1) we are dealing with a type of relative tense usage in which the verb refers to an event which is past from a future reference point (R) rather than from the moment of speaking (S). In some cases we are dealing with a quotation that will be uttered in the future (§ 3.4.2). In such cases the event (E) is not being described in relation to the time of the narrator or of the text itself but rather from the quoted speaker's (future) temporal perspective. In other instances we argued that the event (E) referred to is not in fact to be understood as future but rather as past: in some cases it is a past decision (§ 3.4.3) or it occurred in a dream or vision (§ 3.4.4). In some cases *qatal* appears indeed to be used to refer to an event that has not yet occurred (§ 3.4.5). Such "idiomatic tense mismatches" occur in many languages which possess grammaticalized tense and are best treated as exceptions. The use of *qatal* in these cases appears to be exaggerated rhetoric by which a future event is described "as good as done". Finally, we argued that a large number of al-

---

[151] The verb כָּלָה in conjunction with עַד has the sense of a *futurum exactum*; cf. Joüon and Muraoka § 112 *i* and Driver § 17.

[152] This might be similar to Keil's interpretation, though his precise meaning is not entirely clear to me: "The *perf.* נֶעֱשָׂתָה does not stand for the *imperf.* because it is decreed, but in its proper meaning, according to which it represents the matter as finished, settled. Here it accordingly means: 'for that which is irrevocably decreed is accomplished, is not to be recalled, but must be done.'" Rashi argues that כִּי has the sense of כַּאֲשֶׁר here, in which case it would be possible to interpret נֶעֱשָׂתָה as a *futurum exactum* (cf. preceding note): "when what is decreed has (i.e. will have) been done".

leged examples of the prophetic perfect are exegetically uncertain (§ 3.4.6).

The focus in this chapter has been on the prophetic corpus. It has indeed been correctly pointed out that the term "prophetic perfect" is, strictly speaking, a misnomer, since examples are cited in other genres.[153] However, it should be noted that most alleged examples in prose texts are quite possibly performative perfects (§ 4),[154] and most examples in non-prophetic poetic texts are often extremely ambiguous and open to other temporal interpretations (cf. § 1.1). Driver himself admits:

> In some of the passages from the Psalms we may not perhaps feel assured that the perfects are to be understood in this sense, as representing the certainty and confidence felt by the writers as regards the events they anticipate. It is no doubt *possible* that they may simply describe past facts or former experiences ... which the writer desires to refer to... But the 'perfect of certitude' is of such frequent and well-established occurrence, and at the same time so much more forcible and appropriate to the context than the more common-place 'perfect of experience,' that we need not scruple to interpret accordingly.[155]

In my opinion, the fact that the "prophetic perfect" is actually a complex phenomenon consisting of several distinct uses of *qatal* suggests that some "scruples" are very much in order. As this chapter has shown, most alleged examples of the "prophetic perfect" in the prophetic literature are to be explained as past tenses, and the number of instances in which the use of *qatal* is rhetorically motivated is considerably smaller than has generally been supposed. Hence it is by no means self-evident that any particular instance should be interpreted in this way, given an ambiguous context. At the very least, this study indicates that one will need to avoid the blanket term of "prophetic perfect" and specify more precisely what is meant grammatically.

---

[153] Klein (1990: 45, 60), DeCaen (1995: 12).

[154] See the examples cited by Revell (1989: 5f.) and compare Wagner (1997: 109ff.), e.g. Gen 1.29; 9.13; 15.18; 17.20; 23.11, 13; Dt 1.8; 2.24; 3.2; 9.23; Ju 1.2; 2 Sam 9.9; 24.23; 1 K 3.12f.

[155] Driver § 14 β n.1.

§ 4. THE PERFORMATIVE PERFECT

§ 4.1 Previous Discussion

It is now common to use the term "performative utterance" (or *Koinzidezfall*) to designate statements such as the following:

1.   I now pronounce you man and wife.

2.   I hereby dub thee Sir Henry.

3.   I promise to behave myself.

Such utterances have been frequently discussed in general linguistics,[1] and in recent years have received increasing attention in Semitic studies. As some useful surveys of previous works related to the Semitic languages already exist,[2] we will simply focus here on the discussion as it relates to the semantics of the Hebrew verbal system.

---

[1] See e.g. Partridge (1982), Levinson (1983: ch.5), Recanati (1987), Verschueren (1995). The term "performative utterance" was coined by Austin (1976), though the basic concept had been discussed earlier by Koschmieder, who referred to such cases as *Koinzidenzfall* and, significantly, drew attention to this function of *qatal* in e.g. Gen 17.20 בֵּרַכְתִּי אֹתוֹ "I (hereby) bless him" (1930: 352ff.). With a number of other scholars, I view Austin's "explicit performative utterance" and *Koinzidenzfall* as referring to essentially the same concept and use the terms synonymously (cf. Johanson 1971: 57, Mayer 1980: 304, Partridge 1982, Pardee and Whiting 1987, Hillers 1995: 758ff.; contrast Wagner 1997: 51ff.).
[2] E.g. Pardee and Whiting (1987), Zatelli (1993), Wagner (1997: 58ff.). Most recent studies use Austin's terminology (cf. Schneider § 48.6.2, Pascual 1993: 190, Talstra 1982, De Regt 1983: 270, Zatelli 1993, Hillers 1995, Wagner 1997, Warren 1998: 81ff.; Van der Merwe-Naudé-Kroeze 1999: 146), whereas Koschmieder's term has found wide acceptance among German-speaking Semitists (e.g. Brockelmann 1956: §41 *d*, Rundgren 1961: 90f., Heimpel and Guidi 1969, Mayer 1976: 189f., Richter 1978: 141, Bartelmus 1982: 53, Müller 1988: 79, 1998: 148, Schüle 2000: 140ff.). Earlier grammarians noticed the phenomenon, of course, but did not employ the same terminology (cf. Davidson § 40 *b*, Joüon 1923: § 112 *f*, Cohen 1924: 212, Gesenius-Kautzsch-Cowley § 106 *i*, Driver § 10, Bergsträsser § 6 *e*).

A number of scholars attribute the performative *qatal* to perfective aspect.[3] Wagner, in his extensive study on speech-act analysis of the Old Testament, adopts the understanding of the Hebrew verb proposed by Michel:

> Im Hebräischen ist eine Zeitbedeutung der Tempora nicht gegeben; Tempora scheinen hier eher die Funktion zu haben, die Handlung hinsichtlich ihrer Gewichtigkeit zu unterscheiden; als syntaktische Form zum Ausdruck selbstgewichtiger Aussagen dient im Hebräischen dabei die Afformativkonjugation. Kaum eine Äußerung ist aber selbstgewichtiger und unabhängiger vorstellbar als eine explizit performative Äußerung, in der die im Verb liegende Proposition als Handlung im Moment des Aussprechens verwirklicht wird; kein Wunder also, wenn im Hebräischen die Afformativkonjugation als syntaktische Grundform der explizit performativen Äußerung eintritt.[4]

Bobzin, who is also influenced to some degree by Michel, explains it somewhat differently: "Daß der Koinzidenzfall nur im Ḥameṭ[5] ausdrückbar ist, wird ... unmittelbar evident sein, da es sich bei ihm soz. um eine einmalige Handlung kat' exochen [sic] handelt!"[6]

There are various explanations of the performative perfect in terms of temporal deixis. Some scholars argue that *qatal* can have a present tense value,[7] and if such is the case then the performative perfect would not

---

[3] E.g. Waltke and O'Connor § 30.5.1 *d*, Hendel (1996: 156), Tropper (1998: 183), Gentry (1998: 18f.); cf. Zatelli (1993: 64f.).

[4] Wagner (1997: 291); cf. Michel (1960).

[5] I.e. *qatal* or the short *yiqtol* (**yaqtul*).

[6] Bobzin (1974: 38). It should be noted that he denies that Ḥameṭ marks a situation as "vergangen" or "abgeschlossen" (1974: 35): "Wesentlich ist allein die Tatsache, daß die betreffende Handlung als *einmalig*, d.h. nicht wiederholt, und vor allem als *nicht notwendig so geschehen* (oder zu geschehen), sondern eher als *kontingent* oder *akzidentiell* gekennzeichnet werden soll. Kurz gesagt: Das Ḥameṭ bezeichnet jede Art von individuellen Sachverhalten." This description is primarily indebted to Rössler (1962), though it also includes elements found in Michel (1960). Given this explicit rejection of a temporal value to *qatal*, it is difficult to see why Rainey (1988) thinks that Bobzin's views regarding the Hebrew verb are amenable to his own.

[7] E.g. Blake (1951: 17). According to Rundgren (1961), Isaksson (1987: 25) and Eskhult (1990: 17ff.) the proto-Semitic verbal system marked a stative::fientive "aspectual" opposition (but Creason 1995: 6 n.14 rightly points out that this is more properly a description of *Aktionsart* rather than aspect) which, in Hebrew, corresponds to the opposition between *qatal* and *yiqtol* (**yaqtulu*). Despite the fact that *qatal* has to a large extent undergone a process of fientization, the use of *qatal* for *Koinzidenzfall* is attributed to its "archaic stative value". Thus e.g. Eskhult considers the verb in such cases to be "*essentially* stative, or put in a construction that signals 'state' as opposed to 'action'" (1990: 23, see also 21, 110; cf. Rundgren 1961: 90f. and Isaksson 1987: 84f.). Cf. also Meyer § 101 2b. However, as we will see below (§ 4.4.2), semantically stative verbs cannot occur in performative utterances, and hence it is not fitting to describe the verb form used in a "performative" (!) utterance as signaling a *state* rather than an *action*. Joosten (1989: 157) likewise calls the performative perfect a trace of an earlier stage of the verbal system in which *qatal*

appear to present any difficulty in regard to the semantics of the form. Other scholars, who understand *qatal* to be a past tense, attempt to explain this use in different ways. Revell views it as a subtype of the "perfect of certainty" (cf. § 3), i.e. a *qatal* "used to present an event which has not occurred at the time of speaking, but which is known, or believed, to have been initiated by a decision made in the past".[8] Bombeck, in his study of Targum and Peshitta translation technique, writes:

> [Das Perfekt] kann in Rede für Handlungen der 1. sg. verwendet werden, die mit dem Akt der Rede zusammenfallen ("Koinzidenz"), also spätestens mit dem Ende der Rede beendet sind. Sie liegen eigentlich in [Gleichzeitigkeit]; trotzdem wird fast immer schematisch (in [Neofiti] öfter mit Zusatz von הא) übersetzt. Da aram. [Perfekt] Koinzidenz nicht bezeichnet, ist anzunehmen, daß die Aramäer in diesen Fällen leicht übertreibend die gemeinte [Gleichzeitigkeit] mit [Perfekt] als [Vergangenheit] dargestellt haben: was ich jetzt sage, ist damit auch schon geschehen. Dasselbe darf man für das Hebr. vermuten; dann wäre [Perfekt] für Koinzidenz keine eigene Funktion, sondern ein stilistisch bedingter Sonderfall von [Perfekt] zur Bezeichnung der [Vorzeitigkeit].[9]

Joüon and Muraoka state that "qatal is used for an instantaneous action which, being performed at the very moment of the utterance, is assumed to belong to the past."[10] Joosten postulates a "post-terminal" meaning for *qatal* in performative utterances: "what is represented as anterior to the moment of speaking is not the entire action expressed by the verb, but its significant 'term'." Thus with the utterance of נתתי "the main component of the action is past."[11]

Finally it should be mentioned that some scholars argue that no attempt should be made to relate performativity to the semantics of *qatal*. For example, Talstra writes: "performative speech in Hebrew should not be explained as an aspect of any 'basic function' of the perfect tense, such as: indication of a completed action."[12] We will return to this question below (§ 4.6).

---

had present tense functions, though he does not think it possible to reconstruct this stage in detail. (N.B. he proposes a somewhat different explanation in his 1997 article, see below.)

[8] Revell (1989: 5f.); cf. Hughes (1993: 134): "the perfect is an assertative form which can be used to express certainty about a future (or present) event... In Biblical Hebrew, נתתי can mean 'I have (certainly) given', 'I (certainly) give', or 'I will (certainly) give'."

[9] Bombeck (1997: 74).

[10] Joüon and Muraoka § 112 *f.*

[11] Joosten (1997: 62f.); cf. Rundgren (1961: 90f.). Precisely what Joosten means by "main component of the action" is not clear to me.

[12] Talstra (1982: 27); see also DeCaen (1995: 253ff.) and Warren (1998: 83f.).

118

§ 4.2 Post-Biblical Hebrew

A clear diachronic development from the use of *qatal* in performatives in Biblical Hebrew to the use of the participle in the post-Biblical period can be observed. See the appendix for documentation.

§ 4.3 Comparative Semitics

We encounter performative perfects in Ugaritic,[13] Egyptian Aramaic,[14] Phoenician,[15] Ethiopic[16] and Classical Arabic,[17] as well as performative *iprus* and *iptaras* in Akkadian.[18] No consensus has emerged, however, as to how this performative use is to be explained.[19] Moreover, it should also be noted that we find some performative participles in Aramaic,[20]

---

[13] M. Smith (1995: 795f.), Tropper (1999: 109; 2000: 714); cf. Hoftijzer (1995-96: 78f.).

[14] Hug (1993: 116f.), Muraoka and Porten § 51 *b*.

[15] Friedrich-Röllig-Guzzo § 262 6.

[16] Weninger (2000).

[17] Denz (1982: 71), Fischer (1972: § 181 *c*; 1994: 81f.).

[18] Heimpel and Guidi (1969), Mayer (1976: 183ff.), Von Soden § 79 *b* and § 80 *c*. It should be noted that these studies are weakened by a confusion of epistolary and performative verb usage; see the criticisms of Pardee and Whiting (1987) and Streck (1995: 91ff., 155ff.) and cf. Rogland (2000).

[19] We find a variety of explanations which are, generally speaking, similar to those proposed for the performative perfect in Classical Hebrew (cf. § 4.1). Fischer (1994: 81 n.5) attributes the Arabic performative perfect to perfective aspect. Cuvalay-Haak, who thinks that the perfect has no past time reference in such instances, states (1997: 134 n.103): "The use of the suffix set in performative expressions can be explained on the basis of its function of indicating Perfect Aspect ('I am hereby in the state of having sold you this') or Factual Mood ('I am hereby definitely selling you this')." However, it is important to note that she distinguishes "Perfect Aspect" from "Perfective Aspect". The latter belongs to the perfective-imperfective opposition (1997: 134f.; cf. § 1.3), whereas the former indicates the resultant state of a completed situation (1997: 135), i.e. she appears to understand it in a way similar to the English present perfect (on the debate over the English perfect see above, p. 5 n.26); cf. also Kurylowicz (1972: 82). By "Factual Mood" she refers to the assertion of the factuality of a proposition (1997: 139f.): In such cases the perfect "expresses the 100% validity of a known fact or a presupposition. This function of the suffix set is often explained as resulting from a metaphorical extension of the Past Tense meaning. Since we can be sure of what happened in the past, we can present future events as certain by describing them with the verb form ordinarily used for Past Tense." Aartun (1963: 43f.) explains such cases as analogous to certain instances of the Greek aorist: "Endlich können auch Verben des *Sagens*, des *Befehlens*, des *Anratens*, des *Schwörens*, obwohl sie auf die Gegenwart bezogen werden, durch den *Aorist* ausgesprochen werden, wenn der Ausspruch als ein *unabänderlicher, ein für allemal gültiger* nachdrücklich bezeichnet werden soll. Denn was der Vergangenheit angehört, lässt sich nicht ändern." According to Denz (1982: 71) the perfect is used "da mit dem Aussprechen des Satzes die durch das Verbum bezeichnete Handlung auch schon vollzogen, d.h. zeitlich abgelaufen ist". See also the quote by Streck in n.22 below.

[20] E.g. Qumran Aramaic and Classical Syriac; see Rogland (1999), *idem* (2001).

imperfects in Classical Arabic and Phoenician,[21] and performative *iparras* in Akkadian.[22]

§ 4.4 Criteria for Performative Utterances

§ 4.4.1 *Formal Criteria*

Five markers of an active voice performative sentence are commonly mentioned.[23]

§ 4.4.1.1 *Non-negative*

Performatives cannot be negative. As Partridge points out, *I don't promise I'll be there on time* "cannot be used to perform an act of not promising, but only to state that one is not promising."[24] This is to be sharply distinguished from e.g. *I promise not to make a fool of myself*, which does constitute an act of promising.

§ 4.4.1.2 *Subject*

Performative utterances typically occur with a first person subject,[25] but a third person subject can occur if it refers to the speaker or if the speaker is acting as a representative of another person.[26]

---

[21] According to Reuschel (1996: 291), there are no performative perfects attested in the Qur'an; I have located a number of performative imperfects, however: e.g. 11:54 "I call Allah to witness (*'ushidu*)", 19:7 "We give thee glad tidings (*nubaśśiruka*) of a son". Cf. also Khalil and McCarus (1999: 10), who claim that the "overwhelming majority" of performatives in Modern Standard Arabic occur in the imperfect. For Phoenician see *KAI* 89.2 אתך אנכי מצלח ית אמען[ש]תרת "I, Meṣliḥ, commend to you Amastarte" and, if Krahmalkov's reading is correct (2001: 183), *KAI* 48.2-3 לאלנם אשאל [תב]ורך ית ארבעת בני "I ask of you gods: Bless ye my four sons!"

[22] Streck (1995: 91ff.), Müller (1986: 372), Mayer (1976: 205ff.). Streck argues (1995: 191 n.441) that the use of both past and present tense forms in Akkadian performatives is "semantisch begründbar und der Ausdruck der Koinzidenz somit als Nebenfunktion der jerweiligen Form interpretierbar": "entweder gilt als Relationswert ein Zeitpunkt innerhalb des durch die Aussage bezeichneten Sachverhalts, woraus sich Gleichzeitigkeit ergibt, oder ein Zeitpunkt am Ende dieses Sachverhaltes, woraus Vorzeitigkeit folgt. ... In vielen Sprachen treten beide Perspektiven nebeneinander auf. Dies erklärt im Akk. den Gebrauch von *iparras* einerseits, von *iprus* und *iptaras* andererseits, im Deutschen des Präsens (*hiermit ernenne ich dich zum Ritter*) und des Perfekts (*hiermit habe ich dich ernannt*)."

[23] See e.g. Leech (1981: 322), Talstra (1982: 28), Partridge (1982: 18), Schneider § 48.6.2, Warren (1998: 82ff.). Performatives can also occur in the passive voice (e.g. "You are hereby notified..."), but these will be not be examined here.

[24] Partridge (1982: 22); see also Brandt *et al.* (1990: 365f.).

[25] Koschmieder (1965: 28).

§ 4.4.1.3 Indirect object

If an indirect object occurs then it refers to the addressee (provided that the addressee is not the direct object).[27]

§ 4.4.1.4 "Hereby"

Performative utterances tolerate the addition of the adverb "hereby". In fact, this test is not foolproof,[28] though it is often helpful in distinguishing performative presents from habitual, iterative or narrative presents.

§ 4.4.1.5 Verb form

It is frequently claimed that one of the formal criteria for a performative utterance is that the verb form is in the simple indicative present; moreover, according to some scholars this is a perfective present.[29] This touches on the chief interest of the present investigation and will be discussed in detail below (§ 4.6).

§ 4.4.2 Semantic and Pragmatic Criteria

Performative utterances cannot be identified by formal criteria alone. Compare the following:[30]

---

[26] See Koschmieder (1930: 353), Talstra (1982: 28), Streck (1995: 93), Warren (1998: 83).

[27] Warren (1998: 83). This is a more careful formulation than the usual statement that the indirect object is second person (e.g. Leech 1981: 322). This rule, incidentally, is one reason why the formula כה אמר יהוה ("thus has YHWH spoken") should not be understood as performative (as argued by e.g. Mayer 1976: 189, Müller 1986: 369, Wagner 1997: 156f.). Krispenz (1998: 137) points out that in some cases the formula occurs with אלי "to me" (Is 8.11; 18.4; 31.4; Jer 13.1; 17.19; 25.15; 27.2) and aptly comments: "Versucht man, die Botenformel in dieser Gestalt als Koinzidenzfall zu verstehen, so ergibt sich, daß dann nicht nur Sprechen und Handeln sowie Sprecher und Subjekt identisch sind, sondern daß hier Sprecher, Subjekt und Angeredeter in eins fallen. Der Prophet spricht in der Rolle Jahwes den Propheten an—eine bizarre Konstruktion!" Consequently I agree with those scholars who take this simply as a past tense which reflects the prophet's awareness of having received a message from YHWH; so e.g. Pardee (1983: 39), Gibson § 57 rem. 3, DeCaen (1995: 248), Bombeck (1997: 76), Krispenz (1998).

[28] Partridge (1982: 20).

[29] See e.g. Koschmieder (1930: 352; 1965: 28), Koschmieder-Schmid (1967: 179f.), Sørensen (1949: 167f.), Warren (1998: 84), Leech (1981: 322), Partridge (1982: 18).

[30] See Levinson (1983: 232); cf. Partridge (1982: 20), Liedtke (1990: 515f.).

4.   I now pronounce you man and wife.

5.   I now beat the eggs till fluffy.

Semantic and pragmatic factors also play a role: An utterance must be capable of performing an act of some sort. Consequently, performative utterances are non-stative.[31] Partridge argues that performatives are limited to *verba dicendi*,[32] and Koschmieder likewise limits them to "alle solche Verben ... die eine durch Sprechen realisierbare Tätigkeit meinen".[33] However, two qualifications must be made. Firstly, not all *verba dicendi* can be used performatively: e.g. "to mumble", "to recite", "to speak", "to remark", "to insinuate".[34] Secondly, performative utterances which are part of a ritualized act do not necessarily have to be *verba dicendi* in the strict sense, provided that a particular utterance is considered necessary for the felicitous performance of a prescribed ritual.[35] For example, "to baptize" is hardly a *verbum dicendi*, yet the utterance of *I baptize you in the name of the Father, and of the Son, and of the Holy Spirit* is nonetheless a necessary part of the baptismal rite: without it there is no baptism. The felicity conditions of these types of ritual utterances are governed by various conventions and institutions (social, legal, religious, etc.),[36] and it would be an enormously complicated task to determine such conditions even with the help of native speaker informants. When dealing with a dead language such as Classical Hebrew the task is naturally even more difficult. The examples below (§ 4.5) will consist of non-ritual utterances, i.e. *verba dicendi* in the narrow sense.

§ 4.5 Examples

A large number of examples proposed in the literature do not meet the criteria discussed above (§ 4.4) and consequently should be eliminated. Talstra notes that the syntactic criteria presuppose that act and utterance coincide,[37] yet it is just this coincidence that can be the most difficult to

---

[31] Partridge (1982: 46f.), Warren (1998: 83); cf. n.7 above.

[32] Partridge (1982: 20, 42ff.).

[33] Koschmieder (1965: 28); see also *idem* (1935: 287f.).

[34] Cf. Partridge (1982: 20), Leech (1981: 323), Vendler (1972: 207f.), Verschueren (1995: 312ff.). One factor, it seems to me, is whether or not a verb has durative *Aktionsart*: If something is to be accomplished by a verbal utterance then it would appear that a durative situation is excluded. E.g. one cannot say **I hereby recite...*, since "reciting" necessarily indicates a process of some duration.

[35] Fraser (1974) and Partridge (1982: 82) distinguish between "institutional" and "non-institutional" performatives; see also Verschueren (1995: 313).

[36] Recanati (1987: 74ff.).

[37] Talstra (1982: 28).

122

determine with certainty in a large number of cases.[38] It is not our intention here to attempt to provide an exhaustive list of examples, nor is it necessary to do so. There are enough cases of *verba dicendi* (cf. § 4.4.2) in which a performative interpretation of *qatal* is clearly the most probable one. The following list is merely intended to be illustrative, not complete.[39]

6.   Ps 75.2

הוֹדִינוּ לְּךָ אֱלֹהִים הוֹדִינוּ

"We praise you, O God, we praise you."

7.   Dt 4.26

הַעִידֹתִי בָכֶם הַיּוֹם אֶת־הַשָּׁמַיִם וְאֶת־הָאָרֶץ כִּי וגו'

"I call heaven and earth as witnesses against you this day, that..." (Vulgate: *invoco*; LXX: διαμαρτύρομαι).[40]

8.   Dt 26.3

הִגַּדְתִּי הַיּוֹם לַיהוָה אֱלֹהֶיךָ כִּי וגו'

"I declare today to Yhwh your God that..." (LXX: ἀναγγέλλω; Vulgate: *profiteor*).[41]

9.   2 S 17.11

כִּי יָעַצְתִּי הֵאָסֹף יֵאָסֵף עָלֶיךָ כָל־יִשְׂרָאֵל מִדָּן וְעַד־בְּאֵר שֶׁבַע

"For I advise: All Israel should be gathered to you, from Dan and unto Beer-Sheva" (Peshitta: ܐܢܐ ܡܠܟ).[42]

10.   2 S 19.8

כִּי בַיהוָה נִשְׁבַּעְתִּי כִּי וגו'

"For I swear by Yhwh that..." (Vulgate: *iuro*).[43]

---

[38] Hillers (1995: 758); cf. Groß (1977: 32).

[39] For a very extensive – though not necessarily exhaustive – list of possible examples, see Wagner (1997).

[40] So also Dt 8.19 (הַעִידֹתִי); 30.19 (הַעִידֹתִי); Jer 42.19 (הַעִידֹתִי). Greek and Latin both use the present tense in performative utterances (Anscombre and Pierrot 1984, Fanning 1990: 187ff., 202ff.). The present tense renderings in the LXX are all the more noteworthy, since it tended to translate performative *qatals* "mechanically" with a Greek aorist or perfect (see Rogland 2001: 244f.).

[41] So also Dt 30.18 הִגַּדְתִּי (LXX: ἀναγγέλλω; Vulgate: *praedico*).

[42] The Peshitta is particularly striking here, as it typically renders performative *qatals* in the Hebrew text with the Syriac perfect; see Rogland (2001: 245) and cf. n.40.

[43] So also Gen 22.16-17 נִשְׁבַּעְתִּי; Jer 44.26 נִשְׁבַּעְתִּי.

11.   Cant. 2.7 (= 3.5; 5.8; 8.4)

הִשְׁבַּעְתִּי אֶתְכֶם בְּנוֹת יְרוּשָׁלַ͏ִם וגו'

"I charge you, O daughters of Jerusalem..." (Vulgate: *adiuro vos*).

12.   Gen 17.20

הִנֵּה בֵּרַכְתִּי אֹתוֹ וְהִפְרֵיתִי אֹתוֹ וגו'

"Behold, I bless him, and I will make him fruitful..."[44]

13.   Arad 16.1-2

אחך חנניהו שלח לשלם אלישב ושלם ביתך

"Your brother Hananyahu sends greetings to Elyashib and to your house."[45]

14.   2 S 19.30

אָמַרְתִּי אַתָּה וְצִיבָא תַּחְלְקוּ אֶת־הַשָּׂדֶה

"I order: You and Ziba will divide the field."[46]

§ 4.6 Discussion

The question of how the Hebrew performative perfect is to be understood in relation to the semantics of the verbal system as a whole is closely connected to the question of verb tenses used in performative utterances. As mentioned above (§ 4.4.1.5), it is often claimed that performatives require the simple indicative (perfective) present tense. As a matter of fact, cross-linguistic evidence indicates that this is not the case. We find

---

[44] This is often taken as a "prophetic perfect" (e.g. Klein 1990: 48f., Tropper 1998: 185 n.106, T. Andersen 2000: 55), and such an analysis has a certain amount of plausibility due to the following *weqataltis* and *yiqtols* (though note LXX: εὐλόγησα; Peshitta: ܒܰܪܟܶܬ; Vulgate: *benedicam*). However, a performative interpretation is possible (Wagner 1997: 104) and seems more probable in light of other examples of ברך which do not appear to have any future reference: e.g. Ps 118.26 בֵּרַכְנוּכֶם מִבֵּית יְהוָה "We bless you from the house of Yhwh", Ps 129.8 בֵּרַכְנוּ אֶתְכֶם בְּשֵׁם יְהוָה "We bless you in the name of Yhwh", Arad 16.2-3 ברכתך ליהוה; Arad 21.2 [ברכתך ל]יהו[ה]; 40.3 ברכתך ליהו[ה] (cf. Schüle 2000: 141f.).

[45] Also Arad 21.1-2 שלח לשלם; Arad 40.1-3 [שלחו לשלם]; papMur 17.1 [ש]לח שלחת את שלם. I have argued elsewhere that this is indeed performative and not epistolary, since we are dealing in this case with an abstract object ("greetings") which can in fact be "sent" by a verbal utterance. It is an alternative to the clearly performative "I greet you" which is limited to letters. See Rogland (2000: 198), *pace* Pardee (1983: 35f.).

[46] For other possible examples of אָמַרְתִּי see Wagner (1997: 100ff.).

modal verb forms used in performatives,[47] as well as aspectual imperfectives.[48] Regarding the use of tense forms, one could certainly get the impression from various definitions for "performative utterances" that there is an inherent connection between performativity and the present tense. Note, for example, Fanning's description:

> A performative action is one which is accomplished in the very act of speaking: it is not one which is about to happen or in the process of happening or which has just occurred; it is an action *identical* with and thus simultaneous with the act of speaking.[49]

Similarly Comrie:

> it is relatively rare for a situation to coincide exactly with the present moment, i.e. to occupy, literally or in terms of our conception of the situation, a single point in time which is exactly commensurate with the present moment. Situations of this rare type do, however, occur, and of course the present tense is an appropriate form to use in locating them temporally. One set of examples falling under this rubric would be performative sentences, i.e. sentences where the act described by the sentence is performed by uttering the sentence in question... Although these situations are not strictly momentaneous, since it takes a certain period of time to utter even the shortest sentence, they can be conceptualised as momentaneous, especially in so far as the time occupied by the report is exactly the same as the time occupied by the act, i.e. at each point in the utterance of the sentence there is coincidence between the present moment with regard to the utterance and the present moment with regard to the act in question.[50]

The fact that many languages use the present tense in performative utterances would seem to support this notion. However, there are enough exceptions to this that it appears to be impossible to maintain that the pre-

---

[47] See especially Hinrichs (1985, 1986); see also Koschmieder (1965: 27). In English non-modal performatives appear to be limited to fairly strict conditions. Cf. Partridge (1982: 120ff.), Fraser (1975: 187f.). For further discussion of modality and performativity see Wörner (1978: 61), Partridge (1982: 120f.) and Brandt *et al.* (1990: 361ff.).

[48] Mihailovic (1962: 40f.), Koschmieder-Schmid (1967: 179ff.), Bartschat (1977), Hinrichs (1985; 1986), Van Leeuwen-Turnovcová (1986: 12). We even encounter English progressive forms on occasion (e.g. *I'm warning you not to do that*); see Hinrichs (1985: 140), Bartschat (1977: 631 n.10), Vendler (1970: 82, 1972: 10); compare Bache (1985: 274, cf. 235). Cf. Hirtle (1967: 37), Verschueren (1995: 302). Thus Verschueren (1995: 316) appears to be justified in stating that there is little evidence to indicate that "the perfective choice occupies a significant proportion of the performative spectrum."

[49] Fanning (1990: 187f.).

[50] Comrie (1985: 37); cf. Sørensen (1949: 167f.): "On ne peut rien imaginer de plus présent que cette sorte de procès."

sent tense is the "proper" one for performatives.[51] In a survey of the Balkan languages, Hinrichs found past, present and future tenses attested in performative utterances and concluded: "Für den Vollzug des [Koinzidenzfall] ist es strenggenommen ganz unbedeutend, welches Tempus gebraucht wird".[52]

> Sprachkontrastiv gesehen ist die grammatische Form für die Koinzidenz beliebig, arbiträr, konventionell. Es gibt keine 'kausale' Verbindung zwischen Grammatik und Koinzidenz.
> Traditionelle Grammatik und Koinzidenz-Forschung sind sachdarstellerisch orientiert, gehen deshalb von der grammatischen Form zur Koinzidenz und wollen beide integrativ und kausal erklären. Dieser Ansatz führt sprachkontrastiv zu Aporie, einzelsprachlich zu Spekulation.
> Koinzidenz ist Vollzug, Handlung, Performance, Metakommunikation, steht über der Grammatik und gehört zur Kommunikations-Steuerung. Sie ist nicht Sachdarstellung. Die Forschung muß deshalb umgekehrt von der Koinzidenz ausgehen, die Grammatik relativieren, Sprechakt-Semantik und -Pragmatik treiben und kann dann nach der Wort-Form fragen.[53]

In a similar vein, Bache argues that performative utterances "do not locate situations in temporal relation to the speech situation but constitute an important part of the speech situation itself" and that "performatives are by definition outside the scope of temporality".[54] Partridge, on the other hand, is opposed to a purely pragmatic approach to performativity, arguing that syntactic, semantic and pragmatic factors need to be taken into account in the analysis of performatives.[55] His point is well taken, but it should be emphasized that it is not in fact being claimed that *all* formal features are irrelevant to the study of performatives. Most of the formal criteria discussed above (§ 4.4.1) remain valid; the cross-linguistic evidence only demonstrates that there is no inherent connection between performative utterances and the semantics of tense, aspect and mood. Consequently, it would be a mistake to interpret the use of *qatal* in performative utterances as an indication of a non-past function of the verb form.

---

[51] Cf. Hinrichs (1985, 1986), Kißling (1960: 154), Koschmieder (1965: 31f., 46f.), Koschmieder-Schmid (1967: 191 n.35), Johanson (1971: 55ff., 122ff.), Menges (1995: 130). According to Streck (1995: 191 n.441) the German perfect can occur in performative utterances; on the ancient Semitic languages see § 4.3 above.

[52] Hinrichs (1986: 173).

[53] Hinrichs (1986: 183). Compare also p.179: "Der Annahme der kommunikativen 'Wichtigkeit' von Tempus, Modus, Aspekt oder Person im [Koinzidenzfall] gehört wahrscheinlich mit zu jenen sprachwissenschaftlichen Mythen, die von der Situation der Sprachanalyse produziert werden oder vom statistischen Normalfall suggeriert werden."

[54] Bache (1985: 108); see also *idem* (1986 b: 83, 1995: 290f.).

[55] Partridge (1982: 15ff., 23).

This use simply appears to be a convention and has no bearing on the semantic analysis of *qatal*.

APPENDIX II:
DIACHRONIC DEVELOPMENT IN HEBREW PERFORMATIVES

In Hebrew one can see a diachronic development from the use of the perfect to the use of the participle in performative utterances.[56] We have already seen a number of examples of performative perfects in Classical Hebrew. I have located only one possible case in Qumran Hebrew:

15. 4QWords of the Luminaries (4Q504) fr. 1-2, col. 6, lines 4-6

ועתה כיום הזה אשר נכנע לבנו רצינו את עוננו
ואת עוון אבותינו

García Martínez translates, "And now, on this very day on which our heart has been humbled, we atone for our sin and the sin of our fathers."[57] Although רצינו is not a *verbum dicendi*, it is possible that this is a ritual utterance of some sort (cf. § 4.4.2). However, it is just as possible that this is simply a past tense referring to a previous situation, thus: "Et maintenant, comme aujord'hui où s'est humilié notre coeur, nous avons expié notre iniquité et l'inquité de nos pères."[58]

There are three alleged performative perfects in Ben Sira:[59]

16. Ben Sira 51.12 (ms. B)

על כן הודיתי

"Therefore I give thanks."

17. Ben Sira 51.25 (ms. B)

פי פתחתי ודברתי בה

"I open my mouth and speak of her."

---

[56] An analogous development can be observed in Aramaic; see Rogland (2003: 426f.).
[57] García Martínez (1997-98: 1017).
[58] Baillet (1982: 149).
[59] Van Peursen (1999: 64f.).

While example 16 seems possible, a performative interpretation for 17 seems dubious on semantic grounds (§ 4.4.2).[60] It is doubtful whether the phrase פִּי פָתַחְתִּי is semantically capable of being used performatively, and the verb דבר has durative *Aktionsart* and should probably be excluded for that reason.[61] It is quite possible that these should be understood as past tenses referring to the immediately preceding section of praise.

Mishor provides a number of examples from Mishnaic Hebrew, but most of them do not meet the criteria given above (§ 4.4.1) and cannot be considered performative.[62] In fact, only one of his examples does meet the criteria, and one could question whether it absolutely requires a performative interpretation:

18.   Sifre Numbers 92

מה שביקשתה נתתי לך

"What you have asked for, I give/have given (?) to you."

It thus appears that the performative perfect has all but disappeared by the Mishnaic period.

When we turn to examine the performative use of the participle, it should be noted that some scholars have argued that even in Biblical Hebrew the participle can have this function. Groß mentions, for example,

19.   Gen 9.12

זֹאת אוֹת־הַבְּרִית אֲשֶׁר־אֲנִי נֹתֵן ... לְדֹרֹת עוֹלָם

"Dies ist das Zeichnen der b°rit, die ich hiermit für ewige Geschlechter gebe."[63]

Groß does not attempt to relate this use of the participle to the verbal system as a whole nor to the semantics of the participle itself.[64] As a matter

---

[60] Note LXX (ἤνοιξα τὸ στόμα μου καὶ ἐλάλησα) and Peshitta (ܡܒ ܐܠܠܬܗܡ, ܗܡܒ ܐܘܣܐ).

[61] Joüon and Muraoka § 111 *d*; cf. n. 34 above. "To speak" is certainly not used performatively in English.

[62] Mishor (1983: 36ff.).

[63] Groß (1978: 107f.); see also Mayer (1980: 304 n.6) and cf. Joosten (1989: 150f., compare 157). Hatav (1997: 158) even claims that "most of the performative speech acts in the Bible use the *qotel* form", though she provides no evidence whatsoever to support this statement. On the other hand, it does not appear that Wagner, who claims that only *qatal* is attested in performative utterances in his corpus, even took the participle into consideration (1997: 98).

[64] Groß (1978: 108 n.25): "Nun ist das hebräische Partizip aspektuell nicht festgelegt, es bezeichnet in unterschiedlichen syntaktischen Konstellationen imperfektiven wie

of fact, most of the alleged examples of "performative participles" in Biblical Hebrew could just as easily be understood as indicating the progressive present or *futurum instans*.[65] However, the following examples are noteworthy:

20.　1 C 29.13

וְעַתָּה אֱלֹהֵינוּ מוֹדִים אֲנַחְנוּ לָךְ וּמְהַלְלִים לְשֵׁם תִּפְאַרְתֶּךָ

"And now, O our God, we thank you and praise your glorious name."

21.　Zech 9.12

גַּם־הַיּוֹם מַגִּיד מִשְׁנֶה אָשִׁיב לָךְ

"Even today I declare: I will restore to you double."

22.　Mal 3.15

וְעַתָּה אֲנַחְנוּ מְאַשְּׁרִים זֵדִים

"And now we declare the arrogant happy."

In all of these cases a performative interpretation seems the most probable, and it should be noted that they all occur in Late Biblical Hebrew.[66]

There are a few possible examples of performative participles in the Qumran documents, though perhaps they could be taken as progressive presents:

23.　4QTobit[e] (4Q200) fr. 4 lines 4-5

ועתה מבקש [אני אות]כה אבי אשר תשלחני והלכתי אל אבי

"And now I beg you, my father, that you send me off so that I may go to my father."[67]

24.　1QWords of Moses (1Q22) 1.6-7

מגיד אנו[כין] אשר יעזבו[ני]

"I announce that they will desert me."[68]

---

[65] Cf. Warren (1998: 85f.). Gen 41.9 אֶת־חֲטָאַי אֲנִי מַזְכִּיר הַיּוֹם is one possible example, depending on the meaning of the verb. If it means "to mention" (so Brown-Driver-Briggs 270b-271a) in the sense of "to confess" (Vulgate: *confiteor peccatum meum*) then it could be performative, yet this seems rather odd in the context. The Peshitta (ܡܕܟܪ ܐܢܐ) and LXX (ἀναμιμνῄσκω) could perhaps be taken in this sense as well, yet they could also mean "to bring to remembrance, recall to memory," and Prof. Muraoka has suggested (personal communication) that מַזְכִּיר could mean "to recollect", which could hardly be taken as performative (cf. § 4.4.2).

[66] Perhaps also Dan 8.19 (הִנְנִי מוֹדִיעֲךָ), although this could be indicating the *futurum instans*.

[67] Fitzmyer (1995: 68).

In the following example it is difficult to decide whether it is a performative or a general present; either interpretation seems possible in the context:

25. 4QShir[a] (4Q510) frag. 1 line 4

ואני משכיל משמיע הוד תפארתו ולב[ן הל] כול רוחי מלאכי חבל

"And I, a Sage, declare the splendour of his radiance in order to frighten and terr[ify] all the spirits of the ravaging angels..."[69]

In the Bar Kochba letters we find:

26. PapMur 43.3-4

מעיד אני עלי ת שמים

"I swear by the heavens."[70]

The participle is abundantly attested in performative utterances in Mishnaic Hebrew:[71]

27. Taanith 3, 8

נשבע אני בשמך הגדול וגו'

"I swear by your great name..."

28. Eduyoth 7, 6

אני מעיד שהיתה לנו פרה זבחי שלמים וגו'

"I testify that we had a heifer that was a peace offering..."

It thus appears that the performative participles which we begin to encounter in Late Biblical Hebrew have completely ousted the perfect in performative utterances by the Mishnaic period.[72]

---

[68] García Martínez (1997-98: 59).

[69] García Martínez (1997-98: 1029).

[70] See Pardee (1982: 130). On ת instead of את see Benoit (1961: 120).

[71] Azar (1991: 17); cf. Bendavid (1967: 543f.).

[72] Warren somewhat strangely suggests that the use of the perfect הוֹדִינוּ in Ps 75.2 (example 6), as opposed to the participle מוֹדִים in 1 C 29.13 (example 20), indicates that the psalm is "relatively late" (1998: 87). The diachronic evidence presented here in fact suggests just the opposite. Although Eskhult does not notice the performative use of the participle in Late Biblical Hebrew, he does think that the performative perfects we find in Chronicles (1 Chr 21.23; 29.3; 2 Chr 2.9) are "formulaic" (2000: 86).

§ 5. Conclusion

The results of this study are easily summarized: It is possible to understand fientive *qatal* as an aspectually unmarked relative past tense in Classical Hebrew, in poetry as well as prose. To demonstrate this we examined the apparent exceptions to such a view, namely the so-called gnomic, prophetic and performative perfects, and we argued that these should not in fact be understood as disproving this theory.

In regard to the gnomic perfect, an examination of proverbs in various languages led to a number of important observations. Firstly, it was noted that proverbs are not limited to the present tense but can utilize past tenses as well. Secondly, proverbs are not always intended to make general statements but are sometimes to be understood as the report of a particular, and often extraordinary, experience or observation. Thirdly, it is possible to make general statements concerning the way things have typically occurred in the past. These factors make it unnecessary to postulate a general present ("gnomic") meaning for fientive *qatal*.

In regard to the prophetic perfect, it was argued that we are not dealing with one blanket phenomenon but rather several distinct uses of *qatal*, most of which are to be explained in terms of temporal deixis. In some cases the examples were understood as expressing a past relative to a future reference point. Other examples involved quoted speech which would be uttered at a future point in time. In other cases the speaker's use of the past tense was due to the nature of the event being described: In some instances the verb referred to a past decision, and in other instances the verb referred to events that had occurred in a dream or a vision. It was also observed that in a small number of cases a past tense is used to refer to events which are still future. Such examples admittedly form an exception to the idea that *qatal* is marked as a past tense. However, it was argued that the significance of these cases should not be overstated, as it was pointed out that such exceptions or "idiomatic tense mismatches" occur in a wide variety of languages which possess grammaticalized tense. It is, therefore, illegitimate to take such exceptions as necessitating a "tenseless" analysis of Hebrew (or any other language). Given the cross-linguistic evidence it is just as possible simply to treat these cases as exceptions and to explain them in terms of exaggerated rhetoric.

Finally, in regard to the performative perfect, it was argued on the basis of cross-linguistic evidence that this use is purely conventional and that there is no inherent connection between performativity and the semantics of tense, aspect and mood. Past, present and future tenses are attested in performative utterances in various languages, as are aspectual perfectives and imperfectives and various forms marked for modality. The performative use of *qatal* thus has no bearing on the question of the semantics of the verbal form.

It thus appears that our working theory is sufficient for analyzing the indicative functions of fientive *qatal*. The idea that *qatal* is marked as a past tense is of course not new. However, we believe that the present study has been able to place it on a firmer footing by demonstrating that most of the alleged exceptions are in fact better understood as past tenses. Those exceptions that remain (§ 3.4.5) should not be understood as disproving this theory. Moreover, the results of this study indicate that a temporal understanding of *qatal* applies not only to prose but to poetry as well. There remain some passages in which the use of the tenses is obscure or uncertain, but these would hardly provide sufficient justification for the notion that the morphosyntactic oppositions of the Hebrew verbal system have different semantic values in prose as opposed to poetry.

There is one respect in which our working theory does require modification. Although we have provided analyses of *qatal* in terms of both absolute and relative tense when possible (cf. § 1.2), we have seen some alleged examples of the gnomic (§ 2.5.4) and prophetic perfects (§ 3.4.1) which can only be understood in terms of relative tense. The latter group of examples consists of subordinate clauses, while the former group of examples consists of both main and subordinate clauses. Hence it would appear that, regardless of clause type, *qatal* is to be understood as a relative past tense.[1] Of course, in most cases it is possible to analyze *qatal* as an absolute past tense, since the speaker's "now" is the reference point.

We believe that the results of this study can be fruitfully applied to a number of other vexed questions concerning the verbal system of Hebrew and other Semitic languages. In regard to the semantics of *qatal* itself, one immediately thinks of the so-called "precative perfect", which A. Müller called "eine der bestrittensten der auf den Tempusgebrauch bezüglichen Fragen",[2] and this description remains valid despite the fact that more than a century has passed since it was written.[3] As this use

---

[1] This is also the case with the Hebrew "epistolary perfect", as I have argued elsewhere; see Rogland (2000). These examples, which occur in main clauses, cannot be understood in terms of absolute past tense but must be analyzed as expressing the relative past.

[2] A. Müller (1877: 201).

[3] On the subject generally in the Semitic languages see Müller (1988: 185f., 1984b: 121f., 1983: 38f.) and Marcus (1970: 6ff.). Though it is clearly attested in e.g. Classical Arabic, it remains a disputed point in other languages. On Amarna Canaanite see Rainey (1996:

should be analyzed as an expression of deontic modality it fell outside of the bounds of our study of the indicative functions of *qatal*.[4] Nevertheless, many scholars view the prophetic and precative perfects as related phenomena,[5] and hence our discussion in chapter 3 could have some bearing on this question.

In regard to the indicative functions of other Hebrew verbal forms, the results of our study could certainly be of use in the analysis of alleged examples of non-past *wayyiqtol*. As with *qatal*, there are a number of instances cited in the grammatical literature of *wayyiqtol* with either a present or a future meaning.[6] We have already encountered some of these in chapters 2 and 3, and it seems to me that in many cases our explanation of *qatal* applies, *mutatis mutandis*, to these examples as well. A more systematic investigation of such instances is clearly called for.[7]

Finally, I believe that the results of this examination could prove useful for the study of the Semitic suffix conjugation more generally. As we have noted in the preceding chapters, similar "gnomic", "prophetic" and

---

364f.). It is accepted by several scholars of Ugaritic (Gordon § 13.28, Fenton 1973:39, Cunchillos 1986, Verreet 1988: 119, M. Smith 1994: 43ff., 1995, Sivan 1997: 98, 1998: 91f., Tropper 2000: 726f.), though it is denied by Marcus (1970: 18ff.). It does not occur in Egyptian Aramaic (Muraoka and Porten § 51 *e*), and only in the syntagm ܐܒ݂ ܡܐܠ in Syriac (Muraoka 1997: § 87, Nöldeke § 260). According to Blau (1975-76: 474b) and Tropper (1993: 85, 236) it occurs in the Hadad inscription (line 24, ודלח נתן לה), though other analyses of נתן have been proposed: Koopmans (1962: 38) takes it as an infinitive, Donner and Röllig (1964: 221) as an active participle, Dion (1974: 296) and Gibson (1975: 74) as a passive participle with a precative meaning (though Gibson suggests that it is a scribal error for לתן, also with a precative meaning). Opinions regarding Classical Hebrew are especially divided; see e.g. Warren (1998: 89ff.), Meister (1994), Provan (1991), Waltke and O'Connor § 30.5.4 *c-d*, Marcus (1970: 4 n.4), G. R. Driver (1936: 147ff.; 1969: 52ff.), Lambert (1925), Driver § 20, A. Müller (1877: 201ff.).

[4] See above, p. 10 n.50.

[5] The precative and prophetic perfects are generally understood as distinct though related (cf. e.g. Provan 1991: 173, 175), but there is some disagreement whether the precative is to be understood as an extension of the prophetic perfect or vice versa. Although Driver rejects the existence of the precative in Biblical Hebrew, he nonetheless states (§ 20): "If the usage exists, it is but an extension of the same manner of speech which has been already explained, § 14, viz. the perfect of certitude"; cf. Gottlieb (1978: 60) and Hendel (1996: 171): "the [precative perfect] is used to indicate a perfectivity of wishful expectation, with the event conceived as complete and bounded, hence expressing confidence in its accomplishment". Blau (1972: 113), on the other hand, believes that the prophetic perfect was an extension of its precative use. In any event, precisely how the precative use is to be related to the semantics of *qatal* remains an open question. For example, it is interpreted by Tropper (1998: 184, cf. 176) and Hendel (1996: 171) as supporting a perfective analysis of *qatal*, whereas T. Andersen (2000: 34ff.) thinks that it supports an imperfective analysis (cf. also Müller 1998: 146).

[6] E.g. Driver §§ 80-82, G. R. Driver (1936: 141), Isaksson (1987: 100), Joüon and Muraoka § 118 *o-s*, Waltke and O'Connor § 33.3.1 *b, d*, Gibson § 82.

[7] A large number of *wayyiqtols* with an allegedly present meaning were examined in the important study by Groß (1976); cf. also Birkeland (1935).

"performative" uses of the verb are attested in other Semitic languages[8] and – perhaps not surprisingly – also play a significant role in the semantic analysis of these various verb systems.[9] Each language must of course be treated as its own system of morphosyntactic oppositions, yet it is possible that some of our arguments regarding Hebrew *qatal* are applicable to the suffix conjugation in these other languages as well. Thus, for example, it seems to me that some of the possible examples of the "gnomic perfect" in Egyptian Aramaic could be explained by the categories discussed in chapter 2. Moreover, given the conventionality of tense usage in performative utterances, the existence of "performative perfects" in e.g. Arabic, Aramaic, Ugaritic, etc. provides no support for a tenseless analysis of the verb form. Hence a more comprehensive examination of allegedly non-past perfects in other Semitic languages would be in order.[10]

[8] See § 2.3, § 3.3, § 4.3.
[9] See e.g. T. Andersen (2000: 34ff.), Tropper (1998: 158ff.; 2000: 702), Mayer (1992: 390), Cohen (1924: 29f., 243f.).
[10] On some possible non-past uses of the Aramaic suffix conjugation, see Rogland (2003: 422ff.).

BIBLIOGRAPHY

Aalders, G. Ch., *Obadja en Jona* (Commentaar op het Oude Testament; Kampen: Kok, 1958).
_____., *Daniel* (Commentaar op het Oude Testament; Kampen: Kok, 1962).
Aartun, K., *Zur Frage altarabischer Tempora* (Oslo: Universitetsforlaget, 1963).
Agam, J., "Ein nicht-'emphatisches' anfangliches *sḏm.n.f* als Perfectum Propheticum?", in: S. Israelit-Groll (ed.), *Scripta Hierosolymitana 28: Egyptological Studies* (Jerusalem: Magnes Press, 1982) 187-202.
Aistleitner, J., *Die mythologischen und kultischen Texten aus Ras Schamra* (Biblioteca Orientalis Hungarica 8; Budapest: Akademiai Kiado, 1959).
Alonso-Schökel, L., *A Manual of Hebrew Poetics* (Subsidia Biblica 11; Rome: Editrice Pontificio Istituto Biblico, 1988).
Andersen, F., *The Sentence in Biblical Hebrew* (The Hague/Paris: Mouton, 1974).
_____., "Linguistic Coherence in Prophetic Discourse", in: A. Beck, A. Bartelt, P. Raabe, and C. Franke (eds.), *Fortunate the Eyes that See: Essays in Honor of David Noel Freedman in Celebration of His Seventieth Birthday* (Grand Rapids: Eerdmans, 1995) 137-156.
_____., and D. Freedman, *Hosea* (Anchor Bible 24; Garden City: Doubleday, 1980).
_____., *Micah* (Anchor Bible 24E; Garden City: Doubleday, 2000).
Andersen, T., "The Evolution of the Hebrew Verbal System", *Zeitschrift für Althebraistik* 13.1 (2000) 1-66.
Anscombre, J.-C., and A. Pierrot, "Y-a-t-il un critère de performativité en latin?", *Linguisticæ Investigationes* 8.1 (1984) 1-19.
Austin, J., *How to Do Things With Words*[2] (Oxford: Oxford University Press, 1976).
Auvray, P., *Isaie 1-39* (Sources bibliques 8; Paris: Gabalda, 1972).
Azar, M., תחביר לשון המשנה (Jerusalem: Academy of the Hebrew Language/University of Haifa, 1995).
Baayen, R., "The Pragmatics of the 'Tenses' in Biblical Hebrew", *Studies in Language* 21.2 (1997) 245-285.
Bache, C., "Aspect and Aktionsart: Towards a Semantic Distinction", *Journal of Linguistics* 18 (1982) 57-72.
_____., *Verbal Aspect. A General Theory and its Application to Present-Day English* (Odense: Odense University Press, 1985).
_____., review of Comrie (1985), *Journal of Literary Semantics* 15.1 (1986) 66-70.
_____., "Tense and Aspect in Fiction", *Journal of Literary Semantics* 15.2 (1986 b) 82-97.
_____., "Verbal Categories, Form-Meaning Relationships and the English Perfect", in: C. Bache, H. Basbøll, and C.-E. Lindberg (eds.), *Tense, Aspect and Action. Empirical and Theoretical Contributions to Language Typology* (Berlin: de Gruyter, 1994) 43-60.
_____., *The Study of Aspect, Tense and Action: Towards a Theory of the Semantics of Grammatical Categories* (Frankfurt a.M.: Peter Lang, 1995).
Bacher, W., *Abraham Ibn Esra als Grammatiker* (Strassburg: K. J. Trübner, 1882).
Baillet, M., *Qumrân Grotte 4. III. (4Q482-4Q520)* (Discoveries in the Judaean Desert 7; Oxford: Clarendon, 1982).

136

Barr, J., "Limitations of Etymology as a Lexicographical Instrument in Biblical Hebrew", reprinted in: *Comparative Philology and the Text of the Old Testament* (reprint with additions and corrections; Winona Lake: Eisenbrauns, 1987) 412-436.

Bartelmus, R., *HYH. Bedeutung und Funktion eines hebräischen »Allerweltswortes«* (Arbeiten zu Text und Sprache im Alten Testament 17; St. Ottilien: EOS, 1982).

Barth, J., *Die Nominalbildung in den semitischen Sprachen*[2] (Leipzig: J. C. Hinrichs, 1894).

Bartschat, B., "Aspektgebrauch und Performativität", *Zeitschrift für Slawistik* 22 (1977) 629-637.

Barucq, A., *Le livre de Proverbes* (Sources bibliques 2; Paris: Gabalda, 1964).

Bauer, H., "Die Tempora im Semitischen, ihre Entstehung und ihre Ausgestaltung in den Einzelsprachen", *Beiträge zur Assyriologie und semitischen Sprachwissenschaft* 8.1 (1910) 1-53.

Bauer, H., and P. Leander, *Grammatik des biblisch-Aramäischen* (Halle: Max Niemeyer, 1927).

Bendavid, A., לשון מקרא ולשון חכמים (2 vols.; Tel-Aviv: Devir, 1967-71).

Ben-Ḥayyim, Z., זמני הפעל בלשון המקרא ומסורת השומרונים בהם, in: *Sefer Dov Sadan* (Tel-Aviv: Hakibbutz Hameuchad, 1977) 66-86.

Benoit, P., J. Milik, and R. de Vaux, *Les grottes de Murabbaᶜât* (Discoveries in the Judaean Desert 2; Oxford: Clarendon, 1961).

Berggrün, N., זָכַר = הזכיר, הוציא דבר בפיו, *Lešonenu* 21 (1957-58) 279-282.

Bergsträsser, G., *Hebräische Grammatik* (2 vols., reprint; Hildesheim: Olms, 1962).

Berlin, A., *Zephaniah* (Anchor Bible 25A; New York: Doubleday, 1994).

Bewer, J., Smith, J., and W. Ward, *A Critical and Exegetical Commentary on Micah, Zephaniah, Nahum, Habakkuk, Obadiah and Joel* (International Critical Commentary; Edinburgh: T. & T. Clark, 1912).

Bezer, Z., על מערכת הזמנים במגילה החיצונית לבראשית, *Lešonenu* 41 (1976-77) 196-204.

Binnick, R., *Time and the Verb. A Guide to Tense and Aspect* (Oxford: Oxford University Press, 1991).

Birkeland, H., "Ist das hebräische Imperfectum consecutivum ein Präteritum?", *Acta Orientalia* 13 (1935) 1-34.

Blake, F., *A Resurvey of Hebrew Tenses* (Scripta Pontificii Instituti Biblici 103; Rome: Pontificium Institutum Biblicum, 1951).

Blau, J., "Reste des I-Imperfekt von *ZKR*, Qal. Eine lexikographische Studie", *Vetus Testamentum* 11.1 (1961) 81-86.

_____., "Marginalia Semitica I", *Israel Oriental Studies* 1 (1971) 1-35.

_____., תורת ההגה והצורות (Tel Aviv: Hakibbutz Hameuchad, 1972).

_____., review of Dion (1974), *Kirjath Sefer* 51 (1975-76) 474-476.

_____., "Marginalia Semitica III", *Israel Oriental Studies* 7 (1977) 14-32.

_____., "Minutiae Aramaicae", in: W. Conrad and E. Newing (eds.), *Perspectives on Language and Text* (Winona Lake: Eisenbrauns, 1987) 3-10.

Bobzin, H., *Die 'Tempora' im Hiobdialog* (Ph.D. diss., Philipps-Universität Marburg; Marburg/Lahn: Görich & Weiershäuser, 1974).

Bombeck, S., *Das althebräische Verbalsystem aus aramäischer Sicht. Masoretischer Text, Targume und Peschitta* (Europäische Hochschulschriften. Reihe 23, Theologie 591; Frankfurt a.M.: Peter Lang, 1997).

_____., "Die Verwendung der Präformativkonjugation im Aramäischen des Buches Daniel", *Biblische Notizen* 83 (1996) 5-8.

Borbone, P., *Il libro del profeta Osea. Edizione critica del testo ebraico* (Quaderni di Henoch 2; Torino: Silvio Zamorani Editore, 1987).

Böttcher, F., *Ausführliches Lehrbuch der hebräischen Sprache* (2 vols.; Leipzig: J. A. Barth, 1866-68).

Brandt, M., G. Falkenberg, N. Fries, F. Liedtke, J. Meibauer, G. Öhlschläger, H. Rehbock, and I. Rosengren, "Die performativen Äußerungen - eine empirische Studie", *Zeitschrift für Phonetik, Sprachwissenschaft und Kommunikationsforschung* 43 (1990) 355-369.

Brockelmann, C., "Die 'Tempora' des Semitischen", *Zeitschrift für Phonetik und allgemeine Sprachwissenschaft* 5 (1951) 133-154.

_____., *Hebräische Syntax* (Neukirchen-Vluyn: Neukirchener Verlag, 1956).

Brown, F., S. R. Driver, and C. A. Briggs, *A Hebrew and English Lexicon of the Old Testament* (original 1907; reprint: Peabody: Hendrickson, 1979).

Buth, R., "The Taxonomy and Function of Hebrew Tense-Shifting in the Psalms (*qatal-yiqtol-yiqtol-qatal*, antithetical grammatical parallelism)", *Selected Technical Articles Related to Translation* 15 (1986) 26-32.

_____., "The Hebrew Verb in Current Discussions", *Journal of Translation and Textlinguistics* 5.2 (1992) 91-105.

Buttenwieser, M., *The Psalms Chronologically Treated With a New Translation* (New York: KTAV, 1969).

Bybee, J., R. Perkins, and W. Pagliuca, *The Evolution of Grammar. Tense, Aspect, and Modality in the Languages of the World* (Chicago: University of Chicago Press, 1994).

Bybee, J., and Ö. Dahl, "The Creation of Tense and Aspect Systems in the Languages of the World", *Studies in Language* 13.1 (1989) 51-103.

Caquot, A., and A. Lemaire, "Les textes araméens de Deir 'Alla", *Syria* 54 (1977) 189-208.

Caquot, A., M. Sznycer, and A. Herdner, *Textes ougaritiques. I: Mythes et legendes* (Paris: Editiens du Cerf, 1974).

Chaine, M., *Grammaire éthiopienne* (Beyrouth: Imprimerie Catholique, nouvelle édition 1938).

Charles, R., *A Critical and Exegetical Commentary on the Book of Daniel* (Oxford: Clarendon, 1929).

Chomsky, W., *David Kimhi's Hebrew Grammar (Mikhlol)* (New York: Bloch Publishing Company, 1952).

Chung, S., and A. Timberlake, "Tense, Aspect and Mood", in: T. Shopen (ed.), *Language Typology and Syntactic Description. III: Grammatical Categories and the Lexicon* (Cambridge: Cambridge University Press, 1985) 202-258.

Clark, D., "Wine on the Lees (Zeph 1.12 and Jer 48.11)", *Bible Translator* 32 (1981) 241-243.

_____., and H. Hatton, *A Translator's Handbook on the Books of Nahum, Habakkuk and Zephaniah* (Helps for Translators Series: Handbooks; New York: United Bible Societies, 1989).

Clines, D., *Job 1-20* (Word Biblical Commentary 17; Dallas: Word Books, 1989).

Cohen, M., *Le système verbal sémitique et l'expression du temps* (Paris: Imprimerie nationale, 1924).

Cohen, D., *La phrase nominale et l'évolution du système verbal en sémitique. Études de syntaxe historique* (Collection linguistique publiée par la Societé de Linguistique de Paris 73; Leuven/Paris: Peeters, 1984).

Collins, J. J., *Daniel* (Hermeneia; Mineapolis: Fortress Press, 1993).

Comrie, B., *Aspect: An Introduction to the Study of Verbal Aspect and Related Problems* (Cambridge Textbooks in Linguistics; Cambridge: Cambridge University Press, 1976).

_____., "On Reichenbach's Approach to Tense", *Papers from the 17th Regional Meeting of the Chicago Linguistic Society* (1981) 24-30.

_____., *Tense* (Cambridge Textbooks in Linguistics; Cambridge: Cambridge University Press, 1985).

138

Cook, E., "The Aramaic of the Dead Sea Scrolls", in: P. Flint and J. VanderKam (eds.), *The Dead Sea Scrolls After Fifty Years: A Comprehensive Assessment* (2 vols.; Leiden: E. J. Brill, 1998) 1:359-378.

Craigie, P., *Psalms 1-50* (Word Biblical Commentary 19; Waco: Word Books, 1983).

Creason, S., *Semantic Classes of Hebrew Verbs: A Study of Aktionsart in the Hebrew Verbal System* (1995 Ph.D. diss., University of Chicago).

Cunchillos, J. L., "Que tout aille bien auprès de ma mère! Un *qatala* optatif en ugaritique?", in: D. M. Leon (ed.), *Salvacion en la Palabra* (Madrid: Ediciones Cristiandad, 1986) 259-66.

Cuvalay-Haak, M., *The Verb in Literary and Colloquial Arabic* (Functional Grammar Series 19; Berlin/New York: de Gruyter, 1997).

Dahl, Ö., "On Generics", in: E. Keenan (ed.), *Formal Semantics of Natural Language* (Cambridge: Cambridge University Press, 1975), 99-111.

_____., "Temporal Distance: Remoteness Distinctions in Tense-Aspect Systems", *Linguistics* 21 (1983) 105-122.

_____., *Tense and Aspect Systems* (Oxford: Basil Blackwell, 1985).

Dahood, M., *Psalms* (3 vols.; Anchor Bible 16, 17; Garden City: Doubleday, 1966-70).

_____., "Eblaite I-Du and Hebrew 'Ed, 'Rain Cloud'", *Catholic Biblical Quarterly* 43 (1981) 534-538.

Dammron, A., *Grammaire de l'araméen biblique* (Strasbourg: Editions P. H. Heitz, 1961).

Davidson, A. B., *Hebrew Syntax*[3] (Edinburgh: T. & T. Clark, 1902).

Davies, G., *Hosea* (New Century Bible; Grand Rapids: Eerdmans, 1992).

DeCaen, V., *On the Placement and Interpretation of the Verb in Standard Biblical Hebrew Prose* (Ph.D. diss., University of Toronto, 1995).

_____., "Ewald and Driver on Biblical Hebrew 'Aspect': Anteriority and the Orientalist Framework", *Zeitschrift für Althebraistik* 9 (1996) 129-151.

Delitzsch, F., *Psalms* (3 vols., reprint; Grand Rapids: Eerdmans, 1949).

_____., *Proverbs, Ecclesiastes, Song of Solomon* (2 vols., reprint; Grand Rapids: Eerdmans, 1985).

_____., *Biblical Commentary on the Prophecies of Isaiah* (2 vols., reprint; Grand Rapids: Eerdmans, 1950).

Dempsey, D., *The Verb Syntax of Second Isaiah and Deuteronomy Compared* (Ph.D. diss., Catholic University of America, 1988).

Denz, A., *Die Verbal Syntax des neuarabischen Dialektes von Kwayriš (Irak) mit einer einleitenden allgemeinen Tempus- und Aspektlehre* (Abhandlungen für die Kunde des Morgenlandes 50.1; Wiesbaden: Steiner, 1971).

_____., "Die Struktur des Klassischen Arabisch", in: W. Fischer (ed.), *Grundriß der arabischen Philologie* (3 vols.; Wiesbaden: Reichert, 1982-92) 1:58-82.

Dhorme, E., *A Commentary on the Book of Job* (London: Nelson, 1967).

Dik, S., "Copula Auxiliarization: How and Why?", in: M. Harris and P. Ramat (eds.), *Historical Development of Auxiliaries* (Berlin: de Gruyter, 1987) 53-84.

Dillmann, A., *Grammatik der äthiopischen Sprache* (ed. C. Bezold; Leipzig: Chr. Herm. Tauchnitz, 1899).

Dion, P. E., *La langue de Ya'udi: description et classement de l'ancien parler de Zencirli dans le cadre des langues sémitiques du nord-ouest* (Waterloo: Editions SR, 1974).

Donner, H., and W. Röllig, *Kanaanäische und aramäische Inschriften. II: Kommentar* (Wiesbaden: Harrassowitz, 1964).

Driver, G. R., *Problems of the Hebrew Verbal System* (Old Testament Studies 2; Edinburgh: T. & T. Clark, 1936).

_____., "Hebrew Homonyms" in: *Hebräische Wortforschung* (Vetus Testamentum Supplements 16; Leiden: E. J. Brill, 1967) 50-64.

_____., "Some Uses of *QTL* in the Semitic Languages", *Proceedings of the International Conference on Semitic Studies held in Jerusalem 1965* (Jerusalem: The Israel Academy of Sciences and Humanities, 1969) 49-64.

Driver, S. R., *A Treatise on the Use of the Tenses in Hebrew and Some Other Syntactical Questions*[3] (original 1892; reprint, with an introductory essay by W. Garr; Grand Rapids: Eerdmans, 1998).

_____., *The Books of Joel and Amos* (Cambridge: Cambridge University Press, 1915).

_____., and G. Gray, *A Critical and Exegetical Commentary on the Book of Job* (International Critical Commentary; Edinburgh: T. & T. Clark, 1921).

Ehrlich, A., *Randglossen zur hebräischen Bibel. Textkritisches, sprachliches und sachliches* (7 vols.; Leipzig: J. C. Hinrichs, 1908-14).

Ellenbogen, M., *Foreign Words in the Old Testament* (London: Luzac, 1962).

Elliger, K., *Die Propheten Nahum, Habakuk, Zephanja, Haggai, Sacharja, Maleachi*[3] (Das Alte Testament Deutsch 25; Göttingen: Vandenhoeck & Ruprecht, 1956).

Elmer, H. C., "A Note on the Gnomic Aorist", *Proceedings of the American Philological Association* (1894) lix-lxiii.

Eskhult, M., *Studies in Verbal Aspect and Narrative Technique in Biblical Hebrew Prose* (Studia Semitica Upsaliensia 12; Uppsala: Almqvist & Wiksell International, 1990).

_____., "Verbal Syntax in Late Biblical Hebrew", in: T. Muraoka and J. F. Elwolde (eds.), *Diggers at the Well. Proceedings of a Third International Symposium on the Hebrew of the Dead Sea Scrolls and Ben Sira* (Studies on the Texts of the Desert of Judah 36; Leiden: E. J. Brill, 2000) 84-93.

Ewald, H., *Ausführliches Lehrbuch der hebräischen Sprache des Alten Bundes*[7] (Göttingen: Verlag der dieterichschen Buchhandlung, 1863).

Fanning, B., *Verbal Aspect in New Testament Greek* (Oxford: Clarendon, 1990).

Fensham, F., "The Use of the Suffix Conjugation and the Prefix Conjugation in a few Old Hebrew Poems", *Journal of Northwest Semitic Languages* 6 (1978) 9-18.

Fenton, T., "The Absence of a Verbal Formation *yaqattal from Ugarit and Northwest Semitic", *Journal of Semitic Studies* 15 (1970) 31-41.

_____., "The Hebrew 'Tenses' in the Light of Ugaritic", *Proceedings of the Fifth World Congress of Jewish Studies* (5 vols.; Jerusalem: World Union of Jewish Studies, 1973) 4:31-41.

Finley, T., "The *WAW*-Consecutive with 'Imperfect' in Biblical Hebrew: Theoretical Studies and its Use in Amos", in: J. Feinberg and P. Feinberg (eds.), *Tradition and Testament: Essays in Honor of Charles Lee Feinberg* (Chicago: Moody, 1981) 241-262.

Fischer, W., *Grammatik des klassischen Arabisch* (Wiesbaden: Harrassowitz, 1972).

_____., "Zur Bestimmung der Funktionskategorien des arabischen Verbums", in: D. Bellmann (ed.), *Gedenkschrift Wolfgang Reuschel. Akten des III. Arabistischen Kolloquiums, Leipzig, 21.-22. November 1991* (Abhandlungen für die Kunde des Morgenlandes 51.1; Stuttgart: Steiner, 1994) 59-96.

Fitzmyer, J., *The Syntax of Imperial Aramaic Based on the Documents Found in Egypt* (Ph.D. diss., John Hopkins University, 1956).

_____., et al, *Qumran Cave 4. XIV. Parabiblical Texts, Part 2* (Discoveries in the Judaean Desert 19; Oxford: Clarendon, 1995).

Fleisch, H., "Le verbe du sémitique commun. Les discussions a son sujet", *Semitica* 25 (1975) 5-18.

Fleischman, "Temporal Distance: A Basic Linguistic Metaphor", *Studies in Language* 13.1 (1989) 1-50.

Folmer, M., "Some Remarks on the Use of the Finite Verb Form in the Protasis of Conditional Sentences in Aramaic Texts from the Achaemenid Period", in: K. Jongeling, H. L. Murre-van den Berg, and L. van Rompay (eds.), *Studies in Hebrew and Aramaic Syntax* (Studies in Semitic Languages and Linguistics 17; Leiden: E. J. Brill, 1991) 56-78.

_____., *The Aramaic Language in the Achaemenid Period. A Study in Linguistic Variation* (Orientalia Lovaniensia Analecta 68; Leuven: Peeters, 1995).

Frankenberg, W., *Die Sprüche* (Handbuch zum Alten Testament II, 3.1; Göttingen: Vandenhoeck & Ruprecht, 1898).

Fraser, B., "Hedged Performatives", in: P. Cole and J. Morgan (eds.), *Speech Acts* (Syntax and Semantics 3; New York: Academic Press, 1975) 187-210.

Friedrich, J., Röllig, W., and M. Guzzo, *Phönizisch-Punische Grammatik*[3] (Analecta Orientalia 55; Rome: Editrice Pontificio Istituto Biblico, 1999).

Furuli, R., "The Problem of Induction and the Hebrew Verb", in: E. Wardini (ed.), *Built on Solid Rock* (Oslo: Novusforlag, 1997) 82-90.

Futato, M., "Because It Had Rained: A Study of Gen 2:5-7 with Implications for Gen 2:4-25 and Gen 1:1-2:3", *Westminster Theological Journal* 60.1 (1998) 1-21.

Garbini, G., "L'iscrizione di Belaam Bar-Beor", *Henoch* 1 (1979) 168-188.

García Martínez, F., and E. Tigchelaar, *The Dead Sea Scrolls: Study Edition* (2 vols.; Leiden: E. J. Brill, 1997-98).

Garr, W. R., "Driver's *Treatise* and the Study of Hebrew: Then and Now", introductory essay to 1998 reprint of S. R. Driver's *Treatise on the Use of the Tenses in Hebrew and Some Other Syntactical Questions* (Grand Rapids: Eerdmans, 1998) xviii-lxxxvi.

Gelb, I., "The Origin of the West Semitic *Qatala* Morpheme", in: W. Taszycki (ed.), *Symbolae Linguisticae in Honorem Georgii Kurylowicz* (Warsaw: Polska Akademia Nauk, 1965) 72-80.

Gelderen, C. van, and W. Gispen, *Het boek Hosea* (Commentaar op het Oude Testament; Kampen: Kok, 1953).

Gemser, B., *Sprüche Salomos* (Handbuch zum Alten Testament 1. Reihe, 16; Tübingen: Mohr, 1937).

Gentry, P., "The System of the Finite Verb in Classical Biblical Hebrew", *Hebrew Studies* 39 (1998) 7-39.

Gesenius, W., *Hebrew Grammar*[28] (ed. E. Kautzsch and A. Cowley; Oxford: Oxford University Press, 1910).

_____., and F. Buhl, *Hebräisches und aramäisches Handwörterbuch über das Alte Testament*[17] (Leipzig: Vogel, 1921).

Gianto, A., "Mood and Modality in Classical Hebrew", *Israel Oriental Studies* 18 (1998) 183-198.

Gibson, J., *Textbook of Syrian Semitic Inscriptions. 2. Aramaic Inscriptions* (Oxford: Clarendon, 1975).

_____., *Davidson's Introductory Hebrew Grammar: Syntax* (Edinburgh: T. & T. Clark, 1994).

Givón, T., *Syntax. A Functional-Typological Introduction* (2 vols.; Amsterdam/Philadelphia: John Benjamins Publishing Company, 1984-90).

Goldfajn, T., *Word Order and Time in Biblical Hebrew Narrative* (Oxford: Clarendon, 1998).

Goldingay, J., *Daniel* (Word Biblical Commentary 30; Waco: Word Books, 1989).

Gordon, C., *Ugaritic Textbook* (Rome: Pontifical Biblical Institute, 1965).

Gosling, F., *The Syntax of Hebrew Poetry: An Examination of the Use of Tense in Poetry with Particular Reference to the Book of Job 3:1-42:6* (Ph.D. diss., University of St. Andrews, 1992).

Gottlieb, H., *A Study on the Text of Lamentations* (Aarhus: Aarhus Universitet, 1978).

Gray, G., *A Critical and Exegetical Commentary on the Book of Isaiah* (International Critical Commentary; Edinburgh: T. & T. Clark, 1912).

Gray, J., *The KRT Text in the Literature of Ras Shamra*[2] (Leiden: E. J. Brill, 1964).

Greenstein, E., "Kirta", in: S. B. Parker (ed.), *Ugaritic Narrative Poetry* (Writings from the Ancient World 9; Atlanta: Scholars Press, 1997) 9-48.

_____., "On the Prefixed Preterite in Biblical Hebrew", *Hebrew Studies* 29 (1988) 7-17.

Gropp, D., "The Function of the Finite Verb in Classical Biblical Hebrew", *Hebrew Annual Review* 13 (1991) 45-62.

Groß, W., *Verbform + Funktion. wayyiqtol für die Gegenwart? Ein Beitrag zur Syntax poetischer althebräischer Schriften* (Arbeiten zu Text und Sprache im Alten Testament 1; St. Ottilien: EOS, 1976).

_____., "Zur Funktion von *qatal*. Die Verbfunktionen in neueren Veröffentlichungen", *Biblische Notizen* 4 (1977) 25-38

_____., "Bundeszeichen und Bundesschluß in der Priesterschrift", *Trierer theologische Zeitschrift* 87 (1978) 98-115.

_____., "OTTO RÖSSLER und die Diskussion um das althebräische Verbalsystem", *Biblische Notizen* 18 (1982) 28-78.

Hamann, C., "The Awesome Seeds of Reference Time", in: A. Schopf (ed.), *Essays on Tensing in English. Vol. I: Reference Time, Tense and Adverbs* (Linguistische Arbeiten 185; Tübingen: Max Niemeyer, 1987) 27-69.

Harder, P., "Verbal Time Reference in English: Structure and Functions", in: C. Bache, H. Basbøll, and C.-E. Lindberg (eds.), *Tense, Aspect and Action. Empirical and Theoretical Contributions to Language Typology* (Berlin: de Gruyter, 1994) 61-79.

Harper, W., *A Critical and Exegetical Commentary on Amos and Hosea* (International Critical Commentary; Edinburgh: T. & T. Clark, 1905).

Hasel, G., and M. Hasel, "The Hebrew Term *'ed* in Gen 2,6 and Its Connection in Ancient Near Eastern Literature", *Zeitschrift für die alttestamentliche Wissenschaft* 112.3 (2000) 321-340.

Hatav, G., "Aspects, *Aktionsarten*, and the Time Line", *Linguistics* 27 (1989) 487-516.

_____., *The Semantics of Aspect and Modality. Evidence from English and Biblical Hebrew* (Studies in Language Companion Series 34; Amsterdam/Philadelphia: John Benjamins Publishing Company, 1997).

Heimerdinger, J.-M., *Topic, Focus and Foreground in Ancient Hebrew Narratives* (Journal for the Study of the Old Testament Supplement Series 295; Sheffield: JSOT Press, 1999),

Heimpel, W., and G. Guidi, "Der Koinzidenzfall im Akkadischen", in: W. Voigt (ed.), *XVII. Deutscher Orientalistentag vom 21. bis 27. Juli 1968 im Würzburg* (ZDMG Supplement 1:3; Wiesbaden: Steiner, 1969) 148-152.

Held, M., "The *YQTL-QTL (QTL-YQTL)* Sequence of Identical Verbs in Biblical Hebrew and in Ugaritic", in: M. Ben-Horin, B. Weinryb, and S. Zeitlin (eds.), *Studies and Essays in Honor of Abraham A. Neuman* (Leiden: E. J. Brill, 1962) 281-90.

Hendel, R., "In the Margins of the Hebrew Verbal System: Situation, Tense, Aspect, Mood", *Zeitschrift für Althebraistik* 9 (1996) 152-181.

Hermisson, H.-J., *Studien zur israelitischen Spruchweisheit* (Neukirchen-Vluyn: Neukirchener Verlag, 1968).

Herzberg, H., *Der Prediger (Qoheleth)* (Kommentar zum Alten Testament 16.4; Leipzig: Deichert, 1932).

Hill, A., *Malachi* (Anchor Bible 25D; New York: Doubleday, 1998).

Hillers, D., *Micah* (Hermeneia; Philadelphia: Fortress, 1984).

_____., "Some Performative Utterances in the Bible", in: D.P. Wright, D. N. Freedman, and A. Hurvitz (eds.), *Pomegranates and Golden Bells: Studies in Biblical, Jewish, and Near Eastern Ritual, Law, and Literature in Honor of Jacob Milgrom* (Winona Lake: Eisenbrauns, 1995) 757-66.

Hinrichs, U., "Der Koinzidenzfall in den Balkansprachen (I)", *Zeitschrift für Balkanologie* 21.2 (1985) 136-151.

_____., "Der Koinzidenzfall in den Balkansprachen (II)", *Zeitschrift für Balkanologie* 22.2 (1986) 165-184.

Hirtle, W., *The Simple and Progressive Forms: An Analytical Approach* (Quebec: Les Presses de l'Université Laval, 1967).

Hoftijzer, J., *Verbale Vragen* (Leiden: E. J. Brill, 1974).

_____., *The Function and Use of the Imperfect Forms with Nun Paragogicum in Classical Hebrew* (Studia Semitica Neerlandica 21; Assen: Van Gorcum, 1985).

_____., "A Preliminary Remark on the Study of the Verbal System in Classical Hebrew", in: A. Kaye (ed.), *Semitic Studies in Honour of Wolf Leslau* (Wiesbaden: Harrassowitz, 1991) 645-651.

_____., "Some Notes on the Ugaritic Text KTU 2.42 Lines 1-9", *Jaarbericht van het Vooraziatisch-Egyptisch Genootschap Ex Oriente Lux* 34 (1995-96) 73-80.

_____., "Zukunftsaussagen und Modalität", *Kleine Untersuchungen zur Sprache des Alten Testaments und seiner Umwelt* 2 (2001) 5-45.

_____., and G. van der Kooij, *Aramaic Texts from Deir 'Alla* (Leiden: E. J. Brill, 1976).

Holladay, W., *Jeremiah* (2 vols., Hermeneia; Philadelphia: Fortress, 1986-89).

Hug, V., *Altaramäische Grammatik der Texte des 7. und 6. Jh.s v. Chr.* (Heidelberg: Heidelberger Orientverlag, 1993).

Hughes, J. A., "Another Look at the Hebrew Tenses", *Journal of Near Eastern Studies* 29 (1970) 12-24.

Hughes, J., review of Waltke and O'Connor (1990), *Journal of Semitic Studies* 44.1 (1993) 132-37.

Humbert, P., "Essai d'analyse de Nahoum 1 $_2$ - 2 $_3$", *Zeitschrift für die alttestamentliche Wissenschaft* 44 (1926) 266-280.

_____., "La vision de Nahoum 2, 4-11", *Archiv für Orientforschung* 5 (1928-29) 14-19.

_____., *Problèmes du livre d'Habacuc* (Neuchatel: Secretariat de l'Université, 1944).

Humbert, J., *Syntaxe Grecque* (Paris: Klincksieck, 1945)

Hurvitz, A., "Can Biblical Texts be Dated Linguistically? Chronological Perspectives in the Historical Study of Biblical Hebrew", in: A. Lemaire and M. Sæbø (eds.), *Congress Volume Oslo 1998* (Vetus Testamentum Supplements 80; Leiden: E. J. Brill, 2000) 143-160.

Huwyler, B., *Jeremia und die Völker* (Forschungen zum Alten Testament 20; Tübingen: Mohr Siebeck, 1997).

Ibn Ezra, A., צחות ספר (ed. G. Lippmann; Fuerth, 1827).

Irsigler, H., *Gottesgericht und Jahwetag. Die Komposition Zef 1, 1-2, 3, untersucht auf der Grundlage der Literarkritik des Zefanjabuches* (Arbeiten zu Text und Sprache im Alten Testament 3; St. Ottilien: EOS, 1977).

_____., *Einführung in das biblische Hebräisch* (Arbeiten zu Text und Sprache im Alten Testament 9; 2 vols.; St. Ottilien: EOS, 1978-79).

Isaksson, B., *Studies in the Language of Qoheleth: With a Special Emphasis on the Verbal System* (Studia Semitica Upsaliensia 10; Uppsala: Almqvist & Wiksell International, 1987).

Jastrow, M., *Dictionary of the Targumim, Talmud Babli, Yerushalmi and Midrashic Literature* (original 1886-1903, 2 vols.; reprint: New York: Judaica Press, 1975).

Jenni, E., "Ein Querschnitt durch die neuere Althebraistik", *Theologische Rundschau* 65.1 (2000) 1-37.

Jirku, A., *Kanaanäische Mythen und Epen aus Ras Schamra-Ugarit* (Gütersloh: Gerd Mohn, 1962).

Johanson, L., *Aspekt im Türkischen* (Stockholm: Almqvist & Wiksell, 1971).

Johnson, B., *Hebräisches Perfekt und Imperfekt mit vorangehendem w^e* (Lund: CWK Gleerup, 1979).

Jones, D., *Jeremiah* (New Century Bible; Grand Rapids: Eerdmans, 1992).

Jong, C. de, *De Volken bij Jeremia. Hun Plaats in Zijn Prediking en in het Boek Jeremia* (Diss., Kampen, 1978).

_____., "Deux oracles contre les nations. Reflets de la politique étrangère de Joaqim", in: P.-M. Bogaert (ed.), *Le livre de Jérémie* (Leuven: Peeters, 1997), 369-379.

Joosten, J., "The Predicative Participle in Biblical Hebrew", *Zeitschrift für Althebraistik* 2 (1989) 128-159.

_____., "Biblical Hebrew w^{e}qātal and Syriac hwā qātel Expressing Repetition in the Past", *Zeitschrift für Althebraistik* 5.1 (1992) 1-14.

_____., "The Indicative System of the Biblical Hebrew Verb and its Literary Exploitation", in: E. van Wolde (ed.), *Narrative Syntax and the Hebrew Bible* (Biblical Interpretation Series 29; Leiden: E. J. Brill, 1997) 51-71.

_____., "The Long Form of the Prefix Conjugation Referring to the Past in Biblical Hebrew Prose", *Hebrew Studies* 40 (1999) 15-26.

Joüon, P., "Notes de syntax hébraïque 2: L'emploi du participe et du parfait dans l'Ecclésiaste", *Biblica* 2 (1921) 225-226.

_____., "Les temps dans Proverbes 31, 10-31 (La Femme Forte)", *Biblica* 2 (1922) 349-352.

_____., *Grammaire de l'hébreu biblique*² (Rome: Pontificio Istituto Biblico, 1923).

_____., "Cinq imparfaits (*yiqtul*) remarquables dans l'araméen de Daniel (4, 8. 31. 33; 6, 20; 7, 16)", *Biblica* 22 (1941) 21-24

_____., and T. Muraoka, *A Grammar of Biblical Hebrew* (Subsidia Biblica 14; 2 vols.; Rome: Pontifical Biblical Institute, 1991).

Junger, J., "Aspect and Cohesion in Biblical Hebrew Narratives", *Semitics* 10 (1989) 71-130.

Kautzsch, E., *Grammatik des biblisch-Aramäischen* (Leipzig: Vogel, 1884).

Keil, C., *The Prophecies of Jeremiah* (2 vols., reprint; Grand Rapids: Eerdmans, 1950).

_____., *The Minor Prophets* (2 vols., reprint; Grand Rapids: Eerdmans, 1949).

Keller, C., *Nahoum, Habacuc, Sophonie* (Commentaire de l'Ancien Testament 11b; Neuchatel: Delachaux et Niestle, 1971).

Kelly, F., "The Imperfect with Simple *waw* in Hebrew", *Journal of Biblical Literature* 39 (1920) 1-23.

Kesterson, J., *Tense Usage and Verbal Syntax in Selected Qumran Documents* (Ph.D. diss., Catholic University of America, 1984).

Keulen, P. S. F. van, *Manasseh Through the Eyes of the Deuteronomists (2 Kings 21:1-18)* (Oudtestamentische Studiën 38; Leiden: E. J. Brill, 1996).

Khalil, A., and E. McCarus, "Arabic Performative Verbs", *Zeitschrift für Arabische Linguistik* 36 (1999) 7-20.

Kim, S., *Difficult Uses of the Perfect with Waw-Consecutive in 1 and 2 Samuel* (Th.M. thesis, Dallas Theological Seminary, 1998).

Kissane, E., *The Book of Isaiah* (rev. ed.; Dublin: Brown & Nolan, 1960).

Kißling, H., *Osmanische-türkische Grammatik* (Wiesbaden: Harrassowitz, 1960).

Klein, G., "The 'Prophetic Perfect'", *Journal of Northwest Semitic Languages* 16 (1990) 45-60.

Koehler, L., W. Baumgartner *et al.*, *Hebräisches und aramäisches Lexikon zum Alten Testament*³ (Leiden: E. J. Brill, 1967-96).

König, E., *Historisch-comparative Syntax der hebräischen Sprache* (Historisch-kritisches Lehrgebäude der hebräischen Sprache 3; Leipzig: J. C. Hinrichs, 1897).

_____., *Hebräisches und aramäisches Wörterbuch zum Alten Testament*³ (Leipzig: Dieterich, 1922).

_____., *Die Psalmen eingeleitet, übers. und erklärt* (Gütersloh: Bertelsmann, 1927).

_____., *Das Buch Hiob* (Gütersloh: Bertelsmann, 1929).

Koopmans, J., *Aramäische Chrestomathie, 1: Einleitungen, Literatur, und Kommentare* (Leiden: Nederlands Instituut voor het Nabije Oosten, 1962).

Koschmieder, E., "Durchkreuzungen von Aspekt- und Tempussystem im Präsens", *Zeitschift für Slavische Philologie* 7 (1930) 341-358.

_____., "Zu den Grundfragen der Aspekttheorie", *Indogermanische Forschungen* 53 (1935) 280-300.

_____., "Zur Bestimmung der Funktionen grammatischer Kategorien", reprinted in: *Beiträge zur allgemeinen Syntax* (Bibliothek der allgemeinen Sprachwissenschaft. Reihe 2, Einzeluntersuchungen und Darstellungen zur allgemeinen Sprachwissenschaft; Heidelberg: Winter, 1965) 9-69.

Koschmieder-Schmid, K., *Vergleichende griechisch-slavische Aspektstudien* (Slavistische Beiträge 13; München: Otto Sagner, 1967).

Kottsieper, I., "'... und mein Vater zog hinauf...' Aspekte des älteren aramäischen Verbalsystems und seiner Entwicklung", in: N. Nebes (ed.), *Tempus und Aspekt in den semitischen Sprachen. Jenaer Kolloquium zur semitischen Sprachwissenschaft* (Jenaer Beiträge zum Vorderen Orient 1; Wiesbaden: Harrassowitz, 1999) 55-76.

_____., "*yaqattal* - Phantom oder Problem? Erwägungen zu einem hebraistischen Problem und zur Geschichte der semitischen Sprachen", *Kleine Untersuchungen zur Sprache des Alten Testaments und seiner Umwelt* 1 (2000) 27-100.

Krahmalkov, C., "The *qatal* with Future Tense Reference in Phoenician", *Journal of Semitic Studies* 31.1 (1986) 5-10.

_____., *A Phoenician-Punic Grammar* (Leiden: E. J. Brill, 2001).

Kraus, H.-J., *Psalmen* (3 vols., Biblischer Kommentar zum Alten Testament 15; Neukirchen-Vluyn: Neukirchener Verlag, 1960-1979).

Krispenz, J., "Grammatik und Theologie in der Botenformel", *Zeitschrift für Althebraistik* 11.2 (1998) 133-139.

Kühner, R., *Ausführliche Grammatik der griechischen Sprache. II: Satzlehre*³ (2 vols., ed. B. Gerth; Hannover/Leipzig: Hahnsche Buchhandlung, 1898-1904).

Kurylowicz, J., *Studies in Semitic Grammar and Metrics* (Prace Jezykoznawcze 67; Warszawa: Zaklad Narodowy Imienia Ossolinskich - Wydawnictwo Polskiej Akademii Nauk, 1972).

Kustár, P. *Aspekt im Hebräischen* (Theologische Dissertationen 9; Basel: Reinhardt, 1972).

Kutscher, E., הלשון והרקע הלשוני של מגילת ישעיהו השלמה ממגילות ים המלח (Jerusalem: Magnes Press, 1959).

_____., "The Hermopolis Papyri", *Israel Oriental Studies* 1 (1971) 103-119.

_____., *The Language and Linguistic Background of the Isaiah Scroll (1QIsaᵃ)* (Studies on the Texts of the Desert of Judah 6; Leiden: E. J. Brill, 1974).

_____., *A History of the Hebrew Language* (Leiden/Jerusalem: E. J. Brill/Magnes Press, 1982).

Lamarche, P., *Zacharie IX-XIV: Structure litteraire et messianisme* (Paris: Lecoffre, 1961).

Lambert, M., "Du passé optatif en hébreu", *Revue des études juives* 80 (1925) 218-219.

Laude-Cirtautas, I., "The Past Tense in Kazakh and Uzbek as a means of Emphasizing Present and Future Actions", *Central Asiatic Journal* 18 (1974) 149-158.

Lawler, J., "Generic to a Fault" in: P. Peraneau, J. Levi, and G. Phares (eds.), *Papers from the Eighth Regional Meeting of the Chicago Linguistic Society, April 14-16, 1972* (Chicago: Chicago Linguistic Society, 1972) 247-258.

Leech, G., *Semantics*² (Harmondsworth: Penguin Books, 1981).

Leeuwen, C. van, *Hosea* (Prediking van het Oude Testament; Nijkerk: Callenbach, 1968).

Leeuwen-Turnovcová, J. van, *Illokutive Komposita von Verben des Sagens* (Veröffentlichungen der Abteilung für slavische Sprachen und Literaturen des Osteuropa-Instituts (Slavisches Seminar) an der Freien Universität Berlin 60; Wiesbaden: Harrassowitz, 1986).

Levinson, S., *Pragmatics* (Cambridge Textbooks in Linguistics; Cambridge/New York: Cambridge University Press, 1983).

Liedtke, F., "Performativität, Sprechhandlung, Wahrheit", *Zeitschrift für Phonetik, Sprachwissenschaft und Kommunikationsforschung* 43.4 (1990) 515-532.

Lindblom, J., *Die Jesaja-Apokalypse* (Lund/Leipzig: C.W.K. Gleerup/ Harrassowitz, 1938).

_____., *Prophecy in Ancient Israel* (Oxford: Blackwell, 1962).

Lindenberger, J., *The Aramaic Proverbs of Ahiqar* (Ph.D. diss., The Johns Hopkins University, 1974).

_____., *The Aramaic Proverbs of Ahiqar* (The Johns Hopkins Near Eastern Studies; Baltimore: The Johns Hopkins University Press, 1983).

Ljungberg, B.-K., "Tense, Aspect, and Modality in Some Theories of the Biblical Hebrew Verbal System", *Journal of Translation and Textlinguistics* 7.3 (1995) 82-96.

Lohse, E., *Die Texte aus Qumran*[4] (Darmstadt: Wissenschaftliche Buchgesellschaft, 1986).

Longacre, R., *"Weqatal* Forms in Biblical Hebrew Prose: A Discourse-modular Approach", in: R. Bergen (ed.), *Biblical Hebrew and Discourse Linguistics* (Winona Lake: Eisenbrauns, 1994) 50-98.

Lunde, P., and J. Wintle (eds.), *A Dictionary of Arabic and Islamic Proverbs* (London: Routledge and Kegan Paul, 1984).

Lyons, J., *Introduction to Theoretical Linguistics* (Cambridge: Cambridge University Press, 1968).

_____., *Semantics* (Cambridge: Cambridge University Press, 1977).

_____., *Linguistic Semantics: An Introduction* (Cambridge: Cambridge University Press, 1995).

Macintosh, A., *A Critical and Exegetical Commentary on the Book of Hosea* (International Critical Commentary; Edinburgh: T. & T. Clark, 1997).

Maimonides, M., *The Guide of the Perplexed* (ed. Sh. Pines; Chicago: University of Chicago Press, 1963).

Marcus, I. D., *Aspects of the Ugaritic Verb in the Light of Comparative Semitic Grammar* (Ph.D. diss., Columbia University, 1970).

Marti, K., *Das Buch Daniel* (Kurzer Hand-Commentar zum Alten Testament 18; Tübingen: Mohr, 1901).

Mayer, W., *Untersuchungen zur Formensprache der babylonischen 'Gebetsbeschwörungen'* (Studio Pohl, Series maior 5; Rome: Biblical Institute Press, 1976).

_____., "Ich rufe dich von ferne, höre mich von nahe!", in: R. Albertz, H.P. Müller, H.-W. Wolff, and W. Zimmerli (eds.) *Werden und Wirken des Alten Testaments. Festschrift für Claus Westermann zum 70. Geburtstag* (Göttingen/Neukirchen-Vluyn: Vandenhoeck & Ruprecht/Neukirchener Verlag, 1980) 302-17.

_____., "Das 'gnomische Präteritum' im literarischen Akkadisch", *Orientalia* 61 (1992) 373-399.

McCarter, P. K., "The Balaam Texts from Deir 'Alla: The First Combination", *Bulletin of the American Schools of Oriental Research* 239 (1980) 49-60.

McFall, L., *The Enigma of the Hebrew Verbal System. Solutions from Ewald to the Present Day* (Sheffield: Almond, 1982).

McKane, W., *Proverbs: A New Approach* (Old Testament Library; London: SCM Press, 1970).

_____., *A Critical and Exegetical Commentary on Jeremiah* (2 vols., International Critical Commentary; Edinburgh: T. & T. Clark, 1986-96).

_____., *The Book of Micah. Introduction and Commentary* (Edinburgh: T. & T. Clark, 1998).

Meier, S., *Speaking of Speaking. Marking Direct Discourse in the Hebrew Bible* (Vetus Testamentum Supplements 46; Leiden: E. J. Brill, 1992).

Meinhold, A., *Die Sprüche* (2 vols., Zürcher Bibelkommentare 16; Zürich: Theologischer Verlag, 1991).

Meister, M., *An Investigation of the Precative Perfect in Classical Hebrew* (Th.M. thesis, Covenant Theological Seminary, 1994).

Menges, K., *The Turkic Languages and Peoples*[2] (Veröffentlichungen der Societas Uralo-Altaica 42; Wiesbaden: Harrassowitz, 1995).

Merwe, C. van der, J. Naudé, and J. Kroeze, *A Biblical Hebrew Reference Grammar* (Sheffield: Sheffield Academic Press, 1999).

Mettinger, T., "The Hebrew Verb System: A Survey of Recent Research", *Annual of the Swedish Theological Institute* 9 (1974) 64-84.

Meyer, R., *Hebräische Grammatik* (4 vols.; Berlin: de Gruyter, 1966-72),

Meyers, C., and E. Meyers, *Haggai, Zechariah 1-8* (Anchor Bible 25B; Garden City: Doubleday, 1987).

Michel, D., *Tempora und Satzstellung in den Psalmen* (Bonn: Bouvier, 1960).

146

Mieder, W., S. Kingsbury, and K. Harder (eds.), *A Dictionary of American Proverbs* (Oxford: Oxford University Press, 1992).

Mihailovic, M., *Tempus und Aspekt im serbokroatischen Präsens* (Slavistische Beiträge 5; München: Otto Sagner, 1962).

Mishor, M., התנאים בלשון הזמנים מערכת (The Tense System in Tannaitic Hebrew) (Ph.D. diss., Hebrew University of Jerusalem, 1983).

Mitchell, H., "והיה of the Past", *Journal of Biblical Literature* 33 (1914) 48-55.

_____., J. Smith, and J. Bewer, *A Critical and Exegetical Commentary on Haggai, Zechariah, Malachi and Jonah* (International Critical Commentary; Edinburgh: T. & T. Clark, 1912).

Moran, W., "The Hebrew Language in its Northwest Semitic Background", in: G. E. Wright (ed.), *The Bible and the Ancient Near East: Essays in Honor of William Foxwell Albright* (Garden City, NY: Doubleday, 1961) 54-72.

Múgica, J., "Sentido de pasado de la forma 'yqtl' en algunos textos de Isaías II", *Estudios bíblicos* 30 (1971) 195-204.

Mulder, E., *Die Teologie van die Jesaja-Apokalipse (Jesaja 24-27)* (Ph.D. diss., Rijksuniversiteit Groningen; Groningen: J. B. Wolters, 1954).

Müller, A., review of Driver's *Treatise on the Use of the Tenses*, *Zeitschrift für die gesammte lutherische Theologie und Kirche* 38 (1877) 197-208.

Müller, H.-P., "Die aramäische Inschrift von Deir 'Allā und die älteren Bileamsprüche", *Zeitschrift für die alttestamentliche Wissenschaft* 94 (1982) 214-44.

_____., "Zur Geschichte des hebräischen Verbs. Diachronie der Konjugationsthemen", *Biblische Zeitschrift* 27 (1983) 34-57.

_____., "Der 90. Psalm", *Zeitschrift für Theologie und Kirche* 81 (1984) 265-285.

_____., "Assertorische und kreatorische Funktion im althebräischen und semitischen Verbalsystem", *Aula Orientalis* 2 (1984b) 113-125.

_____., "Polysemie im semitischen und hebräischen Konjugationssystem", *Orientalia* 55 (1986) 365-389.

_____., "Das Bedeutungspotential der Afformativkonjugation. Zum sprachgeschichtlichen Hintergrund des Althebräischen", *Zeitschrift für Althebraistik* 1 (1988) 74-97, 159-190.

_____., "Die Sprache der Texte von Tell Deir 'Allā im Kontext der nordwestsemitischen Sprachen", *Zeitschrift für Althebraistik* 4.1 (1991) 1-31.

_____., "Zu den semitisch-hamitischen Konjugationssystemen", *Zeitschrift für Althebraistik* 11.2 (1998) 140-152.

Muraoka, T., "Notes on the Aramaic of the Genesis Apocryphon", *Revue de Qumran* 29 (1972) 7-51.

_____., "The *Nun Energicum* and the Prefix Conjugation in Biblical Hebrew", *Annual of the Japanese Biblical Institute* 1 (1975) 63-71.

_____., *Emphatic Words and Structures in Biblical Hebrew* (Jerusalem/Leiden: Magnes Press/E. J. Brill, 1985).

_____., "Further notes on the Aramaic of the *Genesis Apocryphon*", *Revue de Qumran* 61 (1993) 39-48.

_____., *Classical Syriac: A Basic Grammar with a Chrestomathy* (Wiesbaden: Harrassowitz, 1997).

_____., "Again on the Tel Dan Inscription and the Northwest Semitic Verb Tenses", *Zeitschrift für Althebraistik* 11.1 (1998) 74-81.

_____., "The Participle in Qumran Hebrew with Special Reference to its Periphrastic Use", in: T. Muraoka and J. F. Elwolde (eds.), *Sirach, Scrolls, and Sages. Proceedings of a Second International Symposium on the Hebrew of the Dead Sea Scrolls, Ben Sira, and the Mishnah, held at Leiden University, 15-17 December 1997* (Studies on the Texts of the Desert of Judah 33; Leiden: E. J. Brill, 1999) 188-204.

_____., and B. Porten, *A Grammar of Egyptian Aramaic* (Leiden: E. J. Brill, 1998).

_____., and M. Rogland, "The *Waw* Consecutive in Old Aramaic? A Rejoinder to Victor Sasson", *Vetus Testamentum* 48.1 (1998) 99-104.

Mussies, G., *The Morphology of Koine Greek as Used in the Apocalypse of John: A Study in Bilingualism* (Novum Testamentum Supplements 27; Leiden: E. J. Brill, 1971).

Nebes, N. (ed.), *Tempus und Aspekt in den semitischen Sprachen. Jenaer Kolloquium zur semitischen Sprachwissenschaft* (Jenaer Beiträge zum Vorderen Orient 1; Wiesbaden: Harrassowitz, 1999).

Nel, P., *The Structure and Ethos of the Wisdom Admonitions in Proverbs* (Beihefte zur Zeitschrift für die alttestamentliche Wissenschaft 158; Berlin: de Gruyter, 1982).

Niccacci, A., "A Neglected Point of Hebrew Syntax: *Yiqtol* and Position in the Sentence", *Liber Annuus* 37 (1987) 7-19.

_____., *The Syntax of the Verb in Classical Hebrew Prose* (Journal for the Study of the Old Testament Supplement Series 86; Sheffield: JSOT Press, 1990).

Nöldeke, T., *Kurzgefasste syrische Grammatik* (reprint; Darmstadt: Wissenschaftliche Buchgesellschaft, 1966).

Nowack, W., *Die Kleinen Propheten*[3] (Handkommentar zum Alten Testament 3.4; Göttingen: Vandenhoeck & Ruprecht, 1922).

O'Connor, M., *Hebrew Verse Structure* (Winona Lake: Eisenbrauns, 1980).

Olmo Lete, G. del, *Mitos y leyendas de Canaan segun la tradicion de Ugarit* (Madrid: Ediciones Cristiandad, 1981).

Otzen, B., *Studien über Deuterosacharja* (Copenhagen: Munksgaard, 1964).

Pardee, D., "Letters from Tel Arad", *Ugarit Forschungen* 10 (1978) 289-336.

_____., "The 'Epistolary Perfect' in Hebrew Letters", *Biblische Notizen* 22 (1983) 34-40.

_____., *Handbook of Ancient Hebrew Letters* (Sources for Biblical Study 15; Chico: Scholars Press, 1982).

_____., and R. Whiting, "Aspects of Epistolary Verbal Usage in Ugaritic and Akkadian", *Bulletin of the School of Oriental and African Studies* 50 (1987) 1-31.

Partridge, J., *Semantic, Pragmatic and Syntactic Correlates: An Analysis of Performative Verbs Based on English Data* (Tübinger Beiträge zur Linguistik 143; Tübingen: Gunter Narr, 1982).

Pascual, C. Herranz, *La Sintaxis Verbal en los Oraculos de Ezequiel* (Ph.D. diss., Universidad Complutense de Madrid, 1993).

_____., "Últimas teorías sintácticas sobre el verbo hebreo bíblico. I: Estado de la cuestión", *Miscelánea de Estudies Árabes y Hebraicos, Sección de Hebreo* 44 (1995) 101-119.

Paul, Sh., *Amos* (Hermeneia; Minneapolis: Fortress, 1991).

Peckham, B., "Tense and Mood in Biblical Hebrew", *Zeitschrift für Althebraistik* 10.2 (1997) 139-168.

Pérez Fernández, M., *An Introductory Grammar of Rabbinic Hebrew* (Leiden: E. J. Brill, 1997).

Petersen, D., *Haggai and Zechariah 1-8* (Old Testament Library; London: SCM Press, 1984).

_____., *Zechariah 9-14 and Malachi* (Old Testament Library; Louisville: Westminster/John Knox, 1995).

Peursen, W. Th. van, "Periphrastic Tenses in Ben Sira", in: T. Muraoka and J. F. Elwolde (eds.), *The Hebrew of the Dead Sea Scrolls and Ben Sira: Proceedings of a Symposium Held at Leiden University, 11-14 December 1995* (Studies on the Texts of the Desert of Judah 26; Leiden: E. J. Brill, 1997) 158-173.

_____., *The Verbal System in the Hebrew Text of Ben Sira* (Ph.D. diss., Leiden University, 1999).

Plöger, O., *Das Buch Daniel* (Kommentar zum Alten Testament 18; Gütersloh: Gerd Mohn, 1965).

_____., *Sprüche Salomos (Proverbia)* (Biblischer Kommentar zum Alten Testament 17; Neukirchen-Vluyn: Neukirchener Verlag, 1984)

Porter, S., *Verbal Aspect in the Greek of the New Testament* (Studies in Biblical Greek 1; New York: Lang, 1989).

Priebatsch, H., "Der Weg des semitischen Perfekts", *Ugarit Forschungen* 10 (1978) 337-347.

Procksch, O., *Jesaia I* (Kommentar zum Alten Testament 9; Leipzig: Deichert, 1930).

Provan, I., "Past, Present and Future in Lamentations III 52-66: The Case for a Precative Perfect Re-examined", *Vetus Testamentum* 51.2 (1991) 164-175.

Qimron, E., "Consecutive and Conjunctive Imperfect: The Form of the Imperfect with *waw* in Biblical Hebrew", *Jewish Quarterly Review* 77 (1986-87) 149-161.

Raabe, P., *Obadiah* (Anchor Bible 24D; New York: Doubleday, 1996).

Rabin, Ch., "The Genesis of the Semitic Tense System", in: J. Bynon (ed.), *Current Progress in Afro-Asiatic Linguistics: Papers of the Third International Hamito-Semitic Congress* (Current Issues in Linguistic Theory 38; Amsterdam/Philadelphia: John Benjamins Publishing Co., 1984) 391-397.

Rainey, A., "Morphology and the Prefix-Tenses of West Semitized El-'Amarna Tablets", *Ugarit Forschungen* 7 (1975) 395-426.

_____., "The Ancient Hebrew Prefix Conugation in the Light of Amarnah Canaanite", *Hebrew Studies* 27 (1986) 4-19.

_____., "Further Remarks on the Hebrew Verbal System", *Hebrew Studies* 29 (1988) 35-42.

_____., *Canaanite in the Amarna Tablets. A Linguistic Analysis of the Mixed Dialect used by the Scribes from Canaan. II: Morphosyntactic Analysis of the Verbal System* (Leiden: E. J. Brill, 1996).

Recanati, F., *Meaning and Force. The Pragmatics of Performative Utterances* (Cambridge Studies in Philosophy; Cambridge: Cambridge University Press, 1987).

Reckendorf, H., *Arabische Syntax* (Heidelberg: Winter, 1921).

_____., *Die syntaktische Verhältnisse des Arabischen* (Leiden: E. J. Brill, 1895-98).

Regt, L. J. de, "Tempus in het Bijbels Hebreeuws", *Glot* 6 (1983) 247-275.

Reichenbach, H., *Elements of Symbolic Logic* (New York: Macmillan, 1947).

Renaud, B., *Michee, Sohponie, Nahum* (Sources bibliques; Paris: Librairie Lecoffre, 1987).

Reuschel, W., *Aspekt und Tempus in der Sprache des Korans* (Leipziger Beiträge zur Orientforschung 6; Frankfurt a.M.: Peter Lang, 1996).

Revell, E. J., "The Conditioning of Stress Position in *waw* Consecutive Perfect Forms in Biblical Hebrew", *Hebrew Annual Review* 9 (1985) 277-300.

_____., "The System of the Verb in Standard Biblical Prose", *Hebrew Union College Annual* 60 (1989) 1-37.

Richter, W., *Grundlagen einer althebräischen Grammatik* I (Arbeiten zu Text und Sprache im Alten Testament 8; St. Ottilien: EOS, 1978).

Ringgren, H., *Sprüche, Prediger*[3] (Das Alte Testament Deutsch 16.1; Göttingen: Vandenhoeck & Ruprecht, 1980).

Roberts, J., *Nahum, Habakkuk, and Zephaniah* (Old Testament Library; Louisville: Westminster/John Knox, 1991).

Robinson, T., and F. Horst, *Die zwölf kleinen Propheten* (Handbuch zum Alten Testament 1. Reihe, 14; Tübingen: Mohr, 1964).

Rogland, M., "A Note on Performative Utterances in Qumran Aramaic", *Revue de Qumran* 19.2 (1999) 277-280.

_____., "The Hebrew 'Epistolary Perfect' Revisited", *Zeitschrift für Althebraistik* 13.2 (2000) 194-200.

_____., "Performative Utterances in Classical Syriac", *Journal of Semitic Studies* 46.2 (2001) 243-250.

_____., "Remarks on the Aramaic Verbal System", in: M. F. J. Baasten and W. Th. Van Peursen (eds.), *Hamlet on a Hill. Semitic and Greek Studies Presented to Professor T.*

Muraoka on the Occasion of his Sixty-Fifth Birthday (Orientalia Lovaniensia Analecta 118; Leuven: Peeters, 2003) 421-432.

Röhrich, L, and W. Mieder, *Sprichwort* (Stuttgart: Metzler, 1977).

Rosén, H., "On the Use of the Tenses in the Aramaic of Daniel", *Journal of Semitic Studies* 6 (1961) 183-203.

Rosenmüller, E., *Scholia in Vetus Testamentum* (8 vols.; Leipzig: Barth, 1795-1826).

Rosenthal, F., *A Grammar of Biblical Aramaic* (Wiesbaden: Harrassowitz, 1983).

Rössler, O., "Die Präfixkonjugation Qal der Verba Iᵃᵉ im Althebräischen und das Problem der sogenannten Tempora", *Zeitschrift für die alttestamentliche Wissenschaft* 74 (1962) 125-141.

Rowton, M., "The Use of the Permansive in Classic Babylonian", *Journal of Near Eastern Studies* 21 (1962) 233-303.

Rubinstein, R., "The Anomalous Perfect with Waw-conjuctive in Biblical Hebrew", *Biblica* 44 (1963) 62-69.

Rudolph, W., *Jesaja 24-27* (Beiträge zur Wissenschaft vom Alten und Neuen Testament 10; Stuttgart: Kohlhammer, 1933).

_____., *Hosea* (Kommentar zum Alten Testament 13.1; Gütersloh: Gerd Mohn, 1966).

_____., *Jeremia*³ (Handbuch zum Alten Testament 12; Tübingen: Mohr, 1968).

_____., *Haggai, Sacharja 1-8, Sacharja 9-14, Maleachi* (Kommentar zum Alten Testament 13.4; Gütersloh: Gerd Mohn, 1976).

Rundgren, F., *Das althebräische Verbum. Abriss der Aspektlehre* (Uppsala: Almqvist & Wiksell, 1961).

_____., *Erneuerung des Verbalaspekts im Semitischen* (Acta Societas Linguisticae Upsaliensis, New Series 1.3; Uppsala, 1963).

_____., "A propos d'une hypothèse nouvelle concernant la provenance du morpheme *qatal-a*", *Orientalia Suecana* 14-15 (1965-66) 62-74.

Ryou, D., *Zephaniah's Oracles Against the Nations* (Ph.D. diss., Free University of Amsterdam, 1994).

Saebø, M., *Sacharja 9-14: Untersuchungen von Text und Form* (Neukirchen-Vluyn: Neukirchener Verlag, 1969).

Sasson, V., "The Book of Oracular Visions of Balaam from Deir 'Alla", *Ugarit Forschungen* 17 (1986) 283-309.

Saydon, P., "The Use of Tenses in Deutero-Isaiah", *Biblica* 40 (1959) 290-301.

Schneider, W., *Grammatik des biblischen Hebräisch*⁸ (München: Claudius Verlag, 1993).

Schoors, A., *The Preacher Sought to Find Pleasing Words. A Study in the Language of Qoheleth. Part I: Grammar* (Orientalia Lovaniensia Analecta 41; Leuven: Peeters, 1992).

Schüle, A., *Die Syntax der althebräischen Inschriften. Ein Beitrag zur historischen Grammatik des Hebräischen* (Alter Orient und Altes Testament 270; Münster: Ugarit-Verlag, 2000).

Scott, R., *Proverbs, Ecclesiastes*² (Anchor Bible 18; Garden City: Doubleday, 1965).

Segal, M., *A Grammar of Mishnaic Hebrew* (Oxford: Clarendon, 1927).

_____., דקדוק לשון המשנה (Tel Aviv: Dvir, 1936).

Segert, S., *Altaramäisch Grammatik* (Leipzig: VEB Verlag Enzyklopädie, 1975).

_____., *A Basic Grammar of the Ugaritic Language* (Berkeley: University of California Press, 1984).

Seybold, K., *Nahum, Habakuk, Zephanja* (Zürcher Bibelkommentare. AT, 24.2; Zürich: Theologischer Verlag, 1991).

Sharvit, Sh., מערכת ה׳זמנים׳ בלשון המשנה, in: G. B. Sarafatti (ed.), *Studies in Hebrew and Semitic Languages Dedicated to the Memory of Prof. Eduard Yechezkel Kutscher* (Ramat Gan: Bar-Ilan University Press, 1980), Hebrew section 110-125.

Simson, A., *Der Prophet Hosea* (Hamburg: Perthes, 1851).

Sivan, D., *A Grammar of the Ugaritic Language* (Leiden: E. J. Brill, 1997).

150

_____., "The Use of *qtl* and *yqtl* Forms in the Ugaritic Verbal System", *Israel Oriental Studies* 18 (1998) 89-103.

Smith, C., *The Parameter of Aspect* (Studies in Linguistics and Philosophy 43; Dordrecht: Kluwer Academic Publishers, 1991).

Smith, J., W. Ward, and J. Bewer, *A Critical and Exegetical Commentary on Micah, Zephaniah, Nahum, Habakkuk, Obadiah and Joel* (International Critical Commentary; Edinburgh: T. & T. Clark, 1912).

Smith, M., *The Origins and Development of the waw-consecutive. Northwest Semitic Evidence from Ugarit to Qumran* (Harvard Semitic Studies 39; Atlanta: Scholars Press, 1991).

_____., *The Ugaritic Baal Cycle* (Vetus Testamentum Supplements 55; Leiden: E. J. Brill, 1994).

_____., "The **qatala* Form in Ugaritic Narrative Poetry", in: D.P. Wright, D. N. Freedman, and A. Hurvitz (eds.), *Pomegranates and Golden Bells: Studies in Biblical, Jewish, and Near Eastern Ritual, Law, and Literature in Honor of Jacob Milgrom* (Winona Lake: Eisenbrauns, 1995) 789-803.

Smith, R., *Micah-Malachi* (Word Biblical Commentary 32; Waco: Word Books, 1984).

Smyth, H., *Greek Grammar* (rev. G. Messing; Cambridge: Harvard University Press, 1956).

Snaith, J., "Literary Criticism and Historical Investigation in Jeremiah Chapter XLVI", *Journal of Semitic Studies* 16 (1971) 15-32.

Soden, W. von, *Grundriß der akkadischen Grammatik*³ (ed. W. Mayer, Analecta Orientalia 33; Rome: Editrice Pontificio Istituto Biblico, 1995).

Solá-Solé, J. M., *L'infinitif sémitique. Contribution à l'étude des formes et des functions des noms d'action et des infinitifs sémitiques* (Paris: Librairie ancienne honoré champion, 1961).

Sørensen, H., *Aspect et temps en slave* (Aarhus: Universitetsforlaget, 1949).

Spieckermann, H., *Juda unter Assur in der Sargonidenzeit* (Göttingen: Vandenhoeck & Ruprecht, 1982).

Spronk, K., *Nahum* (Historical Commentary on the Old Testament; Kampen: Kok Pharos, 1997).

Stipp, H.-J., "*w=haya* für nichtiterative Vergangenheit? Zu syntaktischen Modernisierungen im masoretischen Jeremiabuch", in: W. Groß, H. Irsigler, and T. Seidl (eds.), *Text, Methode, und Grammatik* (St. Ottilien: EOS, 1991) 521-547.

Strack, H., *Grammatik des Biblisch-Aramäischen*⁴ (Leipzig: J. C. Hinrichs, 1905).

Strauss, E. (ed.), *The Dictionary of European Proverbs* (London: Routledge, 1994).

Streck, M., *Zahl und Zeit. Grammatik der Numeralia und des Verbalsystems im Spätbabylonischen* (Groningen: Styx, 1995).

Talstra, E., "Text Grammar and Hebrew Bible. II: Syntax and Semantics", *Bibliotheca Orientalis* 39 (1982) 26-38.

_____., "Text Grammar and Biblical Hebrew: The Viewpoint of Wolfgang Schneider", *Journal of Translation and Textlinguistics* 5 (1992) 269-297.

_____., "Tense, Mood, Aspect and Clause Connections in Biblical Hebrew. A Textual Approach", *Journal of Northwest Semitic Languages* 23.2 (1997) 81-103.

Thorion-Vardi, T., "The Use of the Tenses in the Zadokite Documents", *Revue de Qumran* 12 (1985) 65-88.

Tropper, J., *Die Inschriften von Zincirli* (Abhandlungen zur Literatur Alt-Syrien-Palästinas 6; Münster: Ugarit-Verlag, 1993).

_____., "Die semitische 'Suffixkonjugation' im Wandel. Von der Prädikativform zum Perfekt", in: M. Dietrich and O. Loretz (eds.), *Vom Alten Orient zum Alten Testament* (Alter Orient und Altes Testament 240; Neukirchen-Vluyn: Neukirchener Verlag, 1995) 491-516.

_____., "Althebräisches und semitisches Aspektsystem", *Zeitschrift für Althebraistik* 11.2 (1998) 153-190.

_____., "Ugaritic Grammar", in: W. Watson and N. Wyatt (eds.), *Handbook of Ugaritic Studies* (Handbuch der Orientalistik, 1. Der Nahe und der Mittlere Osten 39; Leiden: E. J. Brill, 1999), 91-121.

_____., *Ugaritische Grammatik* (Alter Orient und Altes Testament 273; Münster: Ugarit-Verlag, 2000).

Tsumura, D., *The Earth and the Waters in Genesis 1 and 2* (Journal for the Study of the Old Testament Supplement Series 83; Sheffield: Sheffield Academic Press, 1989).

Vendler, Z., "Say What You Think", in: J. L. Cowan (ed.), *Studies in Thought and Language* (Tuscon: University of Arizona Press, 1970) 79-97.

_____., *Res Cogitans* (Ithaca: Cornell University Press, 1972).

Verhoef, P., *Maleachi* (Commentaar op het Oude Testament; Kampen: Kok, 1972).

Verreet, E., *Modi Ugaritici* (Orientalia Lovaniensia Analecta 27; Leuven: Peeters, 1988).

Verschueren, J., "The Conceptual Basis of Performativity", in: M. Shibatani and S. Thompson (eds.), *Essays in Semantics and Pragmatics in Honor of Charles J. Fillmore* (Pragmatics and Beyond, New Series 32; Amsterdam/Philadelphia: John Benjamins Publishing Company, 1995) 299-321.

Vet, C., "Some Arguments Against the Division of Time into Past, Present, and Future", in: L. Goossens (ed.), *Bijdragen over Semantiek van het 33ste. Vlaams Filologencongres* (Antwerp Papers in Linguistics 23; Antwerp: Universiteit Antwerpen, 1981) 153-164.

Vlaardingerbroek, J., *Sefanja* (Commentaar op het Oude Testament; Kampen: Kok, 1993).

Vries, S. de, "The Syntax of Tenses and Interpretation in the Hodayoth", *Revue de Qumran* 5 (1964-65) 375-414.

Wagner, A., *Sprechakte und Sprechaktanalyse im Alten Testament. Untersuchungen im biblischen Hebräisch an der Nahtstelle zwischen Handlungsebene und Grammatik* (Beihefte zur Zeitschrift für die alttestamentliche Wissenschaft 253; Berlin: de Gruyter, 1997).

Waltke, B., and M. O'Connor, *Introduction to Biblical Hebrew Syntax* (Winona Lake: Eisenbrauns, 1990).

Warren, A., *Modality, Reference and Speech Acts in the Psalms* (Ph.D. diss., University of Cambridge, 1998).

Watts, J., *Isaiah* (Word Biblical Commentary 24-25, 2 vols.; Waco: Word, 1985-1987).

Watson, W. G. E., *Classical Hebrew Poetry* (Journal for the Study of the Old Testament Supplement Series 26; Sheffield: JSOT Press, 1984).

_____., *Traditional Techniques in Classical Hebrew Verse* (Journal for the Study of the Old Testament Supplement Series 170; Sheffield: Sheffield Academic Press, 1994).

Wehrle, J., *Prophetie und Textanalyse. Die Komposition Obadja 1-21, interpretiert auf der Basis textliniguistischer und semiotischer Konzeptionen* (Freiburg i.Br.: Albert-Ludwigs Universität, 1980).

_____., *Sprichwort und Weisheit* (Arbeiten zu Text und Sprache im Alten Testament 38; St. Ottilien: EOS, 1993).

Weninger, S., "On Performatives in Classical Ethiopic", *Journal of Semitic Studies* 45.1 (2000) 91-101.

Widmer, G. (ed.), *Die Kommentare von Raschi, Ibn Esra, Radaq zu Joel* (Basel: Volksdruckerei, 1945).

Wildberger, H., *Jesaja* (Biblischer Kommentar zum Alten Testament 10; Neukirchen-Vluyn: Neukirchener Verlag, 1965-1982).

Williams, R., *Hebrew Syntax: An Outline*[2] (Toronto: University of Toronto Press, 1976).

Wolff, H.-W., *Dodekapropheton* (Biblischer Kommentar zum Alten Testament 14; Neukirchen-Vluyn: Neukirchener Verlag, 1961-1998).

Wörner, M. H., *Performative und sprachliches Handeln. Ein Beitrag zu J.L. Austins Theorie der Sprechakte* (Hamburg: Buske, 1978).

Woude, A. van der, *Micha* (Prediking van het Oude Testament; Nijkerk: Callenbach, 1976).

_____., *Jona, Nahum* (Prediking van het Oude Testament; Nijkerk: Callenbach, 1978).

_____., *Haggai-Maleachi* (Prediking van het Oude Testament; Nijkerk: Callenbach, 1982).

_____., *Zacharia* (Prediking van het Oude Testament; Nijkerk: Callenbach, 1984).

Young, I., "The 'Archaic' Poetry of the Pentateuch in the MT, Samaritan Pentateuch and 4QExod^c", *Abr-Nahrain* 35 (1998) 74-83.

Zatelli, I., "Pragmalinguistics and Speech-Act Theory as Applied to Classical Hebrew", *Zeitschrift für Althebraistik* 6 (1993) 60-74.

Zerwick, M., *Biblical Greek* (ed. J. Smith; Scripti Pontificii Instituti Biblici 114; Rome: Editrice Pontificio Istituto Biblico, 1990).

Zevit, Z., *The Anterior Construction in Biblical Hebrew* (Society of Biblical Literature Monograph Series 50; Atlanta: Scholars Press, 1998).

Zimmerli, W., "Visionary Experience in Jeremiah", in: R. Coggins, A. Phillips, and M. Knibb (eds.), *Israel's Prophetic Tradition* (Cambridge: Cambridge University Press, 1982) 95-118.

Zuber, B., *Das Tempussystem des biblischen Hebräisch. Eine Untersuchung am Text* (Beihefte zur Zeitschrift für die alttestamentliche Wissenschaft 164; Berlin: de Gruyter, 1986).

INDEX OF PASSAGES

105.8	30	13.1	37
110.5-6	24	13.8	37
111.4-5	30	13.24	45
115.3	17	14.1	24
118.26	123	14.6	25
119.2-3	46	14.18	37-38
119.10-14	36	14.19	38
119.21	41	14.31	44
119.23	36	16.4	28
119.30	41	16.26	27
119.40	24	16.30	44
129.8	123	17.5	44
135.6	30	17.12	27
135.7	29	18.8	38
146.4	24	18.22	26
		19.24	25
Job		20.12	28
3.16	37	21.22	25
3.17	40	22.2	27
3.18	24, 37	22.3	26
4.3	35	22.12	39
5.11	24	22.13	25
5.20	24	22.19	24
6.19-20	33	26.13	25
7.13	24	26.15	25
10.3	24	26.22	39
11.20	24	27.12	26
19.27	53	27.16	44
20.15	44-45	28.1	25
24.2-11	43	29.13	27
28.3-11	33-34	30.7	24
28.7-8	37	30.15-16	37
28.25	28	30.20	32
33.3	41	30.21	39
36.23	24	31.10-31	32-33
36.27	29		
		Canticles	
Proverbs		2.7	123
1.7	38	3.5	123
1.20-33	32	5.8	123
2.17	24	8.4	123
3.13	44		
3.19-20	28	*Qoheleth*	
4.2	3	1.9	39
4.11	24	1.13	39
6.8	38	1.14	39
7.5-27	32	2.17	39
7.26	35	2.23	24
8.1-9.6	32	4.1	39
8.25-26	28	4.3	39
8.35	44	5.10	24
11.2	25-26	6.5	37
11.7	27	7.10	41
11.8	25-26	7.19	21

160

INDEX OF AUTHORS

INDEX OF HEBREW WORDS

N.B. verbs occur in the *qal* stem unless otherwise noted.

Published in the series STUDIA SEMITICA NEERLANDICA

★ Out of print